12·8·04

Normal loan Kimberlin

Please return this item at or before the date shown below.
Fines will be charged if the item is returned after this date.

Item issued subject to reservation recall see Library Guide for details

Renewals/loan information t **257 7043**   Library information t **257 7042**

 **DE MONTFORT UNIVERSITY** LEICESTER • BEDFORD

Return Migration in the Asia Pacific

Return Migration in the Asia Pacific

Edited by

Robyn Iredale

Associate Professor in Geosciences, University of Wollongong, Australia and Secretariat Director, Asia Pacific Migration Research Network (APMRN)

Fei Guo

Lecturer, Demography Program, Department of Business, Macquarie University, Sydney, Australia

Santi Rozario

Senior Lecturer, Sociology and Anthropology, School of Social Sciences, University of Newcastle, Australia

Edward Elgar
Cheltenham, UK • Northampton, MA, USA

Published by
Edward Elgar Publishing Limited
Glensanda House
Montpellier Parade
Cheltenham
Glos GL50 1UA
UK

Edward Elgar Publishing, Inc.
136 West Street
Suite 202
Northampton
Massachusetts 01060
USA

A catalogue record for this book
is available from the British Library

Library of Congress Cataloguing in Publication Data
Return migration in the Asia Pacific / edited by Robyn Iredale, Fei Guo, Santi Rozario.
    p. cm.
  Includes bibliographical references and index.
    1. Return migration—Bangladesh. 2. Return migration—China. 3. Return migration—Taiwan. 4. Return migration—Vietnam. I. Iredale, Robyn R. II. Guo, Fei. III. Rozario, Santi.

JV8753.5.R48 2003
304.8'5—dc21
                                                        2003043909

ISBN 1 84376 303 6

Printed and bound in Great Britain by MPG Books Ltd, Bodmin, Cornwall

Contents

Tables

Contributors

Dr Dang Nguyen Anh
Head, Population Institute of Sociology, Hanoi, Vietnam

Dr John Gow
Lecturer Sociology and Anthropology, School of Social Sciences, University of Newcastle, Australia

Dr Fei Guo
Lecturer, Demography Program, Department of Business, Macquarie University, Sydney, Australia

Associate Professor Robyn Iredale
Associate Professor in Geosciences, University of Wollongong, Australia and Secretariat Director, Asia Pacific Migration Research Network (APMRN)

Professor Luo Keren
Professor and Vice Director, Shanghai International Migration and Development Research Center, Population Research Institute, East China Normal University, Shanghai, China

Professor Huang Ping
Deputy Director, Institute of Sociology, Chinese Academy of Social Sciences, Beijing, China

Dr Santi Rozario
Senior Lecturer, Sociology and Anthropology, School of Social Sciences, University of Newcastle, Australia

Professor Ching-lung Tsay
The Institute of Economics, Academia Sinica, Nankang, Taipei, Taiwan

Acknowledgements

This book is the outcome of a collaborative project across five regions and as such its completion is a major achievement. The editors would like to thank the researchers from each of the countries/regions who contributed so much of their time and energy to the project. These researchers were responsible for writing reports and these reports have formed the basis of Chapters 3 to 6. They have been substantially edited in some instances.

John Gow from the University of Newcastle joined the project somewhat later and was involved in setting up a database and carrying out what comparative analysis was possible. Ellen Kraly from Colgate University contributed a section in Chapter 1 on the paucity of migration statistics and we would like to thank her for this.

The project was funded by the Ford Foundation as part of a large grant to the Asia Pacific Migration Research Network (APMRN). The Ford Foundation generously supported this and a number of other projects: on irregular migration, women and migration and a range of small 'emergency' projects in Indonesia, Fiji, East Timor, Korea and Malaysia. These other publications are available from the APMRN or the APMRN's website.

The APMRN is funded in part by UNESCO-MOST (Management of Social Transformations). This funding has enabled the network to develop and function across the whole of Asia and the Pacific. Collaborative research involving a common methodology is an exciting method of operating and the coordinators of the project wish to thank all of the participants for their cooperation.

Final editing and formatting was carried out by Suzie Wynn Jones and we are deeply grateful for her time and expertise. Kerry Lyon of the APMRN Secretariat also helped with final editing and this is very much appreciated.

Preface

International migration has become a key element in North–South relationships. Although most international mobility is either within the South or within the North, it is the growing migration from South to North which has become a focus for global political concerns. Governments and supranational bodies are making great efforts to stop 'unwanted' migration while effectively managing the types of migration they consider desirable. The authorities cooperate to keep out asylum seekers and undocumented workers – despite the strong need for low-skilled labour in most rich countries. At the same time, virtually all developed countries are eager to attract highly skilled and business migrants – such as Indian IT professionals or nurses and doctors for Britain's troubled National Health System. For many years, analysts have argued that highly skilled migration benefits the developed countries while holding back development in the South, by causing a 'brain drain' of desperately-needed qualified personnel.

But is this really the case? More recently, some migration scholars have argued that many skilled migrants return in time, bringing with them knowledge of advanced technologies, useful network connections and capital for investment. The argument is that initial 'brain drain' is followed by 'brain return' or 'brain circulation' in which skilled people move back and forwards within international labour markets. This is a crucial issue for understanding development and international relations, but unfortunately there has been very little research to find out the real costs and benefits of skilled migration for the people and the countries concerned.

This book fills an important gap. A group of researchers from Australia, Bangladesh, China, Taiwan and Vietnam have come together to study the patterns and effects of return skilled migration in their countries. This is truly transnational research: Robyn Iredale and her colleagues have developed common research questions and methods. They have then used their varied disciplinary backgrounds as anthropologists, economists, demographers and sociologists to carry out research in settings that differ sharply in their economic, cultural and historical characteristics. Locally-based researchers have been able to build up the trust necessary to persuade large numbers of professional transients to talk frankly about their experiences and problems. This has made it possible to make comparisons that cut across cultural barriers.

Do skilled migrants return home because development is leading to new opportunities? Or is it the return of skilled people that makes development possible? Are returnees a bridgehead for foreign investment, or do they stimulate local enterprises? What is the role of social and cultural links with the area of origin in providing the conditions for successful return? This study examines these and many other questions. The differing experiences of the four regions of origin show that the answers are as complex as the migratory phenomena themselves. Social and cultural capital are of crucial importance. So are government policy and the business climate. People decide to return when the opportunities structure is promising, and when they can maintain networks that allow them to stay at the cutting edge of their professions. Return migration can play a crucial role in economic development – as the case of Taiwan demonstrates – but people will not return to a situation of poor governance and stagnation – as the Bangladeshi experience shows. Return migration can help both foreign investment and local enterprises by linking them in transnational business networks. In this process, migration ceases to be a simple one- or even two-way movement, and takes on a circular character as part of the process of economic and cultural globalisation.

The key question, then, is what governments and supranational bodies can do to maximise the development benefits of return migration, while reducing the unequal exchange relationships typified by the notion of brain drain. The study helps to show what practices and policies can help achieve this. It also points out that there is a long way to go: although some countries have clearly achieved development benefits from migration, many others have not. The central issues, as is so often the case, come down to economic capacity and political will.

Stephen Castles
Professor of Migration and Refugee Studies,
University of Oxford
February 2003

1. Introduction

Robyn Iredale, Fei Guo and Santi Rozario[1]

BACKGROUND

The contemporary world is polarised into developed and developing countries, or the North and the South. This distinction is characterised by enormous income and demographic differentials that intensify emigration pressures from the poor nations to the rich. 'Cross-border migration, combined with the "brain drain" from developing to industrial countries, will be one of the major forces shaping the landscape of the 21st century', according to the World Bank (2000, p. 38).

International migration can only be fully understood by referring to socio-economic transformation at a global level, ie. to the global capitalist system.

> Historically, the economic and geopolitical penetration by more developed economies and states into pre-capitalist or less developed areas has led to the disruption of economic systems in the latter and to internal and international migration. In the current phase of global economic restructuring and increasing economic integration, these processes have been intensified (Hamilton and Chinchilla 1996, p. 195).

The various types of international migration include: permanent migration, increasingly of skilled migrants and their families; temporary skilled and unskilled labour migration; irregular movements and asylum seekers and refugees. The International Organization for Migration (IOM) and other similar organisations are increasingly focusing on issues such as how to factor international migration into the development process. This can be explained in a variety of ways. An increasing concern (or perhaps fear?) in recent years on the part of the Western developed nations that they may be flooded with unwanted emigrants from less developed nations is, doubtless, part of the explanation. Yet it is evident from both the historical relations between various sending and receiving nations, and the immigration policies of nations in recent years, that receiving countries have always had much more control over who migrated to their nations than the sending countries.

The receiving countries, that is the developed nations, historically recruited migrants from developing countries, often their former colonies, to maximise their own economic development at the time of industrial expansion. In recent years receiving countries, of which there is an increasing number, have been refining or developing immigration policies to suit their economic needs. The emphasis on attracting highly skilled migrants has become a top priority for most receiving countries.

Thurow (1999) and others refer to what is currently taking place as the 'third industrial revolution'. This third revolution – the information revolution sparked by the widespread use of computers and high-technology – is limited by labour and intellectual capital but no longer by land or capital. Rosenblum (2001, p. 384), in turn, argues that labour and intellectual capital 'are fused into one', a crucial change on how we conceptualised 'land, labour and capital'. He states:

> In the past, innovation occurred within elite research and development divisions of large firms otherwise staffed by unskilled labor. Now innovation *is* labor, and entire firms at the forefront of the information revolution exist for no purpose other than research and development. For this reason, in contrast to the previous periods, access to skilled labor is the primary limited factor that will define the geography and long-term distributive effects of the information revolution (Rosenblum 2001, p. 384).

Traditional receiving countries are refining their policies as high-skilled immigration will be a major factor in their future development. Other countries such as Germany, the UK, France, the Netherlands, Japan, South Korea, Singapore and others are also developing policies to attract high-skilled workers.

Such policies have mixed consequences for the sending countries. On an individual level, they provide expanded opportunities for those with suitable skills to emigrate. But these may be precisely the skilled personnel that are most needed within developing countries. Out-migration obviously has both positive and negative impacts on the economies and on the levels of skilled personnel but, in practice, it is not taken into account systematically in development planning. As Appleyard (1992a, p. 22) has argued, 'if appropriate global development strategies were in place, then international, especially temporary migration, could be factored into, and make an important contribution to, the development process'.

Migration theorists have attempted to develop models of how migration might fit into the development process and how the 'migration transition' will occur. For example, Lim (1996) whose work is based in Malaysia, argues that:

> economic development initially raises agricultural productivity, releasing more workers than can find employment in nascent industries. This leads to emigration, but as economic development continues, fertility tends to fall and demand for labour increases, so that emigration declines until a transition point is reached and immigration commences (quoted in Castles 1999, p. 15).

In Lim's model, development aid geared towards the reduction of out-migration from rural areas would have to take a long-term perspective since its immediate effect is likely to be contrary to the desired goal of reducing such emigration. High emigration from rural Malaysia was eventually stemmed and Malaysia is now one of the main receiving countries for temporary labour migration in Southeast Asia. Such labourers go mainly into the plantation sector of the rural economy. This phenomenon is referred to by demographers as the 'migration transition' when emigration is replaced by immigration.

However, whether all developing countries are going to follow the same pattern as Malaysia, is very questionable. In the case of Bangladesh, which has been heavily dependent on foreign aid since its inception in 1971, the so-called 'transition' point at which emigration will begin to decline and immigration will commence is difficult to even dream about in the year 2002. The reasons will become clear in the following chapters.

MIGRATION AND DEVELOPMENT OR SOCIAL TRANSFORMATION

The generally perceived gains from international migration include remittance payments to sending countries, reduced unemployment in sending countries, and skill acquisition overseas which then may be used by return migrants in the development of their own countries. In the case of Bangladesh, it has gained a fair amount through the remittance of foreign currency by the substantial number of contract labourers who have been working, mainly in the Middle Eastern countries, from the late 1970s. In addition, perhaps there has been a slight reduction in the number of unemployed people in Bangladesh due to this labour migration. But we need to appreciate that the gains in these spheres are temporary and their contribution has made little difference to the overall economic development of the country.

The impact of migrants as agents of development or social change in sending and receiving countries or regions received increasing attention in the 1990s. In a summary of the situation in the early 1990s, Appleyard (1992b, p. 261) stated that 'accumulated evidence suggests, at least, that remittance payments, skill acquisition and reduced unemployment have contributed significantly' to the process of development in labour or migrant sending countries. The focus on less skilled migrant labour and its impact on development gained increased attention in the 1990s, especially between Mexico and the US. In the late 1990s, the growth in skilled migration and competition between countries to attract the 'brightest and best' migrants surged and the debate over 'brain drain' or 'brain circulation' attracted considerable attention.

On the one hand, some argue that the 'brain drain' is robbing developing countries of valuable human resources, thereby hindering the application of new technologies, inhibiting research and development and generally holding back development. Others argue that the problem is being overstated and they stress the positive benefits of skilled emigrants for both the sending and receiving countries (Glaser 1978; Stark 1984, 1991). Clearly there is no single answer and the benefits of skilled emigrants need to be analysed in the context of individual countries/regions.

By the late 1990s, theory in relation to the effects of temporary or permanent emigration had developed further. The mechanisms for migration, especially migration networks and collectives (households, kinship groups or organisations), attracted significant attention. In particular, transnational networks and the concept of 'transnational migration' came to be seen as vital. 'Transnational migration' is a 'process by which immigrants forge and sustain simultaneous multi-stranded relationships that link together their societies of origin and destination' (Glick-Schiller *et al.* 1992, p. 48). Furthermore, Faist (1997, p. 206) stresses that 'leaving and returning may not be decisions taken only once'.

> This suggests that space in international migration is inadequately described by focusing solely on countries of origin and destination. Rather, as international migration proceeds, transnational spaces unfold that cross-cut nation-states. A flow of people, goods, capital and services emerges. In sum, in addition to the interpersonal and inter-group dimension, all these aspects concern the intertemporal dimension of international migration (Faist 1997, p. 206).

The potential benefits of emigration and re-migration are seen as possibly occurring at three different levels: the micro-level for individual migrants, families and communities; the meso-level or intermediate effects on particular industries/areas and the macro-level effects for economies and societies as a whole. The first and last have received most attention to date in the literature.

Possible micro-level benefits are, for example, improvements in individual or family income, the acquisition of capital to invest, the development of skills through training or work experience and an improvement in family security and social status. Benefits at this level will assist families but they may also have flow-on effects to the wider economy and society. The 'new economics of labour migration' body of research has demonstrated the spill-over effects of micro-level benefits (Taylor 1995, 1999).

Meso-level effects include the impact of remittances on investment in agriculture or business activities generally and stimulation to the economies of local regions through investment from remittances or money brought home/ sent home by permanent or temporary/intermittent returnees. The formation of migration networks and collectives provides vital mechanisms through which meso-level benefits may occur. Faist (1997) argues that focusing on networks and collectives provides the most useful analytical tool for analysing migration systems in which 'transfers' and 'retransfers' of financial, human and social capital take place.

Potential macro-level benefits include the use of remittances to improve balance of payments, reduce foreign debt and fund imports; an improvement in human capital at the national level; the contribution of migration networks to international trade and the introduction of innovative attitudes towards economic development through exposure to more industrialised societies. This represents the most difficult area to analyse as the separation of the impact of migrants, from all the other aspects (such as the information revolution, technology, research, etc), on the economy and society is not easy.

PREVIOUS RESEARCH ON RETURN MIGRATION

Most of the research into the effects of emigration, temporary or permanent, has focused on two aspects: the effects of relatively unskilled labour out-migration, and the probability and subsequent impacts of the return of a proportion of these labour migrants. On the first aspect, much has been written about the scale and nature of remittances and the use to which remittances have been put back home. Increasingly, work has also been conducted on the impact of emigration on families left behind. In particular, in countries where the level of female labour out-migration is high, such as the Philippines, the impact on families can be very serious and often goes unattended. This deficit is now being addressed by a range of researchers and organisations, especially non-government organisations (NGOs).

On the question of return, work has tended to focus on the factors promoting or inhibiting return. For example, a study of the return migration of guestworkers from Germany between 1970–89 indicated that return intention probabilities were strongly affected by satisfaction and other time-dependent variables while the influence of personal characteristics was of little importance (Waldorf 1995). Studies of return migration in other regions suggest some similarities. Lindstrom's study (1996) of return migration to Mexico from the United States suggested that the likelihood of return to Mexico decreased when migrants were joined by their immediate families, although economic incentives for return were high. Another study of Mexico/United States migration by Massey and Espinosa (1997) suggested that over the past 25 years, the probability of first, repeat and return migration was linked to forces identified by social capital theory and the new economics of migration. Mexico/United States migration stemmed from three mutually reinforcing processes – social capital formation, human capital formation and market consolidation – and thus the decision to return home was the result of weighing up many factors which themselves vary over time.

On the impacts of return, there has been much less work. A study by Colton (1993) on the return migration of Yemeni after working in Saudi Arabia showed that upon their return, many people invested in small businesses such as convenience stores. Colton found that they had to undergo social reintegration into Yemeni society but the processes or interaction between the returning migrants and the society at large were not analysed. Most work on this aspect has been done or is now being done in Mexico and the Philippines.

Other general studies on return migration have tended to focus on retirement emigration or the return of people to their country of birth after they have finished paid employment. The return of Greeks and Italians from Australia and elsewhere after retirement is a well documented phenomenon. In a recent study in Europe, Kulu and Tammaru (2000) investigated return migration to Estonia in the 1990s. Their study revealed that return migrants to Estonia are mostly those who were born in Estonia and who had recently retired in western countries. Second-generation Estonians who were born in western countries were less likely to return.

THE GROWTH OF SKILLED MIGRATION AND ITS POTENTIAL IMPACTS

Knowledge workers are the modern source of economic growth and development, according to 'new growth' theory (Straubhaar 2001). Cumulative human capital produces positive knowledge externalities that spill over the economy in which they occur and thus countries which have high levels of human capital grow more quickly (Mahroum 2002, p. 9). For this reason, countries are now competing for highly skilled immigrant workers. Skilled migrants do not just bring skills and knowledge but more importantly they bring positive externalities – in terms of increased technological and economic entrepreneurship networks – in and between the sending and the receiving countries (Saxenian 2001).

Thus, highly skilled migrants represent an increasingly large component of global migration streams. The phenomenon is not new but the numbers and trends are changing rapidly. Stalker (2000) estimated a stock of 1.5 million professionals from developing countries in the industrial countries alone and on top of this there is estimated to be another 1.5 million students from developing countries studying in Western countries. There are many types of movement: permanent settlement to major immigrant-receiving countries; temporary migration both within and outside of multinational corporations and refugee flows. Few countries take highly skilled professionals on a permanent basis but many are seeking them on a temporary basis, supposedly to meet skills shortages until they can train their own stock of skilled workers.

The potential benefits of the return migration of professionals and business people, usually from more developed countries, for both the country of original emigration and the country from which the return migration takes place, has received little attention. Much of the early skilled migration was termed 'brain drain' and sending countries tended to see it as a loss of their resources to wealthier countries. At the same time, more industrialised countries were willing to accept these immigrants as they filled labour market shortages and increased the general human capital stock of the nation. Few benefits were seen as emanating from these flows for the sending countries. The possibility of return was also seen as minimal and the lack of data on both emigration and return migration made analysis of the scale of the flows difficult if not impossible.

The earliest work on return skilled migration and the possibility of return migrants being 'agents of change' was carried out by Gmelch (1980, 1987) in Barbados. Thomas-Hope has also conducted research on return skilled migration in the Caribbean region. Much of her work is qualitative in nature and the paucity of data has been an ongoing problem. Thomas-Hope has specifically focused on IOM's *Return of Talent* programme and she found that migration came to be regarded less as a means of permanent escape and more as a mechanism for extending opportunities beyond the resource limitations of small islands. Return became an integral part of the purpose for emigration and this has continued to the present time. Emigration provided the opportunity for migrants to reap the benefits of working abroad. These benefits were measured both in economic terms and in terms of opportunities for social mobility for the migrants themselves and for their children. The return of families was not common in the 1970s and 1980s but has emerged recently. Thomas-Hope (1999, p. 191) concludes that 'only when Caribbean international migration is examined in its entirety will activity at the origin and destination be seen to be intrinsically linked'. She argues that the presence of the migrant abroad must be seen as 'part of the wider transnational system of outflow, interaction and feedback'.

The loss of skilled human resources from Africa has reached alarming proportions with estimates of around one third of skilled personnel leaving between 1960–87 and the trend is expected to increase with the worsening economic and political conditions in most African countries (World Bank 2000, p. 39). This is very concerning for policy makers and they are calling for incentives and policies to encourage skilled people offshore to maintain links with and to perhaps return home. IOM has now developed its *Return of Talent* programme in Africa. A study currently being conducted by Savina Ammassari is focusing on the 'reverse' mobility of the elite to Accra, Ghana and Abidjan, Côte d'Ivoire (Ammassari 2000). Ammassari's work is similar to this project and there has been an exchange of questionnaires and reports.

Little research has been conducted in Asia on return skilled migration. The exception is Taiwan where the government has deliberatley sought to attract Taiwanese students back from the US and elsewhere since the 1960s. Growing interest in this phenomenon in China and India is leading to increased research and policy focus.

Recent reports on overseas Chinese returning to the People's Republic of China have indicated that there is a noticeable trend for more and more overseas Chinese to return. Most of them are professional and business people. For example, a report in the *Far Eastern Economic Review* provided a number of stories of the successful return of overseas professional Chinese who have found their fortune and success in China – which made them feel there is 'no place like home' (Wilhelm and Biers 2000). Another report in *Newsweek International* also suggests that there is an increasing number of Western-educated highly qualified overseas Chinese who have returned to China (Larmer 2000). They often work in law firms and multinational companies and/or establish their own firms. Zweig (1997) conducted a study on the views of Mainland Chinese in the United States on returning to China and found that the majority did not intend to return. Economic factors, such as better income and housing in the United States, as well as professional concerns, such as lack of career mobility and a poor work environment in China, were important. Only a small fraction (9 per cent) of respondents indicated an intention to return but Zweig predicted that if China's economy continued to grow, significant numbers of Chinese would return in the future.

A seminar held by the Organisation for Economic Cooperation and Development (OECD) in June 2001 has resulted in a new publication which addresses the issue of return skilled migration from various angles (OECD 2002). Barrett (2002) analyses the return of highly skilled Irish and demonstrates that skilled returnees may assist in reducing income inequalities. Meyer (2002) shows that the loss of human capital as part of the 'brain drain' may be partially offset by the return of migrants and the development of networks facilitating the circulation of skilled workers between host countries and their country of origin. According to Hugo (2002, p. 9), the 'mobility of skilled workers can also promote investment in training in sending countries and increase inflows of currency through remittances'.

This statement needs to be investigated. First, the Indian case will be outlined in some detail. It shows that while there is a high level of circulation involving Indians living in the US, Canada, Singapore etc there is not a high level of permanent return migration. Further, there is not a high level of investment in base level education in India but in elite education for the middle and upper classes. Thus, Indians offshore have served mostly as 'key middle-men linking US businesses to low-cost software expertise in India' (Saxenian 2001, p. 220).

CASE STUDY OF INDIA AND THE IMPACT OF THE INFORMATION TECHNOLOGY (IT) SECTOR

The impact of the emigration of highly skilled Indian workers has attracted most attention from researchers in recent years. From the 1950s to 1975, most emigration of high-skilled Indians was permanent. In 1975, recognising the trend in greater communication and travel between India and the West, the Indian government created the category of non-resident Indian (NRI) to intro-duce a financial facility to allow persons of Indian origin in the US and the UK to open and maintain foreign currency non-resident accounts in US dol-lars or UK pounds sterling. This led to a rapid increase in remittances. In 1990, a series of economic crises resulted in India's eighth Five-Year Plan promoting an export-led development strategy instead of the previous import-substitution policy. This marked a major change for India and meant the end of state control and the experiment with socialist policies.

From the 1980s, India targeted the IT sector as a priority in its larger devel-opment agenda but 1991 marked the beginning of advancement in India's development strategy, according to US entepreneurial NRIs. The export of software is now the 'fastest-growing sector in the India economy', according to the National Association of Software and Services Companies (Chakravartty 2001, p. 326). A significant portion of India's software exports takes the form of Indian workers employed on short-term contracts with foreign firms in the US, Singapore, Canada, Australia, Japan and elsewhere, by means of a proc-ess known as 'body shopping'. This includes temporary workers admitted to the US under the H-1B visa scheme. Figures for the late 1990s show that Indians comprised 53.3 per cent of the intake under this programme in 1999 – due to an increased emphasis on computer-related occupations (Lowell 2001, pp. 136-41). The proportion of H-1B visa holders remaining permanently in the US reached almost 50 per cent in 1993 and then dropped to a low of 21 per cent in 1998. However, the new *American Competitiveness in the Twenty-First Century Act 2000* has lifted a previous per-country cap that existed and this will enable more Indians to obtain green cards and stay permanently. The remaining H-1B workers either return home or go to another country.

To these temporary workers must be added those who make a transition from a student visa to a H-1B visa or to a green card (permanent residency). This constitutes a significant number, especially among postgraduate stu-

dents. India encourages its students to go offshore to complete high-tech degrees, especially in the US. When they return home 'they bring money, they
bring a tested education, and above all, they come back bitten by the entrepreneurial bug' (Gardner 2000, p. 19). They also become a part of networks that
'have emerged as byproducts' of the attraction of US universities to Asian
students (Mahroum 2002, p. 52). Both students and researchers actively seek
out prestigious institutions in the US and UK, or what Mahroum calls global
'meccas', so that they can join their elite networks (Mahroum 2002, p. 42).

> One way of securing access to such networks, for instance, is through enrolling in
> a doctoral programme at a prominent institution (Mahroum 2002, pp. 55–56).

Other countries have also adjusted their migration policies to make it easier
for former tertiary students and temporary migrants to remain permanently,
without having to return home. Half of the intake in the skilled category in
Australia's immigration intake now has Australian qualifications. An 'Australian degree or diploma' attracts five points in the selection points system
and points for 'occupation in demand', 'age' and 'English language ability'
ensure that young, Australian, tertiary educated students qualify readily.

A study of Indian workers and the IT industry suggests that they serve as
intermediaries for US/Indian outsourcing.

> American NRIs have played a prominent role in the development of India's high-
> tech economy, functioning as economic and cultural brokers in terms of body-
> shopping contracts and establishing offshore software facilities in India
> (Chakravartty 2001, p. 339).

The combination of a large pool of skilled labour along with a relatively small
market for computer services 'translated into a policy environment that encouraged firms to develop software primarily for export', according to
Chakravartty (2001, p. 336). India has a very well developed education system and the elite technology institutes, the Indian Institutes of Technology
(IITs), turn out world class computer scientists and engineers who are actively
headhunted before they have even completed their studies. Thus, the avail-
ability of skilled labour at home made it feasible for NRIs to consider
outsourcing from their own firms, setting up subsidiaries of American companies or establishing their own companies. NRIs act as cultural interpreters and
are best able to negotiate the 'complex and often bewildering bureaucracy and
backward infrastructure of [her] home country' (Saxenian 2001, p. 225).
Saxenian cites the example of Radhu Basu who was invited by the Indian
government to set up one of the first foreign subsidiaries, Hewlett-Packard
(HP) in the mid-1980s. She spent four years setting up HP's software centre in
Bangalore, thereby pioneering the trend of using low-waged Indians for software development. She explained the patience and cultural understanding that

are required to do business in India: 'You have to understand India and its development needs and adapt to them' (Saxenian 2001, p. 225).

Many Indian engineers followed Basu's lead in the early 1990s. They exploited their cultural and linguistic capabilities and their contacts to help build software operations ... Indians educated in the United States have been pivotal in setting up the Indian software facilities for Oracle, Novell, Bay Network, and other Silicon Valley companies (Saxenian 2001, p. 225).

Today, intense competition persists between different Indian states

to draw IT and telecom transnationals to specific cities and regions that are being designed as techno-parks and high-tech cities ... some 160 Fortune 500 companies [now] outsource software projects to India, and they highlight the fact that Silicon Valley-based NRI executives are increasingly turning to India to help fledgling Indian startups (Chakravartty 2001, pp. 340–1).

Now what is happening is that 'the best and brightest Indian IT workers increasingly see advantages to staying in India, a country that is developing its own IT industry, a development that reinforces the value of outsourcing to India' (Salzman and Biswas 2000, quoted in Lowell 2001, p. 152). Indian engineers and computer professionals/technicians now have much greater opportunity of emigrating by working first for a US firm in India.

The 'brain drain' continued unabated throughout the 1990s, according to Saxenian (2001, p. 226). Most Indians who work, or have business interests, in India do not return home permanently. Saxenian (2001, p. 225) argues that this is unlike Taiwanese immigrants 'who have increasingly returned home to start businesses or to work in established companies'. Indians typically return home on a temporary basis – due partly to differences in the standard of living but 'most observers agree that the frustrations associated with doing business in India are equally important' (Saxenian 2001, p. 225).

NRIs and foreign subsidiaries have had some impact on the bureaucratic climate and level of infrastucture in India, mostly in Software Technology Parks (STPs), but 'complex bureaucratic restrictions, corrupt and unresponsive officials and poor infrastructure that causes massive daily frustrations' still prevail (Saxenian 2001, p. 226). For returning Indians, this situation is compounded by feelings of resentment towards them – a resentment that is not unrelated to India's long-standing hostility to foreign corporations. Thus, Saxenian (2001, p. 226) describes Indians as having a 'largely arms-length role connecting US firms with India's low-cost, high-quality skilled labor force'.

Is this a 'diaspora by design', as Visweswaran (1997) suggests? Certainly current attempts by the Indian government to train skilled workers for export supports this notion. Chakravartty (2001, p. 346) describes the 'nationalism of the NRI [as being] based upon a nationalist, Americanized business culture that is pro-nation but anti-state. This version of nationalism resonates with a powerful cosmopolitan, urban, upper-caste elite that is increasingly anxious about its place in a largely low-income democracy'.

The impact of NRIs on the wider society and economy of India is important. One of the aims of our study is to examine the impacts of 'returning' migrants on their families and on the wider society. Few people tackle the class aspects of Indian high-skilled migration, according to Visweswaran (1997), but it is clear from Chakravartty (2001) and Xiang's (2001) work on Indian high-tech workers that they come from upper-caste and upper-class families and that they have benefited very considerably from India's education system. Besides the economic benefits for India mentioned above, they mostly put their resources (money and time) into establishing organisations and networks that benefit other upper-class Indians. One such organisation, The Indus Entrepreneurs (TIE) which was founded in 1992 in Silicon Valley, organises conferences, meetings and other sessions for NRIs in the US and for regional branches in Chennai, Bangalore, Hyderabad and Mumbai (Chakravartty 2001). TIE plans to raise US$1 billion to contribute to IITs, provided that the IITs 'become less beholden to national caste-based affirmative action policies' (Chakravartty 2001, p. 344). That is, the privatisation of India's higher education system is seen as a necessary step for increasing training opportunities for people who will then be able to join the stream of NRIs. Thus, the sector that enabled NRIs to be successful is the same sector that is the subject of their attention. They ignore the 52 per cent illiteracy rate in India and the fact that 40 per cent of the population still live in poverty. They see the contribution of the IT sector in terms of the number of jobs provided – even though they are mostly at a low skill level.

The lack of a trickle down effect from the IT sector to other parts of the Indian economy is highlighted by Khadria (1999). He calls for a major paradigm shift. This would entail replacing the existing focus on expectations regarding the exogenous return of resources (remittances, technology, return migration) with a new focus on enhanced productiveness of the resident work force that 'can be triggered by human development to be brought about through education and health that the expatriates [NRIs] can foster endogenously' (Khadria 1999, p. 217). NRIs' money, materials, skill and vision should be channelled into the health and education sectors, rather than into business and industry, work and living infrastructure or other multifarious development targets, according to Khadria. The development of strategies and institutions to achieve this end is called for. The *World Development Report 1996* supports this position by saying that:

> In the end what matters is people...Labour productivity, critical for economic growth, depends on workers' knowledge, skills, motivation, and health...A well-educated,

healthy workforce is essential for economic growth (World Bank 1996, pp. 66 and 123).

In this way, the resources of NRIs 'would help to restore the human capital taken away from the system and may some day even produce a break to the first generation negative effects of the brain drain' (Khadria 2001, p. 60). This long-term, society and economy wide outlook is quite different in its perspective from the narrow focus on trying to get returnees to invest in businesses. The role of networks and associations of non-resident nationals takes on a new dimension in terms of the contributions that they could be encouraged to make to basic education and health service provision.

This case study provides one example of the relationships between emigrants and their home country. The situations that pertain for Bangladesh, China, Taiwan and Vietnam will be analysed in the following chapters.

THE IMPACT OF RETURN MIGRATION ON THE COUNTRY FROM WHICH PEOPLE RETURN

Research into the impact of return migration on the country from which migrants are returning is also limited. Hugo (1994) completed an important Australian study for the Bureau of Migration, Population and Multicultural Research titled *The Economic Implications of Emigration from Australia*. He estimated an overall settler loss of 20.8 per cent during the period from 1947 to 1991 but also noted the trend towards an increasing number of transients in the intake – in line with the increasing globalisation of highly skilled labour. Hugo documented the increased permanent and long-term departure of Australian-born and Asian-born Australians to Asia with the emergence of rapidly growing economies in Asia in the 1980s and 1990s. Hugo's study was a statistical analysis of the comprehensive data collected in Australia but did not engage in the debate about a 'brain drain' from Australia. He was careful to point out that Australia experiences a net gain of skills rather than a loss, and that Australian-born professionals are becoming part of international skilled migration flows.

Kee and Skeldon's study (1994) of Hong Kong immigrants in Australia confirmed a high return migration rate of 30 per cent for those who arrived in 1990–91. Mak (1997) took this work further and in a statistical analysis of the factors affecting permanent settlement found that work and family factors are important determinants of the intention to settle permanently. Career satisfaction and having school age children constitute a 'parsimonious set of predictors of Hong Kong immigrants' intention for permanent stay' (Khoo and Mak 2000, p. 2).

Pe-Pua *et al.* (1996, p. 70) in a more qualitative Australian study of Hong Kong 'astronauts' (people who have acquired permanent residence elsewhere but continue to work or do business in Hong Kong) concluded that 'returnees to Hong Kong appear to be more an asset than a liability to their adopted country'. They create 'transnational business networks which bind Australia with other parts of Asia and these networks are a form of capital, an asset which can generate returns and expand value of an economic kind' (Wong *et al.* 1994, p. 39). The latter define network capital as a diffused asset that lacks the institutional framework of other forms of capital and 'may take the institutional form of associations of various kinds, but it is generally lodged in reciprocal relations...In order to reduce uncertainty and to reinforce mutual obligations, personal trust is essential as a cementing force in the operation of network capital'.

These networks are normally regarded as being contained within ethnic networks but they may extend across ethnic groups. Pe-Pua *et al.*'s research showed that Hong Kong astronauts had set up businesses in Australia with a range of non-Hong Kong partners and they were all part of the operating network or network capital. Xiang's (2001) research into Indian information technology professionals in Australia also shows that they are very active in forming a bridge in that industry between people back home and those in Australia and many other parts of the world. Outside of business and family networks, however, little research has been conducted into the impacts of 'returning' migrants on countries from which they return or that they re-migrate to (a third destination).

In the late 1990s, Khoo and Mak (2000) partially replicated Mak's 1997 study. They analysed data from the first and second waves of interviews of the *Longitudinal Survey of Immigrants to Australia* (LSIA) conducted by the Department of Immigration and Multicultural Affairs. A sample of 5192 principal applicants who arrived in major urban areas of Australia from September 1993 to August 1995 were interviewed three to six months after arrival. They were re-interviewed one year later and again two years after the second interview. Khoo and Mak used the first two waves of data in their analysis of eight birthplace groups who arrived in the Concessional Family, Independent Skill and Business Migration visa categories that existed at that time.[2]

Of the 530 skilled and business migrants in their sample, 70 per cent were classified as 'having the intention of settling permanently' and the remainder were classed as possible or actual (having been absent for the second interview) returnees. Khoo and Mak found that the highest rate of intention to remain permanently was amongst migrants from China (76 per cent) compared to 62.7 per cent for Taiwan and Korea and 63 per cent for South Asia (India and Sri Lanka). They analysed the relationship between several variables (visa category, reasons for migration, age, English language proficiency, work factors) and the intention to settle permanently. The results varied for each birthplace group but, on the whole, having relatives in Australia and migrating for a better future for the family were important factors in the intention to settle permanently.

The view that return migration (and emigration) from developed countries represents a loss of human capital and a waste of migration administration funds is gaining added impetus. Countries such as Australia, the US and Canada are now themselves talking about a 'brain drain' from their countries. However, there has also been some increasing recognition that the return migration of earlier migrants or the long term or permanent departure from Australia, United States or Canada of their own native-born may actually bring benefits to these countries as well as contribute to social and economic transformation in the countries of destination of these migrants. There have been few studies, however, that have been able to explain or quantify these gains.

A recent book which focuses on high-skilled migration to the US (Cornelius *et al.* 2001) includes some references to benefits for the US when Indians/ Chinese return home (permanently or temporarily). In her case studies of Indian and Chinese ethnic networks in Silicon Valley, Saxenian (2001, p. 221) shows how immigrant entrepreneurs 'are creating transnational communities that provide the shared information, contacts, and trust that allow local producers to participate in an increasingly global economy'. She states:

> As recently as the 1970s, only very large corporations had the resources and capabilities to grow internationally, and they did so primarily by establishing marketing offices or manufacturing plants overseas. Today, by contrast, new transportation and communications technologies allow even the smallest firms to build partnerships with foreign producers to tap overseas expertise, cost-savings, and markets. Start-ups in Silicon Valley today are often global actors from the day they begin operations...

> The scarce resource in this new environment is the ability to locate foreign partners quickly and to manage complex business relationships across cultural and linguistic boundaries....First-generation immigrants...who have the language, cultural, and technical skills to function well in both the United States and foreign markets are distinctly positioned to play a central role in this environment.

> These ties have measurable economic benefits. Research at the University of California at Berkeley has documented a significant correlation between the presence of first-generation immigrants from a given country and exports from California. For example, for every 1 percent increase in the number of first-generation immigrants from a given country, exports from California go up nearly 0.5 percent (Saxenian 2001, pp. 220–1).

The growing relationship between migration, trade and economic development, especially in the 1990s, was the motivation for the UC (Berkeley) research. Intuition would tell us that this occurs but many countries have been either slow to realise it or have not been able to measure it.

This background provides the content within which this research was undertaken. The next section outlines the research method of the study and the comparative framework.

RESEARCH METHOD

The 1998 United Nations Fund for Population Activities (UNFPA) Technical Symposium in The Hague developed a useful concept which broadened the field of analysis from what had previously been considered the factors influencing return migration. Questions that came to be seen as important were 'Do migrants compare the anticipated "comfort level" in the home country with that in the country of residence as part of the return decision-making process?' and 'Which factors among the whole range of social, psychological and economic factors most affect the decision to return?' (Castles 1999). In order to investigate these and other questions, it was decided to conduct fieldwork amongst potential or intending returnees in Australia as well as in four very different return contexts.

The hypotheses that guided the research are:

1. the 'brain drain' is no longer a major problem for countries as return migration and brain circulation have started to become more significant;
2. the stronger the commitment of migrants to social units in the country of origin (not only in terms of strength of social ties – weak and strong – but also regarding the content – 'reciprocity' and 'solidarity'), the more likely it is that return migration of successful migrants takes place (Faist 1997, p. 214). By 'reciprocity' Faist means an obligation to assist those at home, while 'solidarity' is based on a group identity that refers to a unity of wanting and action;
3. the stronger the economic growth and the more 'globalised' the economy, the greater the rate of return migration as skilled émigrés will not feel that they will drop out of the loop of their profession. For professionals, the borders of their profession may now be global, and to remain globally competitive, they must keep up-to-date and in touch with all new developments. Thus the prospect of dropping out of the loop, by going home to a less dynamic environment, is out of the question; and
4. the role of the government in facilitating return migration is as important as the economic, social and political environment of the country.

Aims of the Project

The aims of this project are to:

- describe return migration to Bangladesh, Mainland China, Taiwan and Vietnam and the factors affecting it;
- discuss the processes of decision-making about return migration;
- investigate the patterns of the return of skilled and business migrants to the four countries/regions in the study;
- investigate the impacts of return migration on the economic and social sectors of the destination regions;
- contribute to understanding of the role of transnational communities on social transformation and development;
- explore decision-making processes amongst potential returnees in Australia and migration-based linkages between Bangladesh/China/Taiwan/ Vietnam and Australia in order to examine the importance of transnational communities for social transformation and the possible flow-on effects of return migration on Australia;
- suggest policy options to optimise the benefit of skilled emigrants for home (especially developing) countries.

There are five participating regions in this study: Australia, Bangladesh, People's Republic of China, Taiwan and Vietnam. The last four are all at different stages of economic development and were chosen to provide a range of scenarios of the role of returning skilled and business migrants. Their samples consisted of people who met the following criteria:

- Return skilled migrants – a person with an overseas degree[3];
- Return business migrants – a person who was already a business person overseas or who was intending to establish a business at home.

Australia was incorporated to complete the picture and provide input as to the decision-making process that returning migrants engage in before they actually return home. 'Return' in the study was defined loosely in that it was either seen as permanent or long term departure from Australia or intermittent returning associated with the establishment of a business or some other activity. Return to visit family members was not included as potential return migration.

The research for this project was funded by the Ford Foundation and carried out under the auspices of the Asia Pacific Migration Research Network (APMRN). This network is a UNESCO-MOST funded body that has linked migration researchers in the Asia Pacific region since 1995. The network facilitates communication between migration researchers and policy makers and promotes in-country and collaborative research projects.

Comparative Fieldwork: Four Case Studies

This was a large project, requiring a comparative approach among four countries/regions (China, Taiwan, Vietnam and Bangladesh). They differ from each other in their level of economic development, as well as in their history, cultural and social norms. The Bangladeshi situation, for example, differs drastically from that of Taiwan in both level of economic development and cultural values. These differences understandably posed problems when the team tried to develop a common questionnaire which was to be administered in each country. In an effort to accommodate different aspects of the four regions, the questionnaire that was finally produced took 20 pages in all and included many open-ended questions. It contained seven parts with 103 open/closed questions regarding the general characteristics of interviewees, return decision-making, migration process, job application, working conditions, family living conditions, return impacts and overall opinions of skilled returned migrants on their return. It took around two to three hours to administer one questionnaire thoroughly and this made it difficult to get potential candidates to agree to be interviewed.

Each of the key researchers in Bangladesh, China, Taiwan and Vietnam was asked to interview a sample of 100 returnees using the common schedule. Individuals were free to add questions and this occurred in most cases. In-depth interviews were also conducted to elaborate on the material collected. Researchers also set out to collate whatever data were available on both the out-migration and return migration of skilled nationals.

Comparative research of this type requires agreement upfront about a common methodology, the use of a common data base for entering statistical infomation, methods of analysing data and processes for writing up both individual and comparative findings. Even though such agreements were generally reached at the beginning of the project, variations in method and other aspects subsequently occurred due to the individual circumstances in countries/regions and the skills and disciplines of key researchers. The method adopted in each of the four case studies is outlined here to assist with a fuller understanding of the nature of the material offered in each of Chapters 3 to 6.

Bangladesh
As an anthropologist from Bangladesh, Dr Santi Rozario anticipated some problems with the methodology, namely doing the research only by questionnaire. She asked: 'Is it possible to get a genuine anthropological understanding of what is going on from this kind of data?' Anticipating problems at the

stage of analysis, she added quite a few open-ended questions. In addition, she and her three research assistants carried out 17 in-depth interviews. In all they conducted 125 interviews, including the in-depth interviews. Ten of the 17 interviewees who gave in-depth interviews did not fill out the questionnaire.

Despite the constraints with the research overall, however, the questionnaires did contain useful information – especially on the problems people faced on their return. These included problems relating directly to work but also problems to do with politics, bureaucracy, security and violence, law and order, pollution etc. Data from 108 questionnaires form the basis of the statistical analysis in Chapter 3 but qualitative material serves to provide a deeper understanding of the processes occurring.

Due to transport problems, traffic jams, difficulties with the telephone system, etc. it took much time and energy on the part of the Bangladeshi team to conduct the interviews. In some cases, it was necessary to leave the questionnaires with the interviewees to complete in their own time and then return to collect and check the unclear items.

The snowballing technique was used to find interviewees. In Bangladesh it is difficult to near impossible to do research by the random sampling method. Given the length of the questionnaire the problem was compounded. A major issue in the Bangladeshi context was the problem of finding genuine 'skilled returned migrants'. The sample obtained was spread over five major industries: government service, research and university, NGOs, business, and the industrial sector. As the minimum qualification of our returnees was bachelor level, they came largely from middle to upper class backgrounds.

Another issue is that only 25 per cent of the sample is female. This is despite the fact that all the researchers were women and they consciously tried to find more women in their sample. It is suggested that this imbalance has nothing to do with the bias of the researchers but reflects the overall gender imbalance in the migration pattern, especially those going overseas for higher education, for business or on temporary work permits. Nevertheless, due to the special interest of the chief researcher, much greater emphasis was placed on the gender aspects of the topic for Bangladesh than the other three studies.

China

Fieldwork in China was carried out by a statistician, Professor Luo Keren, and his staff from the China East Normal University in 2000. Some of the 185 questionnaires were distributed at an office for returning Chinese nationals in Shanghai and were later collected after they had been filled out. Other questionnaires were completed by interviewers in the returnees' work places. The sample was 82 per cent male and the majority (85.6 per cent) were married. It is felt that this gender balance reflects the pattern of returnees in general. The prevailing pattern seems to be that in the case of a married couple, the man returns to China while the wife remains overseas. Few singles seem to be returning. Most people had obtained postgraduate degrees overseas and worked for a few years before returning. This method contrasts with that used in the other three case studies and the analysis relies mostly on quantitative data. These data have been supplemented by qualitative information from interviews with resource and policy people.

Taiwan

Professor Ching-lung Tsay, an economist, and his team from Academia Sinica conducted the fieldwork in Taiwan in 2000. The survey of returnees focused on those working in private enterprises, with an emphasis on the Hsin-chu Industrial Park. A total of 124 interviews were completed and in most cases a copy of the questionnaire was distributed prior to the interview by e-mail.

The questionnaire developed for the project was modified quite considerably. Most of the questions were structured with categorised items for easy choice. The structure and categories were developed and modified in the process of pre-tests with almost 30 cases. It was learned from the pre-tests and some other contacts with potential respondents that unstructured open-ended questions should be avoided as much as possible. It was also clear that interviews with business owners are extremely difficult, if not impossible, and definitely not practical. As employees in the high-tech industries are very busy, it was also advised that the questionnaire must be brief and structured. All these points were taken into consideration in developing the questions and in selecting the cases. The results of the 124 respondents were supplemented by in-depth interviews with the human resources managers of eight high-tech companies.

Vietnam

The survey in Vietnam was carried out by Dr Dang Anh from the Asia-Pacific Economic Center in March–May 2001. One hundred interviews were conducted in the two largest cities, Hanoi and Ho Chi Minh City. The sample was evenly split between women and men (50 men/50 women nationwide and 25 men/25 women in each city). The survey subjects were people who had mainly studied or participated in study trips in foreign countries for a period of at least nine consecutive months and who had returned to Vietnam at least two years before the time of survey. There were very few business people in the sample as most business people go overseas for short periods only. Very few Vietnamese business people have been attracted back to Vietnam from overseas – this will take some time, according to Dang Anh.

The study used the personal interview method and a set of semi-structured questions to collect information. The questionnaire used in Vietnam was similar to that used in Bangladesh and China. The interviews were conducted at the work place or in private houses. Due to careful preparation of the survey and the questionnaire, few difficulties were experienced.

Australian Research

Fieldwork was conducted in Australia in order to understand another part of the dynamic of skilled migration flows. In the case of Australia, emigration data are among the best in the world and both migration and survey data can be used to describe the level of out-migration of skilled Australians and the emigration of former settlers from overseas. Data on non-permanent movements are also improving so that there is now a good picture of the level and composition of temporary short-term and long-term flows. These data will be incorporated in the following chapter on Australia.

A second questionnaire was constructed for Australia, and samples of potential returnees to the four regions in the study were interviewed in Brisbane, Canberra, Melbourne, Sydney and Wollongong from May to September 2000. The method of sampling was basically snowballing and the bilingual interviewers were all members of the communities or had close connections with them. The survey was conducted among those who intended to return to their home countries/regions. Some in-depth interviews were also conducted and documented. Table 2.1 in Chapter 2 shows the number of respondents and interviewers' information. Information collected from potential returnees in Australia included:

- demographic characteristics of potential returnees;
- education and employment profile of potential returnees;
- experiences in Australia that led to their intention to return;
- linkages and influence of migration communities in Australia;
- motivation of return and decision-making process;
- plan and expectation of potential returnees; and
- pattern of economic activity of returnees and links with the Australian economy.

STATISTICAL DATA ANALYSIS

The original intention was to supplement the fieldwork data with analysis of existing macro data sets, but this proved difficult. The adequacy of international migration statistics for either national social analysis or comparisons of international and inter-regional population flows has been considered among statisticians and demographers for well over a century (see Kraly and Gnanasekaran 1987; Bilsborrow *et al.* 1997, pp. 1–8). For many countries, data on international arrivals and departures and on the settlement of immigrants exist as the weakest component of national demographic accounts. National statistical definitions of categories of international migration such as long-term immigration and return migration vary widely. Data on emigration of either nationals or non-nationals are unavailable for many countries. These deficiencies are illustrated in the absence of comprehensive tables on international migration in the United Nations Demographic Yearbook since the 1996 volume. The 1998 volume included two tables, one reporting national statistics on categories of international arrivals and the second on international departures. Countries or territories reported some statistical information, if only for total arrivals or departures, or tourists, for the period 1986–95.

In 1995, Australia reported the arrival of long-term immigrants (253 940), short-term immigrants (21 680), Australian residents returning after short-term residence abroad for work (2 579 840), as well as several categories of visitors arriving. Indonesia reported data on long-term immigrants (218 952); and short-term immigrants (95 640). The Republic of Korea reported data on long-term immigrants (101 612); short-term immigrants (105 653); several categories of visitors and Korean residents returning from work abroad (3 746 927); China reported data on long- and short-term immigrants, visitors and refugees for Hong Kong only. India, Pakistan, Bangladesh and Vietnam reported no statistics on international arrivals (United Nations 1998, Table 36).

For the same year, Australia also reported data on long-term emigrants (149 360); short-term emigrants (72 230); persons departing for types of visits abroad and non-residents leaving after short-term residence in Australia for work (3 676 840). Indonesia reported only long-term emigrants departing (57 096). Korea reported data on long-term emigrants (403 522); short-term emigrants (471 428); persons departing for visits abroad and non-residents departing after short-term residence in Korea for work (3 109 077). China reported data on the departure of visitors from Hong Kong. Again, India, Pakistan, Bangladesh and Vietnam reported no statistics on international departures (United Nations 1998, Table 35).

The United Nations Statistical Commission has developed recommendations for both standard definitions of international migration statistics as well as guidelines for data collection to encourage national statistical offices to collect information on international population movements to and from the country (United Nations 1980a, 1986). The UN Statistical Division has also prepared technical documentation pertaining to the collection of statistical information on the out-migration of trained workers from less developed to more developed countries (United Nations 1980b). The degree to which countries follow statistical definitions that conform to the statistical concepts recommended by the United Nations is not known with any precision. For example, referring to the arrival and departure statistics presented above, it is not possible to know from the documentation provided in the *1996 UN Demographic Yearbook* (United Nations 1998) whether the numbers of Australian and Korean nationals returning from work abroad are defined in the same way and thus are directly comparable. Within specific national contexts, however, there have been attempts to document the feasibility of adapting national statistics on international migration to conform with international statistical definitions (Kelly 1987; Kraly and Warren 1991, 1992; United Nations 1986).

Bilsborrow *et al.* (1997) provide a comprehensive perspective on means by which national systems of international migration statistics might be improved to yield better national planning and analysis with regard to international migration and migrants. They review the advantages and disadvantages of different types of data collection, for example, border control practices, population censuses and surveys, population registers, and administrative sources, for the major categories of international migrants, as well as routes to documenting the numbers and characteristics of specific categories such as labour migrants, asylum seekers and refugees. Bilsborrow *et al.* also developed model questionnaires for the collection of data on international migrants as well as data on non-migrants for purposes of comparison. Guidelines for the design of surveys for the analysis of out-migration are presented as well as specific questionnaire items for the analysis of the characteristics and experience of return migrants (Bilsborrow *et al.* 1997, pp. 250–60, 317–18).

In spite of the UN's efforts, migration data remain patchy and flawed. Except for Australia and Taiwan, there is little incorporation of national data sets and the analysis relies on data collected during fieldwork.

STRUCTURE OF THE BOOK

Chapter 2 analyses the data from 48 in-depth interviews, partially based on a questionnaire, conducted in Australia. This aspect is extremely valuable for understanding how people go about making a decision to return home. It provides a context for the following chapters. It shows that Bangladeshis are mostly returning with an ambivalent attitude. The possibility of good and prestigious jobs, as opposed to the reality for many in Australia, is the overriding factor motivating their return. The Chinese are planning to return to China with an ambition to 'play a big role' in Chinese society. Their return is also affected by 'unsatisfactory future job perspective in Australia', rather than their 'current jobs and positions'. The Taiwanese 'return' home on a much more fluid basis in general. Relatively more people anticipate a transnational or astronaut type of existence where they will spend some time in Taiwan and some time in Australia. The return of the Vietnamese is motivated by the fact that many older people who experienced hardship before leaving the country maintain strong emotional ties with Vietnam and want to return. Young Vietnamese people intending to return are aiming to establish businesses and find better job opportunities.

Chapter 3 provides an overview of the situation in relation to return migration to Bangladesh. The situation in Bangladesh is one of little voluntary return and those who do come home are faced with a socio-economic, environmental and political situation which is not conducive to their making a great input into the economy and society. This contrasts with China, Chapter 4, where the opening up of the economy and the booming rate of economic growth provide a new 'gold mine' for skilled returnees. They are sought after and welcomed, in the new era, and in spite of the political situation they often decide to return to China to benefit from the rapid growth and opportunities.

The Taiwan case, in Chapter 5, represents the peak in terms of the contribution of returnees in Asia, and probably around the world. The level of policy development and the effectiveness of those policies in helping to build transnational communities is quite unique. The survey highlights the fact that returnees make decisions that are both economically and personally motivated and their 'value' to Taiwan has never been in any doubt. Chapter 6 covers Vietnam, which is starting to open up in economic terms. Most returnees in the sample are students returning after overseas study so this puts them at the same point as Taiwan was in the 1950–60s. There is, nevertheless, a great sense of nationalism and commitment to Vietnam and to maintaining family and societal values.

Chapter 7 attempts to present comparative findings across the four case studies. This is a difficult exercise as inconsistency in method and the size of the samples impose limitations. Nevertheless, some clear patterns emerge and these are valuable for pointing to possible trends. Chapter 8 draws together all of the threads and incorporates findings in relation to the four hypotheses. A discussion of theory relating to the 'brain drain' and its reversal is incorporated. Possible national and global policies and strategies for emphasising the returns to countries experiencing the loss of vital skilled human resources are put forward. It will be argued that such policies are essential for ensuring that developing countries are not excluded from the gains or improvements to be achieved through what has become the most crucial element in the 'new growth theory'.

NOTES

1 The authors wish to acknowledge the contribution of Ellen Kraly in the section on Statistical Data.
2 The Concessional Family category was changed to the Skilled Australian-linked category in July 1999.
3 The original intention was to include only graduates with overseas work experience or a postgraduate degree, but during the research, it became apparent that this definition could not be fulfilled under all circumstances, particularly due to conditions imposed upon students.

2. The View from Australia

Fei Guo and Robyn Iredale

BACKGROUND

During the second half of the twentieth century, Australia's post-war immigration programme delivered around 5.7 million migrants. The initial motivations for the programme in the 1940s to 1960s were to increase population and to provide low skilled workers for the industrialisation process. As Moore (1994, p.15) points out, the semi-skilled 'son of toil' was preferred to the overseas educated professional or skilled workers in the labour shortage situation that existed after the Second World War. Highly skilled migrants admitted during this period were mainly displaced persons from northern and eastern Europe. This was the first large non-British group to enter and their entry was conditional on a two-year period of indentured labour after arrival. Kunz (1975, 1988) has documented the fate of many of these skilled non-British professionals once they completed their indenture period and tried to return to their professions. Many experienced discrimination in both employment and skills recognition.

During the 1960s, a shortage of highly skilled personnel developed which could not be filled from Europe, and tertiary qualified Indians, Sri Lankans and other Asians gained entry to Australia on the basis of filling identified needs. The intake of skilled migrants from these sources was the result of 'economic expediency and unforeseen events' as the White Australia Policy still existed, according to Ongley and Pearson (1995, p. 771).

A points system was first introduced in 1979 but the emphasis on English proficiency and narrowly defined occupational skills still favoured migrants from traditional source countries (Ongley and Pearson 1995, p. 772). Skilled migrant selection was restructured a number of times in the mid-1980s to fine tune the selection. The changes reflected both the desire to 'reduce Australia's reliance on overseas workers (which was felt by some to be compromising the domestic training effort)' and 'to maximise the economic benefits of future skilled migration' (Baker *et al.* 1994, p. 8). A number of reviews and reports in the late 1980s led Australia to commit itself to a dramatically enlarged skilled migration intake, to a more generic selection rather than trying to select to meet identified needs, and to the inclusion of many professionals from non-English speaking backgrounds.

During the 1990s, further changes were introduced that had the effect of excluding people from migrating permanently in the Independent and Concessional (now Skilled Family Related) categories unless the principal applicant (or partner) possessed recognised qualifications and experience and high levels of English language proficiency. The aim was to reduce the number of people arriving who would subsequently experience problems with qualifications/skills recognition or employment acquisition. High visa application fees, monetary bonds to cover periods of possible unemployment in the first two years, English language testing requirements and costs have all had the effect of excluding many potential professional immigrants.

STUDIES OF SETTLEMENT AND RETURN MIGRATION IN AUSTRALIA AND OTHER COUNTRIES

Since the immigration programme emphasised permanent settlement, immigrants' adjustment after their arrival is seen as an important issue. Studies of immigrant adjustment, especially in terms of participation in the labour market, have become a major component of immigration studies in Australia (Khoo and Mak 2000 p. 1). Immigrants who do not adjust are likely to return to their home country, representing a loss of their human capital to Australia after its 'investment in their recruitment and selection' (Khoo and Mak 2000). The view that return migration represents a loss of human capital and a waste of migration administration funds still pertains but there has been increasing recognition that return migration may actually bring benefits to Australia. However, there have been few studies that have been able to explain or quantify the gains. Four groups of potential returnees to the regions in the study were interviewed in Brisbane, Canberra, Melbourne, Sydney and Wollongong. Table 2.1 shows the number of respondents and locations.

Table 2.1 Respondents and interviews

Group	No of respondents	City where interviews conducted
Bangladeshi	13	Sydney, Canberra
Chinese	10	Canberra, Sydney, Melbourne
Taiwanese	15	Brisbane
Vietnamese	10	Sydney, Wollongong

The data were analysed by Fei Guo (Chinese and Vietnamese) and Robyn Iredale (Bangladeshi and Taiwanese). The analysis was circulated to the other interviewers, where applicable, to check the accuracy of the description and to add to the depth of the analysis by gaining more qualitative comments, given their in depth knowledge of the communities.

DESCRIPTION OF THE SAMPLES

As Table 2.2 shows, the Bangladeshi sample has a narrow age range, from 33 to 45, and consists mostly of married respondents. There is only one single person and all but one married interviewee have (generally two) children. Most interviewees arrived in Australia in the 1990s and ten have obtained Australian citizenship while the remaining three are permanent residents.

Table 2.2 Basic characteristics of respondents

Country	Age		Gender		Marital status		Year of arrival			Total
	Range	Average	F	M	Single	Married	Before '90	91–95	96–00	
Bangladesh	33–45	38	5	8	1	12	1	5	7	13
China	33–49	38	2	8	1	9	1	5	4	10
Taiwan	23–62	37	7	8	6	9	11	3	1	15
Vietnam	24–60	44	4	6	2	8	10	0	0	10

The Chinese sample consists of ten middle aged people, ranging from 33 to 49. All of them are in professional occupations, with an advanced degree (at least a Master's). All but one is married with one child. The sample includes eight males and two females. All but one arrived in Australia in the 1990s. Most of them came to Australia as either students or post-doctoral researchers. Among the ten Chinese, four have obtained Australian citizenship, five have permanent resident status and one is on an academic research visitor's visa.

The Taiwanese sample has a wider age range, from 23–62, and consists of a more diverse group from the point of view of marital status. There are six singles/separated and nine married interviewees. Most families consist of one or two children. Most interviewees arrived in Australia in the late 1980s and 100 per cent have achieved Australian citizenship.

The Vietnamese sample of ten people is aged from 24 – 60. Three of them are business owners, and the rest are in professional occupations. The sample includes six males and four females. All but one arrived in Australia as refugees around the late 1970s and early 1980s when the country was experiencing dramatic political transition to the Communist regime. Among the ten Vietnamese, two are singles and eight are married with two or three children. All ten people have obtained Australian citizenship.

REASONS FOR COMING TO AUSTRALIA

Reasons for coming to Australia among the four groups of respondents reflect different national and international factors. The dramatic political change in 1975 was the most important reason for many Vietnamese fleeing Vietnam to avoid political oppression. Australian migration policies in recent decades that aim to attract skilled migrants have provided opportunities for many skilled and business people from Bangladesh, China and Taiwan to move to Australia.

Bangladeshis in the sample came to Australia in the hope of finding better employment, better education and a safer living environment. Clearly the level of poverty in Bangladesh and the lack of opportunities for gaining a satisfying/adequately paid job are strong motivations. Families were looking for a better future for themselves and their children. The insecure lifestyle, low wages, high level of pollution and 'bad bureaucracy and administration' are all posited as problems in the home country and as posing potential problems for possible returnees.

The Chinese are new arrivals compared with the other three groups. Most Chinese in the sample arrived in Australia in the 1990s as students or researchers. The reason for coming to Australia for the Chinese in the sample was primarily to study or conduct research. The arrival of large numbers of Chinese students in the late 1980s and later partially resulted from the rapid expansion of the private education sector in Australia. We found that many Chinese students who arrived in Australia in the late 1980s tend to want to stay in Australia but those who arrived in Australia at a later stage (1990s) intend to return to China.

The Taiwanese migrated to Australia for reasons associated mostly with a desire for better education for their children and for a better living environment. The Taiwanese did not mention the same level of insecurity about their homeland as Bangladeshis but they were clearly looking for a more open, less congested living space.

Unlike the other three groups, all the Vietnamese in the sample came to Australia as refugees in the late 1970s and early 1980s. Some of them stayed in refugee camps in Malaysia and Hong Kong for a brief period of time, and then were given the choice of coming to Australia. Most older Vietnamese expressed the view that they experienced political uncertainty after the transition of Vietnam to communism and left Vietnam to avoid political oppression. The younger ones moved to Australia with their families or relatives. The two youngest respondents came to Australia as small children and their memories of Vietnam are not strong.

EMPLOYMENT OUTCOMES AND EXPERIENCES IN AUSTRALIA

The survey included information on pre-migration occupation and current occupation. Pre-migration occupations are expected to affect people's after-migration occupation, which in turn may have effects on their decision to return or stay later on. In this study, the employment/occupation patterns are examined to help understand people's motivations for returning and their linkages with home countries, as well as potential impacts on Australia.

The Bangladeshis in the sample held a range of professional positions before migration including three medical practitioners, three researchers and academics, and others. Their current occupational profile indicates a high level of downward social mobility with only three or four people attaining an equivalent level to their pre-migration position. Only one general medical practitioner is practising in Australia and the remaining two are unemployed or have re-qualified (as an epidemiologist). An IT consultant is now working as a computer programmer and a former seafarer has become a shipping administrator. Overall, the profile is negative but this may partly be a function of the recency of arrival of the group as a whole. But even after five years, an agricultural professor with a Ph.D. from the United Kingdom had not been able to find work in Australia. When asked would he keep up with his Bangladeshi contacts in Australia after he returned home he said 'not really, as most of my friends are in similar situations and are now working as labourers in factories'. No Bangladeshis in the sample are involved in family or small businesses which is in contrast to the other groups.

The Chinese in the sample show an interesting employment pattern. It appears that the Chinese sample has over sampled higher degree holders, especially Ph.D. holders. However, what we have found from fieldwork is that those who came to Australia under other categories, such as students (for language schools, etc.) or as family members, tend not to return to China and they are more likely to stay in Australia. Those who possess higher qualifications and experiences in both countries intend to return to China. All the Chinese in the sample held professional positions before migrating to Australia, either as university lecturers, researchers, or editors. Most of them have been able to work in similar occupations in Australia. Seven people gained Australian qualification, two people gained an advanced degree from China and one in the US. All but two people are employed in the public sector as researchers or university lecturers. Although the Chinese are largely known for their entrepreneurial ability, no Chinese in the sample are involved in small and family business. Only one person, the IT firm project manager, expressed an intention to set up his own firm once he returns to China. Almost all people in the sample claimed that they are not satisfied with their current jobs because the possibility of advancing their career in Australia is slim, and they are unable to play any important role, or 'big role' in their own words, in their institutions. It is not their current job or position that encourages them to return to China, but their expectation of better career advancement in China.

The Taiwanese experience has been more positive than that of the Bangladeshis. One person who had his own business in Taiwan retired to Australia while another has maintained his business in Taiwan on an 'astronaut' basis. Nine people have gained Australian university qualifications at either the undergraduate or graduate level since their arrival and this has given them an advantage in terms of being able to qualify for the Australian labour market. On the whole, they were younger on arrival as indicated by the fact that six were students before coming to Australia.

The employment pattern of the Vietnamese in the sample is quite different from the other three groups. All the Vietnamese in the sample came to Australia as refugees. Before migrating, the older people (40 and above) worked as either businessmen, army officers, or social workers under the old government, and the younger ones were associated with the old government through their family ties. Among the older group, three small business owners are doing very well in Australia and have expanded their business by setting up factories in Vietnam. Those who came to Australia as young school or pre-school age children have obtained qualifications in Australia. Three have Bachelor's degrees (IT and English) and one has a Master's degree (Accounting). All but three Vietnamese in the sample are employed in the private sector. Two social workers are employed with Vietnamese communities in New South Wales.

LINKS WITH HOME COUNTRY

The survey was conducted among those who intend to return to their home countries/regions. The questionnaire included various questions, such as number of visits in the past two years, information about home countries/ regions and awareness of governments' intensive programmes and policies through which people's links with their countries/regions can be understood.

Bangladeshis have kept up strong links with their home country. Most interviewees have been home at least once since arriving in Australia. Many visit once a year and keep in touch with events at home via newspapers and personal communication. Some return remittances but on the whole this is not a common feature. Friends and family are ambivalent about the intentions of the 'returnees' indicating that for many there is a feeling of being torn between what is best for their career and what is best for their family. Nobody knew of any specific programmes/ policies to encourage skilled emigrants to return.

The Chinese in the sample also kept close links with their home country. All but two people have visited China at least once in the past two years; about half have visited once a year and one has visited China three times a year. All respondents claimed that they have been following up what is happening in China through various forms of media and through communications with friends and relatives. Most people claimed that they have gathered up-to-date information on their recent trips to China which confirms the idea of returning. One person received a high profile job offer when he visited a city in southern China. It is clear that people's intention of returning was strongly related to their up-to-date information and knowledge about China. Only two people had not visited China in the past two years but they all follow what's happening in China, especially in their previous work units. It has been widely reported that the Chinese government has implemented a series of regulations and policies to attract overseas scholars, business persons and foreign investment (*Shenzhou Xueren* 1999; *Xinhua News Agency* 1999).

The notable programmes for attracting business investments include 'science park' projects in a number of Chinese cities and 'special development zone' projects around the country. Some high profile programmes aiming to attract overseas scholars include 'Chang Jiang Scholars Project' in the higher education sector and 'Hundred Scholars Project' within the Academies of Sciences and Social Sciences. However, from the information we gathered in the survey, people in the sample were not very enthusiastic about responding to the government promoted programmes. Although most of them are aware of the government programmes, they don't think the programmes are directly relevant to their own situations.

The Taiwanese had maintained regular contact, ten through regular visits, but also by means of newspapers, etc. Friends and family are unanimous in their support for the intended 'return' of the respondents indicating a generally positive view about life in Taiwan. No government programmes for encouraging the return of skilled emigrants were known about. Many Taiwanese have family members and close relatives in Taiwan, some of them have family businesses in Taiwan. It is clear that close ties with family members and relatives in Taiwan have played an important role in their decision-making. One import/export manager in Brisbane has planned to return to Taiwan to help his father's business, and he hopes 'to bring to his business a better organisational and management structure, and to help the company develop a marketing plan as well'.

The Vietnamese in the sample have kept some contacts with their home country. Many Vietnamese left the country as refugees with their whole family and relatives, and many of their relatives and family members are also living in western countries, including the US, France and Australia. Most people claim that they have followed what's happening in Vietnam through media and friends and relatives. Except for two business people in the sample, all others have visited Vietnam at least once in the past two years. It seems that their visits only happened in recent years and some have only been back twice since they left the country in the late 1970s. Older people maintain strong emotional ties with Vietnam and some of them are planning to live in Vietnam after their retirement. 'Going home' and 'my country' are the most frequently mentioned phrases by the older Vietnamese when asked why they want to return. For younger people, getting a good job, having a cultural experience and expanding current businesses are the main motivations for visiting Vietnam. Their emotional ties with Vietnam are not as strong as those of their parents' generation.

RETURN INTENTIONS AND EXPERIENCES

Bangladeshis

Nine Bangladeshis intended to return home in 2000 or 2001. Four were planning to return because of their unsatisfactory occupational situation in Australia; they had been employed as a school teacher, agricultural researchers and academics before coming to Australia. 'Difficulty getting a good job', 'no job' or 'no good job' were provided as explanations for going back to Bangladesh. However, there was no firm commitment to the length of stay in Bangladesh among most of these people. They intended to see what happened and perhaps move to a third country (such as the US) at a later date or send their children back to Australia for their education. Three had gained some career benefit from being in Australia, including general education and experience and one had undertaken a Technical and Further Education (TAFE) IT course which would benefit his research work.

The school teacher had not been able to get an appropriate job after five years in Sydney and the completion of a child care course. She is married with three children and wants to return temporarily to Bangladesh to 'get a job, be socially accepted again and put children back into school routine'. The agricultural researcher is unemployed and says it is easier to get a job in Bangladesh but would return to Australia if he could get a good job. Despite the fact that he is unemployed he sees his time in Australia as being of benefit in helping to develop research to 'assist poor farmers in Bangladesh'. A former Agricultural Director has been employed for two years as a process worker in Sydney but wants to return to the IT sector which 'has lots of new developments'. A very good job will be easy to get and culturally it will be easier. As for Australia, he said that 'high status is not here'.

Five others were returning with a more positive motivation in that they saw opportunities to assist with Bangladesh's economic and social development. One person who intends to work in the manufacturing sector to advance Bangladesh's industrial development and international trade has been employed as an executive manager in Australia. He intends to develop strategic alliances with Australian and international universities and promote a 'trade bridge' between Australia and Bangladesh. He said that 'Australia's entrepreneurial culture is somewhat lagging behind the US and this is a barrier to implementation of my knowledge and skill'.

One person, formerly an IT consultant in Bangladesh, intends to reintegrate into the IT sector. He applied for immigration to Australia and was selected and so 'I took a chance to explore the Australian work market'. However, he was 'not satisfied professionally' in Australia and did not see his time in Australia as being beneficial to the software business (partnership with a Bangladeshi) that he is planning to establish in Dhaka. He was 'always inclined to go back but was definitely influenced by a six week visit last year' in which he saw opportunities and approached a firm about forming a partnership. However, his US education (Bachelor's degree) and experience are valuable and 'the transfer of new technologies and IT knowledge could contribute to Bangladeshi computer institutions'. He wants to work in the private sector as he said that the 'Bangladesh Government has been talking about software exports but so far nothing has been done'. He plans to maintain his business links with people in Australia as part of the development of his software exports business.

A man who had been an architect in Bangladesh and has been working as a programme officer in the public service in Canberra plans to return with his wife, who is also an architect, to establish an architectural firm in Dhaka. 'I always wanted to return but the last visit was important' as 'I saw that there are lucrative business opportunities'. The couple plan to use the savings from 12 years of working in Australia and they feel that their time in Australia will also benefit their business in other ways. 'Better communication skills and cultural knowledge will help' and [non-Bangladeshi] 'education degrees will encourage people to trust me more and do business with me'. In response to a question about how their cultural understanding of Australian society would be an advantage to career development at home, the response was 'I have learned to be tolerant. The experience of western society will help me to be creative and more skilled in business dealings'. But the respondent is cautious about 'corruption at every level and dishonesty in the bureaucracy may be a problem'. Even though they are planning to return to Bangladesh permanently he is not sure 'how my children (now four and 11) will feel later on'.

An epidemiologist who is accompanying her husband, a diplomat, back home has achieved her Ph.D. in Australia and says that 'a foreign degree is always useful and will help me to get a good job. My research experience will be very useful'. She has mixed feelings about returning but says that she 'wants to work for Bangladesh'.

Another man who has been working as a development programme officer in the federal government is finally returning home after nine years in Australia on his own. His wife (a university lecturer) and two children remained in Bangladesh when he came in 1991 as they 'did not want to join' him in Australia. He returned home twice yearly but never looked seriously for a job there till 1999. He was interviewed in 2000 and has now received a job offer as head of a USAID funded project in Bangladesh. He is clearly reluctant to leave his job in Canberra and the environment in Australia but hopes that 'seeing the immediate family will compensate'. His time spent in Australia has not led to significant savings and he 'hasn't mixed with Australians' but his contacts 'may help in fund-raising programmes' and his work experience has 'contributed to his outlook and knowledge'. However, he is not looking forward to 'settling down in that very crammed and polluted environment'.

Chinese

Although all Chinese in the sample expressed their intentions of return to China in the near future, only two have a definite schedule for returning. Both of them were offered jobs in China, and planned to return before the end of 2000. In spite of a strong intention to return, eight Chinese are unable to decide when to return. The overall impression gained was that most Chinese were not very sure what exactly they would do after their return, but they had high expectations about the return.

Although all Chinese in the sample work in professional occupations, some in highly regarded research institutes in Australia, many were not fully satisfied with their future job prospects. Two post-doctoral researchers in Canberra felt that although they are satisfied with their current jobs and positions, they think they would not be able to have a promising future here in their research institute. In other words, they felt that it would be very hard, if not impossible, for them to climb to the upper level of the academic ladder or to 'play a big role' in Australia. 'Being able to play a big role' in Chinese research institutes is one important expectation for their return.

All people except one claimed that what they learned or experienced in Australia and other western countries would benefit their career advancement in China. This is particularly true for researchers. They learn research processes, grant application writing and research management in the West which will help them maintain international standards in scientific research. One claimed that what he learned in Australia was not very important for his career advancement once he returned to China, because he thought China was in a leading position in that area.

One researcher with a Ph.D. in Biology from a European country moved to Australia in 1994. He has been doing research as a post-doctoral fellow in the past four years. He has gradually become dissatisfied with his job in Australia, and has decided to return to China before he reaches 45-years-old. He says:

> When we (Chinese researchers in Australia) were young and just got our Ph.D., we were willing to play a role as research associates in projects. We are willing to do others' projects. Gradually when you see people around you all have chance to get promotion, get permanent positions, or get their own projects, you would feel frustrated. In Australia, we work harder than anyone else, but the reward is not good enough. We hardly got promoted in a research institute, and bosses take credit of the work we do.

Although his planned return to China would happen in a few years, he holds a high expectation about the return:

> I expect a much better working environment in a Chinese research institute. What I mean by the 'environment' here is people environment. I would be able to play a big role in an institute in China. Ideally I would be able to lead a project in one of the research institutes in the Academy of Sciences with my own lab. I am sure I would be much happier there.

This researcher visited China once in the last two years. He spent one month and visited a number of research institutes. The information he obtained from his trip to China has helped him to make a decision about returning in the future.

A female university associate lecturer who has just completed her Ph.D. in Australia planned to return to China to advance her career in the media. She worked at a TV station before coming to Australia in 1987 and she majored in communication and cultural studies in Australia. Her ambition is to run her own TV programmes, introducing either Chinese folk cultures or western cultures. She was very enthusiastic about her planned return, in spite of possible objections from her Australian boyfriend.

For the two people who already had job offers in China, return to China is exciting and full of hope. Both were offered well-paid jobs. A university lecturer got a job offer in a high profile and dynamic electronic and IT company on his recent trip to China. He was offered a position as a Managing Engineer in the company's newly established IT department. For him, the new position is not only a challenge, but also a significant reward and recognition of his innovative research in the IT industry in the past years. In many other people's eyes, he has been very successful, having a Ph.D. in electronic engineering, having worked in some highly regarded research institutes in US and Canada for some period of time and having just been promoted to senior lecturer. But he often felt that his current job did not have enough challenge for him. In his words:

> If I stay in Australia, my future is too predictable. I am pretty sure what I would be doing in five years, ten years, and until I retire. I would not face any big challenges and uncertainties in my life. Now I have decided to accept this job offer in China. I know I will shoulder a lot of responsibilities and face a lot of uncertainties. But I also know I will have a lot of opportunities. I couldn't predict what exactly I would be doing in five years or ten years, but the uncertainties would also give me many opportunities. That's what I want for my future.

His high expectations have made him take risks and challenges in China. When he was asked whether his decision was made based on the calculation of income difference between his current and new jobs, he was certain that although his income in China would be much higher, he was not entirely driven by the economic gain. 'The challenges and unpredictability in China are the main driven forces'.

Almost all people in the sample were aware of the Chinese government incentive programmes that aim to attract overseas scholars and businesses, but none of them intended to respond to the programme. None of the ten people in the sample plan to set up a business in China in the foreseeable future, so the programmes for attracting investment and setting up business in one of the 'science parks' were not directly relevant to these people. The other programmes aimed at attracting overseas scholars were too high to reach for many scholars. The 'Hundred Scholars Project' and the 'Chang Jiang Scholars Programme' target established scholars who have already reached leading academic positions overseas. None of the researchers in the sample showed a strong interest in these programmes as they thought it would be unrealistic to aim for these programmes at this stage. However, the improved atmosphere in China has encouraged people to consider returning to seek better opportunities and career options.

It seems that potential Chinese returnees are those who were educated in the West, have worked in Australia in a professional occupation for a considerable period of time and are not fully satisfied with their future career prospects in Australia. Knowing it would be hard to play a big role in the future in Australia, they have to consider other options, and returning to China is one of their options.

Taiwanese

The Taiwanese were much more optimistic about their economic and business prospects on return and generally had the widespread support of family and friends. One businessman, who had been operating on an 'astronaut' basis, was returning home more permanently due to a marriage breakdown. Five others were returning with savings from Australia to invest in various types of businesses, including trading companies and English language training institutions.

One man who had been running a sales/retail operation in Australia was returning to establish a private English tutoring business in Taiwan. Even though he had acquired an Australian Ph.D., he had clearly been unable to gain an appropriate job in Australia and saw better business opportunities in Taiwan. He anticipated setting up a school where students could learn English in a social rather than 'bookish' way and where his knowledge of Australian culture would provide an added advantage in teaching about Western culture. This person was quite pragmatic and said that if the business was not successful in two years he would return with his wife to Australia and 'find another business to run'.

Three other people involved in importing and exporting were returning with quite specific plans. One man was going to restructure his father's trading business that suffers from 'bad management and poor marketing'. He feels that he 'owes his father everything' and his Australian qualification will enable him to 'gain respect and credibility'. Once the business was back on track he would return to Australia to live with his Polish fiancee who does not want to live in Taiwan. He sees himself returning intermittently to maintain the business in Taiwan. The second person was going home to start a branch office in Taiwan and establish a trade consulting firm for both Taiwanese and Australian clients. 'My knowledge and familiarity with both Australian and Taiwanese markets will enable me to offer my clients advice as to how to crack both markets'. She plans to leave her grown-up children in Australia and eventually retire in Australia if she has enough financial security. The other person plans to set up a business for trading with China.

The fifth person with business intentions, plans to diversify from a retail business in Australia and establish a Western style coffee shop chain and go into partnership running a business that manufactures light fittings in Taipei. The good business opportunities in Taiwan and the relatively small impact of the Asian financial crisis have become evident to him in recent trips. Young people in Taiwan want to try new things and 'I think they'll like an Australian/ European style café rather than an American one'. He plans to retire to Australia.

Others saw much better prospects in the labour market than they have been able to find in Australia. One young woman, who has been working for four years as a bank teller in Australia, had been offered a job as the editor of an English magazine in Taipei. She said 'I anticipate better career opportunities in Taiwan. Working as a bank teller is a dead end job…I don't think an opportunity like this would arise for me in Australia. My better understanding of the English language and its cultural context will enable me to ascertain whether translations are accurate or not'. She was also returning because she felt some pressure to marry and 'there are very few Taiwanese men of my age around to choose from [here]'.

Another 36-year-old man with an Australian Ph.D. said 'I'm disappointed I haven't been able to find a position in Australia, but I'm also happy to resume my old position. I think I'll do a better job now I have been exposed to different teaching methods'. A 40-year-old female social worker with a Ph.D. from Australia has been offered a job managing a home for elderly Chinese women in Taiwan. She stated:

> My Ph.D. dissertation was on elderly Taiwanese immigrants to Australia, so I feel I have some understanding of the needs of elderly Taiwanese. My degree will bring the home a good reputation also. …It's an opportunity I can't refuse because I could never find a position with comparable responsibilities in Australia. It will give me enormous job satisfaction because it's an opportunity to put my learning to the test. Even if I don't like my new job after all, I [may well] stay in Taiwan given the more promising career opportunities.

One retired couple in their sixties were returning to Taiwan as their three daughters had all returned to Taiwan for marriage and their son chose to return to pursue his career in telecommunications. Being close to their children and better health treatment, including Chinese herbal medicine and home care, were important factors in their decision to return. Also 'I have properties and assets in Taiwan which enable me to live comfortably'. Nevertheless, they stated that it seemed like 'a real waste' to leave Australia permanently, after ten years.

Vietnamese

Expectations of return for older Vietnamese are quite different from those of the younger ones. People older than 50 experienced dramatic political changes in Vietnam in the mid-1970s. One 57-year-old man was an army officer in the old government, and another professional builder was trained by an American technical school in the early 1970s. Almost all older Vietnamese in the sample spent years in education camps after the new government assumed power. They went through a great deal of hardship before fleeing the country to avoid further political oppression.

In spite of the unpleasant or even tragic personal experiences that they had had in Vietnam in the past, all of them expressed a strong emotional attachment to the country of their birth. One health worker and one office worker, both in their late fifties, were planning to live in Vietnam for good after they retired. One female health worker talked about her motivation for returning in a very emotional way, with tears in her eyes:

> I have a motherland to remember. I think about my country all the time. I have been missing my country a lot in the past years. Some of my family members and relatives have gone back. My aunt went back, and she got her Vietnamese citizenship back. My brothers (in US and France) are thinking to go back. They expect to have a better life in Vietnam with their families together. My husband and I are also planning to go back. We will live in our ancestor's house in a village.

None of their children will go back to Vietnam with them. When asked why she would want to separate from her children, she answered:

> In this country, you live your life. Your children live their own life. You can not expect that one day when you are old your children will look after you. Everyone is busy here. In Vietnam, family members look after each other all the time. If you are sick, they stay with you all day, or several days, until you are OK. You would never expect this could happen in Australia. This is the reason why we want to return to my country.

The health worker has been working in a community health centre for 20 years in Australia. She plans to establish a training programme on reproductive health for village women once she returns to Vietnam. She intends to apply what she has learned and practised in Australia in Vietnam, providing training for poor Vietnamese village women who otherwise do not have adequate knowledge and access to public health services.

One building company owner has set up three factories in Vietnam and has frequently travelled between Vietnam and Australia in the past eight years. He has always had strong feelings towards 'that side (Vietnam)'. In the late 1980s, when Vietnam just started opening up, he visited the country with an Australian official delegation. He also observed what had happened in China in the late 1980s and early 1990s, and has confidence that Vietnam will change one day. Once he had established a good connection with local Vietnamese partners, he went to Vietnam and set up his building business. He is proud of what he did in the early 1990s when very few people were able to see the opportunities in Vietnam. He described his motivation for returning to Vietnam in the following statement:

> I have strong motivation, and I belong to that side (Vietnam). I understand the potential market in there. We (Vietnamese in the West) are the people who know Vietnam and also know western system. We have advantages and social knowledge to do business in Vietnam. But I also know some people who went back with great ideas, but couldn't establish well in Vietnam, and they had to return back to Australia.

Before his return to Vietnam in the early 1990s, he observed the Vietnamese social and political changes very closely. He also visited China to confirm his idea of doing business in Vietnam. He 'saw Vietnam's future in China'. For this building company owner, returning to Vietnam has allowed him to realise two dreams, being in Vietnam where he thinks he belongs, and establishing a profitable business at the same time.

For younger Vietnamese, the memory of the country of their birth was unclear. Although some of them also have strong emotional ties with Vietnam, they don't consider that they 'belong to Vietnam'. They claimed that culturally they were Australians, and ethnically they were Vietnamese. Young Vietnamese intend to return to Vietnam mainly to look for better business opportunities.

One IT firm partner and managing director has expanded his business in Vietnam. The two IT firms in Vietnam are an integral part of his Australian IT business. He travels frequently between the two countries and expects further business expansion in the future. In the very beginning, setting up a company in Vietnam was to help some of his family members who were still in the country. He didn't have a very high expectation when he started in 1993 but he gradually found that his business in Vietnam was expanding rapidly. By that time, the family reasons became less important. He then decided to extend his current IT business in Australia on a larger scale in Vietnam.

Another young accountant also shares the same ambition. She left the country when she was a baby and settled in a European country for a number of years before coming to Australia in 1990. She plans to set up an accounting firm in Vietnam once she has enough capital and experience in Australia. She expressed her concern about the current accounting system in Vietnam as it is not comparable with the international system. It would be very hard for foreign investors to do business in Vietnam as there is not a sufficient international accounting service available. Her ambition is to set up her own accounting firm, and ideally establish an accounting college later on.

FUTURE ANTICIPATED PROBLEMS AND PROSPECTS

Bangladesh

The anticipated problems or negative aspects of returning to Bangladesh can broadly be categorised into two categories: administrative/government aspects and quality of life. The inefficiency, corruption, nepotism and lack of good governance are all difficult for people to deal with, but especially for people who have lived and worked in a system which is more open and where there are legal systems to cover most operations. The large extralegal sector in Bangladesh, as in many developing and ex-communist countries, makes for an environment where bribes, protection rackets and corruption are commonplace.

The quality of life in cities such as Dhaka is problematic. Overcrowding, traffic congestion, pollution, crime and lack of tolerance are all features of large rapidly developing cities where the development of infrastructure and institutions has not kept pace with numbers. Internal migration, as well as natural increase, have led to urban problems that must be addressed.

Four Bangladeshis interviewed had decided to remain in Australia permanently, or at least for some time yet, or until retirement. The reason for these interviews was to try to gain a better understanding of the factors influencing decisions to return. Three people sent remittances home to their families to be used for education, aged care and daily household goods. The fourth was unable to send money because of his unemployment and the high cost of living in Australia.

One medical practitioner who was working in Australia in her profession has decided to stay as she has 'got a better job and more money, even though it is very stressful'. She does not intend to return home but thinks that the factors that could induce professionals to return would be 'good social infrastructure, secure life and good money in job'. She has her family's support in staying in Australia and she wants to 'buy a house and send her children to a good school'.

Another medical practitioner who arrived in 1995 has been able to get her Bangladeshi qualifications recognised but is unemployed and 'does not have enough money to go back'. But 'once my children have completed their Higher School Certificate (HSC) and enrolled in university then I will have done my duty as a parent. Then I can go back to Bangladesh to retire'. She is not able to assist her family at home financially but they 'all respect me as they also get higher status'. In order to attract professionals back to Bangladesh she felt that the government and NGOs should ensure greater security and better administration in government departments.

China

All the Chinese in the sample were well aware of the potential problems they would face if they returned to China. Most people didn't complain about lower living standards, as they know they would be able to have a relatively comfortable life in China if they could earn enough income. However, almost all people expressed their deep concern about the structure and social infrastructure. While they appreciate what the government has been doing in trying to attract more overseas people by offering impressive packages and benefits, they still think that the government should improve social infrastructure, such as grant application procedures, promotion and personnel systems and academic freedom. It's clear that those who intend to return to China are those who possess high credentials, extensive experience in the West and who want to 'play big roles' in their areas. Their concerns are primarily related to their career expectations.

However, it is interesting to see that only two people intended to return to China on a permanent basis. All the other eight people planned to return on a temporary basis or move intermittently between the two countries. For seven married men in the sample, none of their wives were very supportive, some were neutral and some were against their idea of returning. If they returned to China they would return alone, leaving their families in Australia. Only one man claimed that he would be able to convince his wife to return with him. All others had to admit that they would wait and see. It's clear that family separation would be the most significant problem for many people who were planning to return or who had already returned to China. When one interviewee was asked why his wife was unwilling to return, he answered 'she is concerned by my son's education in China'. Strong competition and too much homework in many Chinese schools have discouraged many parents, especially mothers, from returning to China if their children are still of school age.

Taiwan

Economic factors, especially better opportunities for employment and business, and social support networks were strong motivating factors for all potential Taiwanese returnees. But many saw returning as yet another temporary move and anticipated retiring or returning regularly to Australia. The anticipated problems were less substantial than for the Bangladeshi sample and were mostly associated with the less attractive living environment, pollution, overcrowding and the higher cost of living. The faster pace of life and longer working hours were also seen as potential problems after living in Australia. The impact of the education system where 'too much memorisation and competition find emphasis, even in primary school' was also acknowledged as a potential problem. Generally, exposure to the more relaxed, liberal lifestyle of Australia and to the Australian education system was highly valued.

There was a sense of optimism and excitement for most about the positive nature of what they were doing. Numerous comments were made about the good business environment and about being able to utilise the skills that had been acquired in Australia. The sense that they would be highly valued on their return was strong, together with the fact that they would be able to carry communication, cultural and other skills to their life back in Taiwan. They saw themselves as conveyers of new and different attitudes but they were sometimes anxious about being able to transport these back home. One young woman expressed the fear that 'I am not sure if I'll get along with other teaching staff' and that she may perhaps not be able to exert the type of independence that she has had in Australia.

Those who were leaving children or aged parents behind in Australia were concerned about this separation. One person acknowledged this and said 'My younger daughter will probably feel a bit lonely as she's very attached to me, but she can always visit and we can talk on the phone'. She intended to work part-time in Taiwan and said 'I'll be able to take time off to be with my spouse: my children are old enough to look after themselves'.

Vietnam

The Vietnamese in the sample are most concerned about the current social and political system. Although they have a strong hope that the country will be heading towards a market-oriented economic system, they are concerned by the uncertainties in its political system. A number of people in the sample felt uncomfortable when they were asked to participate in the project, mainly being afraid that information disclosure would bring some trouble for them. For those who had decided to return to Vietnam to live after retirement, the social problems were less concerning, as they were able to re-adjust to society. The younger Vietnamese, especially those who were planning to seek business opportunities in the country, were deeply concerned by a number of social problems, such as corruption and inefficiency in all aspects of the society.

OVERALL PERSPECTIVE OF FACTORS ENCOURAGING 'RETURN' TO HOME COUNTRIES

Bangladeshis were returning with an ambivalent attitude, even those who were returning with a positive outlook. The possibility of good and prestigious jobs, as opposed to the reality for many in Australia, was the overriding factor motivating their return. The downward occupational mobility that most had experienced in Australia eventually led to the decision to take their skills back home where they could be utilised. The survey did not ask questions about health and family issues, but according to key informants, the Bangladeshi community in Australia experiences a significant level of health and social problems due to loss of status. Most people tolerate this for some time but eventually must decide between their own long-term career opportunities and the opportunities for their children. Clearly, people who were single were in an easier position in regard to returning home but most in the sample were married, making the choice more complex.

The Chinese were planning to return to China with an ambition to 'play a big role' in Chinese society. Their planned return was motivated by seeking better opportunities to advance their career in China. Their return was also affected by 'unsatisfactory future job perspective in Australia', and their 'current jobs and positions'. For some, unpredictability means 'unlimited potential' in China. For others, return to China is a 'have to' option, as other options, such as staying in Australia, do not hold much promise for the future. Most Chinese in the sample admitted that what they learned and experienced in western countries, including Australia, would benefit their future career development and they would utilise their knowledge and understanding of Western culture in their future jobs. It is understood that although the Chinese government's incentive programmes do not have a direct impact on people's decision-making, people do receive the signal from the government that the social environment and policies in China have been improving.

The Taiwanese were planning to 'return' home on a much more fluid basis. More people anticipated a transnational or 'astronaut' type of existence where they spent some time in Taiwan and some time in Australia. The establishment of a Taiwanese diaspora in Australia in the last 20 years would enable people to retain a foot in both camps, and some will act as a bridge between the economic acitivities of the two communities and other countries/regions. The impression is that families primarily made the move to Australia for the sake of their children. Now that they have given them an alternative base they are free to return home to pursue their own interests, be they retirement, a business, some other type of work or less work.

The return of the Vietnamese is self-motivated. The older generation, who experienced hardship before leaving the country, maintain strong emotional ties with Vietnam and for them return is 'going home'. It is expected that improved living conditions would encourage more people to return to Vietnam in the near future. Younger Vietnamese people intended to return to Vietnam with the ambition of establishing their own business and better job opportunities. Their emotional ties with Vietnam are not as strong as their parents'. Vietnam to them is not simply a 'motherland' but a dynamic market with great potential.

CONCLUSION

This chapter provides a background for the following four chapters. It shows the complexity of the situation and the decision-making processes that most people go through. Decisions are not clear-cut and are made after weighing up many different factors. The potential personal, social and economic gains and losses are weighed up by each individual. The analysis shows that decisions no longer need to be seen as 'life long' in their duration, however, and the possibilities for undoing the decision or re-migrating elsewhere are clearly evident.

The potential benefits for Australia of the return migration of former skilled and business immigrants, are also clearly evident. The links that these people provide between offshore businesses and Australia generally and the international business networks that began to emerge, more noticeably in the 1990s, are a form of cultural capital. In this respect Australia is a long way behind the US–Taiwan partnerships that were described in Chapter 1. It also lags behind in attempts to measure the value of these partnerships but increased awareness of these possiblilities may lead to policies that benefit both ends of the chain. The impact on Australia of the return of skilled migrants is also unrecognised to date but clearly the possibilities for joint research, academic exchanges and ongoing collaboration exist and need to be promoted.

The impact of returnees on their countries of origin comprises the bulk of this study. It is exploratory in nature and the goals that were set out initially have not all been met. Nevertheless, the next four chapters begin to unravel the web of impacts and interactions of skilled and business returnees in their homelands.

3. Bangladesh: Return Migration and Social Transformation

Santi Rozario and John Gow[1]

BACKGROUND

One of the major problems with this study was finding genuine 'returned skilled migrants'. To understand why, we need to consider the whole history of migration from Bangladesh over the last thirty years, as well as the history of migration in the region before the creation of Bangladesh in 1971.

Bangladesh has been a major source of migrants, both permanent and temporary, since it came into existence. However, records on migration from Bangladesh are poor. Ruhul Amin, from the Bangladeshi Ministry of Foreign Affairs, admitted this at the UN Working Group on International Migration in the Netherlands in June 1998 (Amin 1998). The situation is complicated by substantial numbers of irregular and illegal migrants. Data on return migration is even harder to come by.

Bangladesh is one of the world's poorest countries and it ranks 144th out of 175 countries in the UNDP's Human Development Index. Its gross national product (GNP) per capita is a mere $240 (United Nations 1998). About half of the population of the country live below the poverty line. Unemployment is grave. In 1989, only 75 per cent of the active popoulation were employed. The problem is acute amongst even the educated people. In 1978, 48 per cent of the population with qualifications at undergraduate degree level and above were without a job. Again, within this group social science graduates are over-represented. This reflects a serious under-utilisation of highly educated persons, with many in jobs which require skills inferior to their qualifications (Mahmood 1995a, p. 708).

The level of income of employed people is also poor, which is a further incentive for people to emigrate out of the country. 'The average salary is very low. The highest monthly salary earned in the public sector is less than Tk14,650 or US$376. The lowest monthly salary....US$40. Meeting even basic needs becomes difficult for anyone without another source of income' (Mahmood 1995a, p. 714).

Under such conditions, it is only natural that the 'poverty stricken mass of the people, would like to migrate abroad for employment, higher earnings, better quality of life or greater political freedom' (Ahmed 1998, p. 373). Indeed the vast majority of temporary migrants are from this class. With new opportunities for employment in the Middle East, the early 1970s 'marked the beginning of a new era of emigration dynamics' for Bangladeshis. More recently Malaysia, Singapore, Korea, Taiwan and Japan have also become attractive destinations for unskilled or semi-skilled labourers from Bangladesh (Mahmood 1995a, p. 701; Mahmood 1995b). It is estimated that the total cumulative figure for Bangladeshi migrants until 1996 was approximately 2.4 million although no figure is available for return migrants. Most of these migrants (74.5 per cent) are located in the Middle East (Ahmed 1998, p. 373).

The semi-skilled and unskilled temporary migrants in the Middle East and other East and Southeast Asian countries make a major contribution to the Bangladeshi economy,[2] although on the whole, they are unlikely to fall into the categories we are concerned with here. In terms of gaining capital and foreign exchange for Bangladesh, it is the migrant sector of the unskilled and semi-skilled workers from the Middle East and other Asian countries which has contributed the most. The contribution of professional migrants to the West is minimal. According to the Asian Migrant Yearbook 1999, Bangladeshi migrants remit at least US$1.5 billion to the country each year. According to the Asian Development Report of August 2001 (p. 3) 'Bangladesh is one of the few countries in the world where remittances by overseas workers contribute a third to the country's trade deficit and nearly a tenth to the gross domestic product (GDP) (Afsar 1995)' (Pal 2001). The role played by this group of migrants in economic development is significant. Yet the plight of unskilled and semi-skilled migrants is vulnerable and so far the Bangladeshi government has not been able to address this situation.

There are also numbers of illegal Bangladeshi migrants in different countries, with India having about 18 million undocumented Bangladeshi migrants. India, as the country bordering on Bangladesh from all directions, is probably the easiest country for illegal Bangladeshi migrants to gain entry to.

The policy of the government of Bangladesh so far has been to maximise the migration potential of temporary workers. The idea is to earn foreign exchange for the country through the remittances from these migrants and at the same time to solve some of the problems of unemployment in the country. In 1976, the government established the Bangladesh Bureau of Manpower, Employment and Training (BMET). It was their responsibility to monitor the flow of overseas migration: 'labor attaches have been posted to major labor-receiving countries to monitor labor markets and the welfare of workers' (Mahmood 1995b, p. 532). BMET compiles data on the number of people going abroad, their destination, occupational skills as well as sex composition. To June 1994, according to BMET, 6017 workers were female out of a total of 1 491 302, i.e. 0.40 per cent of the total (Mahmood 1995b, p. 532).

BMET only compiles information on the outflow of Bangladeshis and there is no information available on returnees. So it is difficult to determine the trend of net migration, especially with skilled migrants. Skilled returned migrants do not have to register with the BMET or get a No Objection Certificate (NOC).

Bangladesh is a highly stratified society, with great differences of income, education and opportunity between the impoverished majority of the people and a relatively small, often quite wealthy and almost entirely urban elite. There is also a substantial middle class. The skilled and business migrants come overwhelmingly from the upper middle and the elite group. It is this group too, for the most part, who are in a position to travel overseas for study, since they have both the cultural capital and the connections to secure Bangladeshi government scholarships or funding from overseas sources.

Another reason for the middle and upper class to migrate elsewhere is the serious lack of professionalism in every sphere of the country. As Mahmood points out, and this study confirms, 'many ambitious and deserving technical people consider emigration not only as a survial strategy but also as a means to achieve professionalism' (Mahmood 1995a, p. 714).

The lower middle class, and those living below the poverty line, are rarely accepted as permanent migrants by the more developed countries in contemporary times. Historically, when the UK and Western Europe were undergoing industrial expansion and needed extra unskilled labour, many Bangladeshis migrated to these places. The Sylheti community in the UK, which is the largest Bangladeshi migrant community (apart from the Hindu migrants to neighbouring India), and probably also the best-studied, originate from poor and rural backgrounds. This community now numbers nearly half a million in size (Gardner 1995). This resulted from specific historical circumstances, for example, the industrial revolution in the UK and its colonial links to Bangladesh, then part of greater India. Their migration was primarily for economic reasons and they may continue to provide financial support for relations back home. This has a substantial economic impact on their communities of origin, in this case mostly villages in the province of Sylhet in NE Bangladesh. However, unlike more recent non-elite labour migrants to countries such as Saudi Arabia or Malaysia, few of the UK Sylhetis are likely to return to work in Bangladesh. By now, a substantial part of this community is in fact UK-born.

Such a pattern of migration has long come to an end. Migrants who are now accepted as permanent migrants almost always come from middle to upper class backgrounds with professional qualifications. The Bangladeshi community in Australia is quite different in its composition from the British Bangladeshi community, and other Western countries such as the USA or Canada are more similar to the Australian situation. These are attractive destinations for permanent settlement by highly educated and professional people. An estimated 200 000 to 300 000 were said to be living in these countries around 1994 (Mahmood 1995a, p. 702). By contrast with the Middle Eastern, and more recently East Asian countries, western societies, other than the UK, usually admit relatively skilled and educated migrants, along with those migrating temporarily for higher education. A significant proportion of the Bangladeshi community in Australia is made up of students, many of whom will return to Bangladesh after their studies. Australia has also accepted a small number of highly technical and professional people as permanent migrants. The long-term migrant Bangladeshi population in Australia is skewed towards professional and highly-skilled occupations with academics and the medical profession strongly represented. However, as in the UK, these long-term migrants are unlikely to return to Bangladesh though they may move from Australia to similar employment elsewhere.

FEMALE MIGRATION FROM BANGLADESH

The 'feminisation of international migration' which has been a major concern in recent writing on migration is not significant in the context of Bangladesh. Bangladeshi cultural norms have always worked against the migration of single Bangladeshi women. Contract labour migration to the Middle East, Malaysia, Thailand, Singapore, Korea, Japan and elsewhere is still dominated by men and very few are in positions to take their wives and families with them. However, a small percentage of female migrants to these places occupy positions of domestics and are usually lowly paid. In addition, there is the problem of trafficking in women throughout South Asia, as a consequence of which a small number of Bangladeshi women can also be found in distant lands as prostitutes for example.

1995 saw the imposition of the death penalty in Bangladesh for convicted smugglers of humans. The Bangladeshi government banned the deployment of Bangladeshi women (except for doctors and engineers) to the Middle East in 1998. However, this has not had a significant impact on the smuggling and trafficking of children and young women. This is linked to the government's inability or lack of political will to implement these laws. There is also a lack of diplomatic efforts on the part of the Bangladeshi government to ensure the safety and protection of vulnerable migrant workers. According to a study in Dhaka over a period of seven years to 1998, 2600 children went missing, of whom 96 per cent were girls and most were suspected of having been subject to trafficking. Apparently 228 were rescued (Asian Migrant Yearbook 1999, pp. 80–81).

According to the BMET, between 1991 and 1998 about 13 544 Bangladeshi women emigrated from Bangladesh. This figure is rather insignificant, 0.65 per cent, when compared with the total number of migrants, 2 082 272, out of the country during the same period. However, it has been suggested that this official figure is a gross under-representation of the actual number of female migrants to different countries because it does not include the female victims of trafficking. In addition, there is a significant number of women who do not register with the BMET because of a general ban on women's migration to many countries, in particular the Middle East. What is more, the vast majority of these female migrants are from non-professional categories.

Within the professional category too, migration is dominated by men, most of whom, however, are usually accompanied by their wives and families. A significant number of women, single as well as married, travel overseas for higher degrees. The married women are usually also accompanied by their husbands. According to Siddiqui, the percentage of professional female migrants were a mere 5.59 per cent. However, it seems BMET data does not include professional migrants to Western Europe, UK, US, Canada and Australia. The number of the migrants to these countries in recent years has been very small and they are essentially in the professional category (Siddiqui 2000, pp. 91–94).

OVERVIEW OF SAMPLE

A total of 108 survey forms were returned in the Bangladesh study: 64.5 per cent had travelled overseas to Australia, the UK, US, India or elsewhere, for higher degrees and then returned to Bangladesh; 20.6 per cent had been overseas for business and 4.7 per cent had gone to join family members. Most returnees had little choice but to return to Bangladesh after completing their studies, temporary job or business, as 92 per cent had no permanent resident status in their host country. More than 50 per cent of these migrants had been employed before migration and returned to their jobs in government, NGOs and the university system.

Because government jobs, including university teachers, are not well-paid, they were often also involved in consultancy, in business or worked in the informal economy. Most interviewees were from the middle to upper classes. The class dimension of migration is important because it has a bearing on what happens if and when skilled migrants and students return to Bangladesh. They typically return to a social network which helps place them into appropriate jobs, provides them with business opportunities and supports them while they are establishing themselves. Table 3.1 shows the basic demographic characteristics of this group. In spite of efforts to get equal numbers of men and women, only one quarter of the sample is female.

Table 3.1 Age and gender of sample population, Bangladesh

Factor		%	Cumulative %
Age (years)	up to 45	56.6	56.6
	46 to 55	34.0	90.6
	over 55	9.4	100.0
Gender	Male	74.1	74.1
	Female	25.9	100.0

Table 3.2 indicates that the majority of the group had tertiary education before leaving Bangladesh. This was even more the case upon their return. In particular, a significant proportion had upgraded from a Master's degree to a Ph.D.

Table 3.2 Highest qualifications of sample population

Qualification	Bangladesh qualification (%)	Overseas qualification (%)
Up to high school	2.0	*
Vocational school	9.1	4.7
Bachelor's degree	28.3	14.1
Master's degree	55.6	30.6
Doctorate	5.1	34.1
Other	*	16.5

Note: * item not in questionnaire

Table 3.3 indicates that 84 per cent of return migrants sampled worked within the service sector. Professional or managerial level jobs had been aquired by 95 per cent of the sample on their return to Bangladesh.

Table 3.3 Industry and occupational distribution of sample population

Factor		%	Cumulative %
Industry sector	Primary	5.8	5.8
	Manufacturing	10.7	16.5
	Services	83.5	100.0
Occupational sector	Managerial	36.4	36.4
	Professional	58.9	95.3
	Para professional	2.8	98.1
	Clerical	0.9	99.1
	Other	0.9	100.0

Table 3.4 shows that the return migrants worked in a variety of work places with an emphasis on universities (31 per cent) and research institutions, and to a lesser extent NGOs, business services and manufacturing industry (14–15 per cent each). Government, at a little under 10 per cent was a comparatively modest employer of return migrants. Over half worked for comparatively large organisations (over 100 employees).

Table 3.4 Work place distribution of sample population

Work places		%	Cumulative %
Type of work place	Government	9.4	9.4
	Research or university	31.1	40.6
	NGO	15.1	55.7
	Business services	14.2	69.8
	Industry	15.1	84.9
	Other	15.1	100.0
Number of employees	Up to 20	28.9	28.9
	21 to 100	18.1	47.0
	Over 100	53.0	100.0

Table 3.5 shows that within these organisations approximately three-quarters of the return migrants were employees and of these, three-quarters claimed to have managerial responsibilities. When these are combined with the 23 per cent that are either employers or self-employed, it indicates that the return migrants, consistent with their occupational concentration in management or the professions, overwhelmingly assume managerial responsibilities.

Table 3.5 Employment status and managerial role of sample population

Employment		%	Cumulative %
Employment status	Employee	72.9	72.9
	Employer	14.0	86.9
	Self employed	7.5	94.4
	Other	5.6	100.0
Managerial position as an employee	Yes	73.0	73.0
	No	27.0	100.0

The majority of the sample returned from Western European countries while a substantial minority were from Asia and the Middle East, particularly India and the countries around the Persian Gulf. The major reason for moving overseas was for study (nearly two out of three) and business. These two categories accounted for 85 per cent. Over a third of respondents returned within five years while over two thirds returned within 10 years.

Western countries are categorised by socio-economic and cultural considerations and include North America, Western Europe, Australia and New Zealand. Eastern European countries include countries of the former Soviet Union and within the Eastern bloc. Asia and the Middle East is an eclectic category in cultural and socio-economic terms and includes the Middle East, North Africa and other Asian and South Asian countries, including Singapore and Japan.

PROCESSES OF MIGRATION

Why people leave Bangladesh may seem quite straightforward: for economic and other personal self-advancement. However, there is perhaps more to be said on this question. Bangladesh, like other South Asian societies, has developed what could be termed a 'migration culture' where migration to developed countries has become widespread. Most of the young people, especially young educated men, go overseas to find work and settle in another country. Even those whose official reason for going overseas is study, generally intend to find a job overseas rather than return. The common refrain is 'there is no future in this country' and people see the only way to build up a promising career and future for themselves and their family as being to emigrate elsewhere.

These young people are not from the bottom of the social hierarchy but rather from middle class backgrounds. Even if they did not emigrate, they could look forward to a much brighter future than those who cannot dream about international migration: the poor peasants, the day labourers, the slum dwellers, the garment workers and so on. Yet both groups, the middle class potential overseas migrants and the lower classes with no such possibilities, are caught up within the same global structural processes.

While the poor cannot dream about international migration, they too migrate internally out of sheer economic necessity. Most slum dwellers in Dhaka and Chittagong have migrated from villages due to flood, riverbank erosion, cyclone, drought and lack of employment opportunities. 'An estimated 1 million persons are made homeless each year as a result of such natural calamities' (Mahmood 1995a, pp. 710–11). Beside these, the exploitative relations between the rich and the poor peasants in rural Bangladesh drive away the landless and poor to cities in search of employment. Morever, the development-related factors, such as the introduction of cash crops, monoculturalism, the green revolution and construction of large dams, often have adverse effects on the employment prospect of poor villagers. Other people migrate from rural areas to urban centres in search of better opportunities and better education for their children. Many people from this group, including rickshaw pullers and petty businessmen, also migrate to neighbouring parts of India, especially to Calcutta. Such migration is restricted and mostly illegal at present. Historically, particularly in the pre-partition period, there was much freer movement throughout the South Asian region, including Burma. Many people took advantage of this for labour migration. In other words, people have always migrated in response to their circumstances and desires.

However, contemporary migration, internal or international, is different. There is desperation, linked to the poor economic situation of Bangladesh, as well as its deteriorating socio-political situation. For the lower classes, economic factors are undoubtedly paramount. The economic situation of the rural population is progressively worsening. As Mahmood points out: 'based on a head-count ratio – percentage of population unable to consume a 'minimum consumption bundle' as of 1985–86', a maximum 51 per cent of the rural population were living in poverty. Based on calorie intake, 48 per cent of the population were living under absolute poverty in 1988–89 and 29 per cent were living in 'hard-core poverty' (Mahmood 1995a, p. 711). The percentage of landless rural population is well over 50 per cent.

Although in most ways the middle class are much better off than the rural poor, they have been particularly badly affected by rising unemployment in the cities. The young educated middle class especially suffer from acute unemployment and underemployment. A very large number of young men with Bachelor's and Master's degrees are still dependent on their parents for their livelihood.

The educated middle class feel there is a distinct lack of opportunities for them in the country. While this is linked of course to the deteriorating economic circumstances, it is also related to other wider factors which affect their day-to-day lives. Civil society is fraught with violence. The ongoing political violence that has characterised the country ever since its liberation from Pakistani rule now touches most ordinary people, whether they are directly involved in politics or not. The culture of mastans (thugs supported by political parties) is widespread. Even in rural areas this culture has become a problem and a threat to children's lives.

A common refrain with people who are seeking to leave the country is that 'there is no law and order here'. Potential violence and lack of law and order makes it understandable why most people are concerned about their family's security.

Another major concern is the state of education in Bangladesh. The education system is in chaos. It is now taken for granted that teachers will not do any real teaching in the classroom but will compel parents to pay for private tuition after school hours. This problem is universal across the country but no constructive step is being taken to address the situation. University education is worse. In universities, people believe that students are not there to learn, but to engage in politics. Campuses are regularly closed for demonstrations or as a result of other political turmoil. A three-year university degree often takes five or six years because of the frequent interruptions to study. Consequently, it is not only the students who suffer but parents have to bear their expenses for an additional number of years. In western countries, students can often take care of some of their expenses through part-time or casual employment. These opportunities are almost non-existent in Bangladesh. So university students are fully dependent on their parents during their study and until they find a job after they complete their study.

Members of the upper middle class who can afford it are sending their children to residential private schools in neighbouring India. Most of these children will then be sent to a western country for a higher degree and very few of them will return to Bangladesh.

Bureaucratic hassles and lack of efficiency is another reason for leaving the country: getting electricity or telephone lines, paying bills, applying for jobs, opening a bank account, getting loans and generally getting anything done that involves government offices, takes much too long. It also involves bribes and an unnecessary waste of energy. Often things never get done, especially for those who do not have prior contacts in the relevant section of the government.

OUTCOMES OF RETURN MIGRATION

Given this context it is important to understand how return migrants integrate and cope with the difficulties. The issues for return migrants relate to work conditions, living conditions, change in social status of migrants within the community and change in their relationship with family members, including gender. The outcomes were predictably mixed.

Working Environment

The majority (73.3 per cent) of respondents were satisfied with their employment while 26.7 per cent were not. The overall response to satisfaction related to a higher degree and training obtained overseas. An overseas degree and training placed many respondents in a more secure position within their jobs; many obtained promotion, had job satisfaction and many said they commanded respect from their colleagues. Many also expressed a sense of satisfaction from being able to do something for the country such as their work with NGOs, development agencies or teaching at universities.

Job satisfaction was greater for returnees who were employed in the non-governmental sectors: private business, NGOs, foreign banks and other foreign organisations. An increase in salary was also more significant with this group of returnees. University teachers also expressed a high level of satisfaction in terms of being able to use their knowledge and skills effectively in teaching and research.

Just over half (52.4 per cent) of respondents had problems in adjusting to the working conditions in Bangladesh. The problems explained by respondents varied but the problems that were common to most work situations were: low salary; moving from affluence to subsistence; moving from open to closed culture; moving from freedom to loyalty in office; obstacles against innovative work; problems with red tape; too many formalities; spending too much time on paper work; knowledge and skills gained overseas unused because of lack of facilities or equipment; social pressure; lack of professionalism; exploitation by employers (expecting you to work overtime without pay) and lack of employee rights.

One university teacher had this response:

1.   lack of better academic atmosphere;
2.   lack of research facilities;
3.   traditional educational system;
4.   politicisation of academic institutions;
5.   lack of applied education;
6.   low standard of educational course and curriculum;
7.   lack of morality;
8.   lack of economic incentive.

Another returnee commented:

The concept of work ethics is very different here. There is less trust among colleagues; a lot of unhealthy competition, politics, nontransparencies. I find it strange
to observe that above everything else, the personality at work is different from the
personality outside work for most of the people. The reason being the majority of
the people feel insecure and not so confident about their ability, stability or future.

Those working with private and donor-funded organisations usually had
better access to IT and other information facilities than the government and
university employees. University employees had difficulty accessing up-to-
date research material in the form of books, magazines and journals as well as
to functional computer and internet facilities. Universities are starting to provide computer and internet access for their university employees. However, in
most government offices these facilities are beyond the reach of even officials.

Living Conditions

Answers to the questions in this section are significant in understanding not
only why migrants are reluctant to return to Bangladesh, but also why Bangladeshis are oriented to emigration. Some problems, such as climate and adjusting to the Bengali language, can be explained by migrants' length of time
spent abroad. However, most of the other problems mentioned again and again
by the interviewees had nothing to do with being away for so long but with the
overall dysfunctional nature of Bangladeshi society. Problems are both structural and social.

Most interviewees mentioned lack of law and order and social security as a
big concern. Generally, there was no scope to assert one's own rights as a
citizen. There was a fear of general security in life. It was very common for
children to be kidnapped or people's lives to be threatened by *mastans* (thugs).
Government measures are ineffective. Understandably, returnees are concerned
about their own, and more importantly their children's safety in Bangladesh.

One returnee said 'I always feel there is a shortage of scope of establishing my rights, privilege as a citizen like other developed countries. Deterioration of law, i.e. the degraded law and order situation, is alarming'.

Returnees have an on-going hassle in day-to-day living with the tradition of bribes, without which nothing gets done in Bangladesh. Bribery and corruption in every sphere of Bangladeshi life is a perennial problem. The problem of corruption came up in response to many of the open-ended questions asked. One respondent said the following were the major adjustment problems they faced: 'Bribery to facilitate any action; lack of security of life and property; irregular services (electricity, gas water supply); adulteration in everything (most harmful in food stuffs and medicine)'.

Hartals or strikes are very common in Bangladesh. The ones which are of most concern are the ones organised by the two major political parties. Typically, the party in opposition will pick issues or policies of the governing party and call for nation-wide strikes.

The dysfunctional education system is a problem which answers why people leave Bangladesh. Given the gravity of the situation, it is not a surprise that migrants with children are reluctant to return to Bangladesh. A number of Bangladeshi Australian families often cite the lack of appropriate educational facilities in Bangladesh as one of the many reasons why they cannot go back. They usually say 'there is no way we can go back now, what will happen to our children?'.

Most interviewees expressed anxiety about not having suitable, clean and effective hospitals adequately equipped and staffed by qualified medical personnel. Several interviewees said that they, and their friends, usually go to India, Bangkok or Singapore for medical attention. However, in emergency situations, this is not an option. In any case, being treated outside Bangladesh is not possible for most of the Bangladeshi population and only a limited number of the upper middle class can resort to this option.

Returnees find lack of convenient and suitable public transport a problem. Travelling in public buses and local trains is very trying. These are very crowded and often do not run on time. Traffic jams almost always interfere with being on time. Most middle class people do not use these types of transport. If they do not have their own car, they take rickshaws or baby taxis everywhere and this can be an expensive affair. Some might have access to transport facilities through work but then they still have to cope with traffic jams and pollution. Women, in particular, find it almost impossible to travel in public buses and trains for fear of being harassed and pushed around by the male crowd.

Air and environmental pollution is another very common problem mentioned by most interviewees. Cities are crowded with too many cars, buses, *tampoos* (extended rickshaws to carry extra passengers), baby taxis, rickshaws and van pullers. The fuel used is often mixed with something else to make it last longer and hence the fume generated is lethal for one's eyes, ears and nose and its long-term effect, especially on children, is disastrous.

There are slum dwellings everywhere in the urban centres and they usually have no water or other sanitary facilities. In addition, the lack of regular garbage collection from most parts of the metropolis is a huge problem. There is rubbish everywhere and plastic bags get washed away during the flood season and clog up whatever functional sewerage system there is.

Some returnees were also very bothered by sound pollution. The problem is aggravated by overpopulation of urban centres, as well as most people having their radio or cassette players on full volume as a general practice. On public buses on inter-district journeys loud music is a must and is appreciated by the general public, and yet there are others who suffer from this intrusion of unwanted sound. Those having spent any length of time abroad, used to a sense of privacy and different forms of music, find sound pollution a special problem.

A few returnees commented on the problem of overpopulation. This is not news, but the problem in urban centres is aggravated as the displaced and needy rural population keep migrating to cities in search of a source of living. Other problems mentioned include social adjustment, for example having to eat rice everyday; having to live in a joint family; political instability and work conditions. Many other problems mentioned relate to the low level of income, inability to maintain a decent standard of living and inefficient bureaucracy.

Social Environment

The overwhelming response among returnees was that they were happy to be re-united with their family and friends and to be back in their own country. Being back in their own cultural environment and to belong to one's group was as important as being back with one's family. Several returnees mentioned that they were enjoying their status as first class citizens again. Responses to the questions on this topic revealed the concern of returnees with issues of identity and a sense of alienness when they lived abroad. Typical responses to being home were:'proud to stay in my own country, to meet my friends, relatives, to speak in my own language and to be in Bengali environment', 'I am serving my country and also I am living with my family members', 'we are living in our society. Our children will grow up in our own culture. They will have love for our country and work for the development of the same', 'first, I am happy that I returned to my homeland. Here in my own country, I can afford servants, care-taker/security guard to have a comfortable standard of living which is never possible in a foreign country', 'I came back to my own land, culture, people, values, music and to my work and community', 'no ethnic problem here for me', 'emotionally positive', 'enjoying my life as a first class citizen and my own cultural environment', and 'the people in my country do not ridicule or underestimate me and family'.

Most respondents said their status had increased within their families, workplaces and the wider community. Their increased status was mainly from higher education in the form of a Ph.D., other training from abroad and increased income.

Most respondents said they had no real 'culture shock' upon returning to Bangladesh. This may be because most returnees did not emigrate permanently but went overseas to study or on temporary working visas. It is also likely that they socialised largely with other Bangladeshis abroad and very much kept to themselves except on occasions when they had to interact with non-Bangladeshis, such as in business or as students in universities. So, although they were exposed to foreign culture and ideas, their tendency to stick together also contributed to perpetuating and clinging to the Bangladeshi culture: food habits, language, music and gender values. Nevertheless, on the whole women tended to suffer from cultural shock to a greater extent than men.

IMPACTS OF RETURN MIGRATION ON ECONOMIC, SOCIAL AND POLITICAL SPHERES

The impact of return migration on economic, social and political aspects of the country so far is minimal. The responses of the interviewees to the relevant questions in this regard, however, highlight the potential impact returnees could make if their number was higher, but more importantly if Bangladesh was ready for them.

The potential impacts include the way returnees could contribute to their work place through the skills, knowledge and training they received overseas. This also includes the use of capital gained overseas in some productive way. However, the vast majority of respondents did not bring back any substantial capital from overseas as they were students. Most brought back small amounts of capital and they used it mostly on consumption items, including housing, rather than in business. There are some who invested their capital in business. Migrants returning from the Middle East after some years of employment there, were usually able to invest their capital beyond merely consumption items.

Most respondents had gone overseas for higher degrees, usually to undertake Ph.D. or Master's degrees (public health). On the whole, most (89.5 per cent) of them found the knowledge and skills gained overseas useful back in their job. These interviewees usually had jobs at a university, NGO or another institution. Often they were supported by their relevant organisation, either directly by paying scholarship, or in keeping their job with pay during their absence. On return, those working at universities usually found their degree very useful in teaching, research, other analytic work or special fields of their expertise. Some returnees also said their business connections from abroad were useful in their current business activities in Bangladesh. Ninety-one per cent of returnees felt their skills, overseas degrees and knowledge were highly valued by their colleagues and their employers. Their opinions were actively sought by their colleagues and employers, and they were given autonomy at work, including decision-making.

However, a significant number of returnees had difficulty in applying their skills or training in their present jobs in Bangladesh. When respondents said their skills were not valued, this seemed to be related to their responsibilities at work and not to their skills and qualifications gained overseas.

Given the general dysfunctional nature of the educational system in Bangladesh, most people trained overseas are more capable than those trained in Bangladesh. This is the case with most jobs, but those returnees employed as university teachers find their degrees and training especially useful. Those with higher degrees improved not only their analytic skills, but their communication and interpersonal skills which help them with team work, etc. Some of the comments were:'I introduced the students to new ideas, new books and effective way of conducting research';'I introduced new methods of treatment', 'I have introduced modern computerised technology in the pre-press sector and now it is very popular in Bangladesh', and 'as a medical manager in the leading pharmaceutical company of Bangladesh, I started the Medical Services department'.

Many (73 per cent) of the respondents held managerial positions and played a role in decision-making at different levels of the organisation they worked in. Even those not in a managerial position found ways of influencing decision-making indirectly as their opinions were highly valued. Altogether 82.5 per cent of the respondents said they played a significant role in decision-making at their work place. These returnees have the potential to bring about significant changes to work place related problems including lack of professionalism, bureaucratic hassles and lack of commitment to one's role in an organisation. However, given that their number is minute in the whole country and because they are spread out in different organisations, this is not a likely outcome within the present circumstances.

Economic impact was evaluated at two levels: at the level of returnees bringing back substantial capital for investment purposes and at the level of the family's overall economic well-being. Student respondents either did not remit any money back home during their study time or sometimes they only sent small amounts for their parents or siblings. Very few brought back substantial capital. As most respondents were students, they did not bring back large amounts of capital. Of the total respondents, 66.2 per cent brought back less than US$10 000, 23.4 per cent said they brought between US$10 000 and 50 000. Only 10 per cent said they brought over US$50 000. Those who did bring back a substantial amount of capital were able to invest in business activities, thus generating employment for siblings and sometimes for others in the community.

Although most returnees did not bring back substantial capital, the majority of the respondents felt their family's economic position improved either because they were able to bring back at least some capital or because they now enjoyed a much higher salary than when they had gone overseas. The last point applies to most student returnees because they essentially went overseas to obtain a higher degree which, in turn, helped them gain promotion and higher salary. Most student returnees responded that their economic position was clearly better than before they went overseas because they had no income as students previously.

The majority, 64.4 per cent, said they sent no remittances. Many returnees sent some money to their relatives (wives and parents) for household related expenses. Some were able to work part-time and save some money to bring back to invest in consumption goods for the household. Those who worked in the Middle East or other Asian countries often were able to invest in business. Many improved their house, bought land to build a house on and built a house, lent it to their father or supported siblings' education. Given that housing is so expensive in metropolitan centres, the middle and upper middle classes see having their own house as one of the most desirable outcomes when there is any capital to spare.

Many respondents said they saw no real differences in their consumption pattern with those who never lived abroad. Many others, however, saw significant differences in the priority they placed on their spending. They said they paid more attention to books, computers and children's education. One respondent said: 'I like to use sophisticated equipment in my house like a PABX, computers, a microwave oven, different electronics etc'.

Another respondent said: 'Generally I would like to purchase quality products, preference is given to purchase of local products. If not available then to purchase foreign products'. One respondent thought those who did not go overseas were prone to saving money while the returnees spent it: 'I like to spend money but the people who didn't go abroad like to save money in the bank.'

The statements about changes in the consumption habits of the returnees reflect a change in their values. Migrants pick up positive values and ideas as well as some negative ones from their time overseas. Buying foreign goods and modern gadgets is not necessarily a good thing, nor is it a good thing to spend whatever money you have, rather than saving some. Such habits, until recently more a feature of advanced industrialised population, contribute to the flourishing of capitalist industries at the global level and do not necessarily contribute to the development of a poor country like Bangladesh. We see a tendency towards the valorisation of consumerism with some returnees – consumerism is the ideal quality for capitalism to flourish in a country without necessarily contributing to the country's overall development in a positive manner. For example, such consumerism is not going to generate more employment or address the problems of the poor in any way. On the other hand, putting more emphasis on personal development and children's education in the form of buying books and computers may have long-term benefit for all.

A significant proportion of the respondents said they were better off because they were able to save and bring some capital back home to invest in business or to spend in other ways. This group were mainly returnees from the Middle East or other Asian countries, who went there with jobs rather than to study. A handful of student returnees were also able to save a little but that did not have a substantial impact on their financial position. Others said their position was better off because they had an increase in their salary and/or earned a promotion.

An increased interest in events outside Bangladesh reflected the respondents' level of awareness of and the value they place on their connection with the outside world. Most respondents maintained some contact with their Ph.D. supervisors, colleagues or friends overseas. Many also read English publications, such as newspapers and research material in their field. They also watched foreign programmes on television and some listened to foreign radio programmes.

Most respondents said they were trying to contribute to the community through the particular work they were involved in. For example, academics usually commented that they were trying to guide their students to delve into innovative research and to think critically. Those working with NGOs usually felt they were doing their utmost to help improve the conditions of the poor in the country. Most returnees were also involved in community work not related to their specific jobs. Some returnees were regularly invited to social events to give speeches, while others said their opinions were actively sought out by neighbours. Others said that they tried to be involved in charitable work when they could.

Hardly any returnees showed any interest in involving themselves in politics. 'Politics' seems to be a dirty word to most. Everyone would like things to change, but found that in the present structure it was a waste of time trying to join one political party or another. There was clearly potential for returnees to contribute to the community. However, because their numbers are so small and the because of unfavourable circumstances in the country, they have had little or no sustainable social or political impact on the communities around them.

IMPACT ON FAMILIES

Overwhelmingly, respondents' experience in western societies made them value the Bangladeshi style extended family much more. They were critical of the way elderly people in the West live in isolation on their own or in homes. Some respondents realised the benefit of being surrounded by extended family especially as they had had to cope with small children in isolation. Others simply said they were attached to their own cultural values in relation to the family and saw no need to change.

There were, however, some respondents, especially women, who learnt to appreciate the value of independence from the extended family. They saw some value both within the extended family and within the nuclear family structure. Some comments were: 'we have a traditional society and a family structure which is very much part of our social/economic/cultural/poltical order'; 'it is very hard to live in a joint family. I don't like so many things which is allowed in our culture but those are just in my view' and 'I have become somewhat individualistic. I would definitely perform my duties to my extended families, but at the same time, would like to have a life of my own'.

About 14 per cent said they consult their parents before making a decision and 5.6 per cent said that the husband makes decisions by himself. 72 per cent of the respondents said decisions were made jointly by the husband and wife. That the overwhelming majority make decisions jointly is not a surprise: in most cases both husband and wife are employed and the influence of western values may also have played a part.

Bangladeshi families experience a totally different lifestyle when living in western countries. For the first time, husband and wife are allowed to spend time together away from the pressure of joint family members. Within joint family structures, the custom is for the husband to give priority to the opinions and ideas of his parents, or siblings rather than his wife. So once they were on their own in a new place, this pattern changed. The husband gradually began to consult his wife until it became a routine.

However, coming from largely educated and middle to upper middle class backgrounds many respondents would have already had an influence on the family's decisions before they went aboard, although women's decision-making role would have been reinforced during their time overseas. The cases where husbands continued to make decisions alone essentially fall into the category where husbands went overseas (mainly to the Middle East and to other Asian countries) on their own to work while their families remained in Bangladesh. These are also the families where very little change took place in gender relations.

Almost all (96.8 per cent) respondents replied 'yes' to the question about control over household income, many adding that they control their income jointly with their spouse. The overwhelming response affirming control over their own income is not surprising in that the majority of female respondents were also employed. For example, some female respondents said 'yes' to this question, but added 'because I am earning'. Moreover 75 per cent of the respondents were men, some of whom responded that they had full control as the breadwinner of the family. Some respondents, however, misinterpreted the question to be asking whether they could manage their income properly or whether they had any say over their income in relation to their employers. Therefore when they said yes, they often meant that they had managed their finances well. This also does not mean that the money is managed jointly by the husband and wife. So not much significance can be attached to their answers.

Predictably, female respondents had faced more problems with parents and parents-in-law than the male respondents. Changes in the role of women, in some ways, is more challenging to the Bangladeshi family values than changes in the role of men, for example women engaging themselves in non-traditional jobs like business, women becoming more assertive and taking an active role in decision-making concerning family matters.

One of the questions was designed to find out if children growing up outside Bangladesh, and therefore, understandably with different values to Bangladeshi culture, faced any real difficulties adjusting to Bangladeshi family life in Bangladesh. Many said they were single, or if married, had no children while overseas. Others said their children were too small to matter. Yet others said their children remained in Bangladesh studying while they were overseas, so there was no problem. Many of those with teenage children, however, identified some problems. A case study of a teenage daughter of one of the returnees is presented as an example.

One female respondent, Suraya, spent seven years in Australia doing her masters and PhD degrees. She related the tragic story of her teenage daughter after her return from Australia. Her daughter Nomita was only about four years of age when Suraya arrived in Australia for her studies. Suraya's husband and her daughter Nomita joined her six months after her arrival. Suraya and her husband had marital problems from the beginning. Nomita thrived and loved everything about Australia: school, games, toys, food and her friends. By the time Suraya finished her studies and the family returned to Bangladesh, Nomita was about thirteen. Suraya tells me that from the beginning Nomita resented her relatives trying to make her into a 'little woman'. She was no longer to play freely with boys and behave in ways she did in Australia. Her hairstyle; the way she dressed; how she talked and laughed all were to be controlled strictly. She was not to go out to see her friends. Nomita also craved Australian food and missed the variety; was sick of having to eat rice and curries all the time. She found it difficult that her friends at her new expensive private school were all so much better off than her parents, their parents had a car but hers didn't. The marital problems between Suraya and her husband continued and eventually led to divorce. This did not help the situation. Eventually Nomita began to take drugs with her friends and schooling was delayed.

Suraya lost the custody of Nomita to her husband on the grounds that she could not look after her properly. Nomita was also somewhat attracted to the idea of being with her father who by then got himself a car and built a nice big house.

What Nomita's story tells us is not that all teenage children of returnees can expect to face the same fate, but that one has to guard carefully against such problems. The above story indicates that there will always be potential problems because of the great difference in the consumption patterns, lifestyle, but more importantly in the value system of Bangladesh from other western countries. This problem is compounded in the case of female teenagers because of conflict between western and Bangladeshi gender norms.

IMPACT ON GENDER RELATIONS

On the whole returnees experienced some changes during their time abroad and many tried to perpetuate these new changes when they returned home. However, it was not always possible, and it was easier for male returnees to slot in within the traditional Bangladeshi patriarchal system, than it was for female returnees. Table 3.6 shows that nearly three quarters of respondents reported changing their attitude to gender relationships, but over 90 per cent of women reported doing so.

Table 3.6 Changed attitudes to gender

Changed attitude to gender?	Male %	Female %	Total %
Yes	65.8	90.5	74.6
No	34.2	9.5	25.4
Total	100.0	100.0	100.0

Many said they changed their ideas about gender relations in that they now believed in equality between men and women. Some added that this equality should not mean that they do not have to respect their own cultural norms.

Many also said that gender relations should be based on religious ideals, and for most Bangladeshis, it should be the Islamic ideal. Some returnees said they were not influenced by any foreign cultures as they valued their indigenous culture and believed this to be good for gender relations. Many others said their experience overseas means they now understand that women can be just as good as men in every sphere given the opportunity. Many female respondents began to value their increased freedom and independence during their time abroad.

On their return, most women found at least some restriction in their physical mobility or faced some discrimination, but some faced more problems than others. Bangladesh is still essentially a men's society despite the fact that women have been much more visible in the public sphere since the 1980s. Things are changing very slowly. While Bangladeshi women at all levels are experiencing substantial changes in their lives at present, as a result of the general socio-economic and political changes within Bangladeshi society, there appears to be a disjunction between these broader (structural) changes and persisting Bangladeshi gender values or ideologies. Some sample responses of returnees: 'I work for establishing women's equal rights in the society but often I cannot take the correct steps due to outlook and attitude of the people with whom I interact, for example government officials; policymakers and other influential people'; 'my mobility is restricted. People's attitudes towards women are negative, 'my mobility is less. Interactaction with male intellectual is restricted', and 'I have to continually prove my worth in a predominantly 'male' profession'.

Many male respondents acknowledged the problems faced by female returnees or rather women in general in Bangladesh. But many others simply thought 'there isn't any kind of differentation between the two genders'; 'they usually get more facilities than male returnees' or 'I have no idea regarding this issue' and so on.

The vast majority (88.6 per cent) responded 'no' to the question about conflict with their spouse due to a change in values while living abroad. This quantitative response can be misleading unless we examine their open-ended answers closely. For example, having answered 'no', respondents added things like 'No, because I do not force my wife to do anything with the knowledge and ideas which I gained abroad', 'No significant change in my values occurred during my stay in abroad'. It is difficult to know what the wives of these male respondents would say. Moreover, even when female returnees say they are not facing any real conflict, they might say that 'I think my values have not changed'. So it's difficult to know what these answers mean without some in-depth interviews. In-depth interviews with some female returnees revealed that they all had some conflicts, some more than others, but the conflicts arose from the fact that female returnees had changed their attitude to gender relations more than their husbands were prepared to accept. For example, when respondents were asked, through another question, if their attitude to gender relations had changed much, 90.5 per cent of the female returnees said 'yes' while only 48.3 per cent of male returnees said 'yes'. Admittedly, 48.3 per cent is a significant indication that male returnees have also changed their attitude even if only half of these really mean what they said. The returnees' class and educational background is a factor here, that is, most returnees are from the middle to upper middle class with at least some university education. Therefore, female returnees can be expected to have some leeway with their husbands which may not be available to women from poorer sections of society.

CHANGES IN GENDER RELATIONS: MARRIED VERSUS SINGLE WOMEN

Imtiaz Ahmed (2000) argues that when South Asians (which include Bangladeshis) go to Japan as a family, the traditional gender relations rarely undergo any changes. He suggests that while the South Asian migrants are already socialised with their respective gender values, life in Japan which is also essentially a 'masculine' culture, does not in any way challenge these values. However, he suggests that those women migrating to Japan on their own as students, trainees or temporary workers, are less constrained by these values and enjoy relatively greater freedom in their day to day lives compared to female migrants with families. Unfortunately the sample size of single women in our survey was insufficient to pursue this analysis with quantitative data.

Ahmed's argument is convincing in that observation confirms this. When Bangladeshi women go abroad accompanied by their husbands they are still largely dependent on their husbands and therefore have to abide by their wishes. This is not to say that nothing changes at all in the gender relations under such circumstances, but to say that changes are much more limited compared to the changes experienced by women on their own. There is a tendency for most Bangladeshis in Australia, and I suspect the same for Bangladeshi migrants elsewhere, to socialise amongst themselves over weekends. There is very little interaction with non-Bangladeshi Australians. What is more, even when women are educated with a Bachelor's or Master's degree, the main type of occupation they are able to engage in is community baby-sitting. This again means that they have no interaction with the outside world. Their husbands remain principal breadwinners, even when their income might not be that much higher than their wives'. This also has implications for any potential changes in gender values and gender relations. It is usually not in the interest of a husband to encourage his wife to change her values drastically. Although most Bangladeshi men accommodate some changes in terms of helping their wives in the household duties, such as shopping, looking after children and sometimes cleaning, very few engage in cooking activities. Cooking continues to remain the domain of women. Perhaps it is no surprise when they return to Bangladesh after some years in a country like Australia, the US or Canada, that their gender values have not changed much. It is not very common for temporary migrants (on a working visa) to the Middle Eastern countries to take their wives and children with them. But when they do, changes in gender relations are even more unlikely because Middle Eastern gender relations are tilted even more in favour of men than is the case in Bangladesh.

It is very uncommon for Bangladeshi single women to migrate overseas on their own, although it does happen and it happens more with non-Muslim communities than with Muslim communities. A significant number of single women, however, manage to gain scholarships to study abroad and many parents are now willing to allow these women to travel on their own.

When abroad, single women, unlike their married counterparts, have to fend for themselves and in the process become relatively independent, confident and assertive. They are more likely to drive, do their own shopping, pay all the bills and interact more widely with non-Bangladeshis. A married woman can only become more independent if her husband is away from her for any length of time.

It is very difficult for married women to become independent or to challenge Bangladeshi gender values even when they are educated, unless their husbands are favourable to the changes. When women do try to defy their husbands' wishes a situation of conflict inevitably arises. The case (mentioned earlier) of a female Ph.D. student, Suraya, and her husband, Shahin, can be cited here. Suraya had come to Australia for higher education (first a Master's followed by a Ph.D.). Her husband and their four-year-old daughter joined her after six months. Suraya was already a confident and independent type of woman before Shahin's arrival. Their conflict perhaps pre-dated their arrival in Australia, but the major source of conflict was that Suraya's Ph.D. degree meant that she was going to be more educated than her husband. It is very rare in Bangladeshi culture for wives to be more educated than their husbands. In some cases a wife might decide to go for further education and get this opportunity after her marriage, but Bangladeshi men find this situation difficult to handle.

Shahin showed his resentment towards Suraya in different ways, including enrolling himself to do a Master's degree at the same university as Suraya. Despite much conflict throughout their eight years in Australia, they kept their relationship going. According to Suraya, this was largely because Shahin's visa was dependent on his being married to her, but also because he was essentially dependent on her scholarship although he also undertook some part-time work. However, soon after their return to Bangladesh Shahin began to take a hard line and eventually they separated and got divorced. Suraya said she had no support from any of her relatives. Even her own parents blamed her for not being a 'good' wife to Shahin. According to Suraya, Shahin used whatever savings he had from his work in Australia to build a big house for himself while Suraya herself had no savings whatsoever. Suraya ended up having to rent a flat of her own. Initially their daughter was with her, but she lost custody of her to her husband. Suraya continues to face much harassment from her relatives, and she is finding it very difficult to rent places on her own in a society where mature single women living on their own is still an alien concept. Among other problems, she is a very convenient target for the local thugs, which is a very common problem for most middle class Bangladeshis these days.

One can perhaps further hypothesise that Western European, US, Canadian, British and Australian cultures might have greater potential than the cultures of the Middle East, and East Asia, to have a liberating influence on the traditional oppressive gender values of Bangladesh.

This hypothesis is borne out by the comments of some male returnees from the Middle East. One returnee was really puzzled and surprised that a researcher should ask a question about whether his stay aboard had any impact on his attitude to his family and gender relations. A few said there were no changes because basically their host country and Bangladesh were both Muslim countries. Many returnees (again from Middle Eastern or Asian countries) were annoyed that a researcher should ask them if they had any form of 'culture shock' after their return because of their long absence from Bangladesh.

FEMALE RETURNEES AND THEIR IMPACT ON SOCIETY

One category of returnees trying to make the best use of their experience, knowledge and skills gained overseas are perhaps female academics. In a way, it is this group who benefit most from their experience abroad. Bangladeshi middle class women are socialised to be humble, timid, dependent on their husbands and forever willing to live by the wishes of their husbands or male guardians. Indeed, as already observed above, when Bangladeshi women migrate overseas as dependants of their husbands the likelihood of them changing their gendered behaviour drastically is slim, although even here some changes are bound to occur. However, women who go abroad to study with a scholarship, with or without their husbands, often have a different experience. In a number of cases, it was clear that these women felt they learnt a lot from their experience of living somewhere else as mature women, able to be independent. They were able to enjoy the freedom of movement, freedom of expression, freedom of language, freedom of body movement (such as not having to look down in order to avoid eye-contact with non-related males; laughing openly and wearing their hair as they liked).

These experiences sometimes initially led to conflicts with their husbands. For example, in one case, it led to a divorce of the couple after they had returned to Bangladesh and the wife refused to adopt a more 'Bengali' attitude, being a good, obedient wife again. However, in many cases the women were able to convince their husbands that they should see things differently in terms of gender relations. After finishing their studies, as they returned to Bangladesh, they sometimes had a new struggle to face in relation to joint families.

In one case, a university lecturer persuaded her husband to move away from his joint family so that they could bring up their children in the way they liked, inculcating their new values, having some space to themselves, etc. The husband moved with her to a new house, but she had to engage in numerous consultancies in order to supplement their limited university income so that they could afford their rental home, away from the husband's ready-made luxurious household. The husband refused to do anything extra in addition to his own university job, but was later appreciative of his wife's role. After some years of struggle, this female academic reported being very happy with the decisions she made and implemented despite financial problems and initial protests from her husband and his family. She gives the example of her own sister being totally absorbed by her husband's joint family and not able to enjoy any meaningful relationship with her children or her husband.

In another case, a female returnee professor (Suraya) was able to initiate new gender studies courses for the first time on campus after she returned from doing her Ph.D. in Australia. This is a really significant achievement. In addition, this professor said she is proud to have been able to train a couple of male colleagues in this area so that now they too do teaching in gender studies. This same female teacher has been able to help her students (male and female) in mobilising and starting a university-wide students' movement against various forms of sexual harassment and some rape incidents on campus. This movement gained much public support, including that of various women's organisations and intellectuals. Although, because of the alliance of the culprits with high-placed politicians, the punishment handed down to them was nominal, it is clear that this kind of students' movement against sexual assault on university campuses is very new.

Indeed this movement has influenced other university students to mobilise around similar issues. Gradually, awareness is being raised, and female students are being made to feel they do not have to suffer in silence so as not to ruin their honour and reputation. While the achievements of these female academics may add little in a pure economic sense to Bangladesh, there is no doubt they are playing a very significant role in trying to make an impact in the gender values that continue to subordinate women in Bangladeshi society.

FACTORS AFFECTING RETURN MIGRATION AND POLICIES TO ENCOURAGE RETURN MIGRATION

Despite the potential for returnees to contribute to the development of Bangladesh in a significant manner, it is perhaps not surprising that few genuine migrants actually return. This is also borne out of a knowledge of the Bangladeshi migrant community in Australia. People talk frequently about how they would like to go back to Bangladesh, and often complain about aspects of life in western societies, and they frequently visit family in Bangladesh if they can afford to do so. However, very few actually go back permanently.

The story of Mr Ahmed, a Bangladeshi expatriate interviewed in Australia and who had recently spent two years back in Bangladesh as a training adviser to one of the government ministries, is revealing in this regard. His story is not atypical but rather common to most returnees in many respects.

Mr Ahmed's problems started from the very beginning as he tried to get his unaccompanied luggage released. It initially took him six weeks before the unaccompanied personal belongings he had sent from Australia were finally released. Mr Ahmed said that there were four government departments involved in the process of releasing his belongings. First he had to apply to the Director General of the Ministry of Shipping, he was referred to the External Resources Division (ERD), and then to the National Board of Revenue (NBR) who in turn wrote to the Airport Customs officer. Then he was told that because his belongings were in storage for more than five days, he would need to pay demurrage. However, the relevant person refused to accept his demurrage fee until he was paid a bribe, an amount much higher than the actual demurrage. Yet there was apparently a memorandum of understanding between his sponsor, the Commonwealth Secretariat, and the Bangladesh government that his belongings would be released quickly and duty free. Mr Ahmed said 'I was chasing up this matter continuously since my arrival in the country and even then it took me six weeks. What a waste of time and resources. We are simply talking about some personal baggage, nothing else'.

When Mr Ahmed finally started work, he received no cooperation whatsoever in conducting his job. For the entire two years he had to do without a telephone, computer or internet connection in his office. During the first few months there were no toilets in his building. Most of all, there were no instructors for him to train, because no new instructors had been employed by the Government for some years. His local colleagues were entirely uncooperative.

He also pointed out the lack of professionalism as being one of the main problems. After two years of his term, he was offered a renewal for another year but he declined and returned to Australia even though remuneration was excellent.

During his two years in the country he faced hassles in every sphere of life. It took him four months to get a telephone line, even after bribing. There were continuous problems with the electricity line, so he had to get a battery to ensure supply of electricity. There was much political bloodshed. There were on-going strikes (hartals) and he was concerned about being caught up in the midst of the mob, who would then smash his car. Mr Ahmed talked about the lack of any human rights in the country. A young male graduate was beaten to death by police in front of his own house and family, but no action has yet been taken against the police.

He had problems with *mastans* (thugs) asking for money, threatening to kidnap his son. Shortly after he left the country, two sons of one of his relatives were kidnapped by some *mastans* and this relative had to pay them 2–3 lakhs takas (around A$7 000 to A$10 000) to get the children returned unharmed.

Mr Ahmed found the pollution problem unbearable. He said that according to some international reports the lead pollution in Bangladesh is supposed to be the worst in the world. He was particularly concerned about his young son's health.

Mr Ahmed talked about bribery problems. He said: 'at least in the past bribes were exchanged secretly, but these days it's all openly negotiated'. He linked the bureaucratic obstacles and the need for as many as hundreds of signatures from numerous government officials to the system of bribing. It is through the need for their signatures that government officials can maintain their power and authority and ensure that a bribe is paid for each of their signatures. As Mr Ahmed correctly pointed out, this bureaucratic bribe system may unfortunately be a by-product of the very low salary that government officials receive.

There are many other examples which show how bureaucratic obstacles prevent skills and capital gained overseas from being used effectively after returning to the country. But for lack of space, further case studies are not included here.

Most of the returnees listed the following problems in relation to settling back in Bangladesh. Indeed, these are the problems that affect most Bangladeshis to a greater or lesser degree, depending on class, gender and work place. The difference is that the returnees had a taste of what life can be like without the following problems.

A normal lifestyle in Bangladesh, even when one has sufficient resources, is a real struggle. Money cannot solve these structural problems for an individual at the economic, legal–political and socio-cultural levels, although it helps sometimes. Respondents found problems in relation to their positions and the duties they are expected to perform; with bureaucracy; the system of bribes and corruption; transport; pollution and traffic congestion. In addition, there is an almost totally dysfunctional educational system and an ineffective health system.

Government-run public hospitals are rarely used by upper middle class Bangladeshis, although many lower middle class people have to visit these hospitals for lack of any other affordable alternatives. The wealthy take their patients to private clinics, or overseas when they can afford it. The government hospitals are unhygienic and treatment of public patients by nurses and doctors is appalling. These hospitals are meant to be free from any charges to patients, but in practice, without some payment, no treatment is usually delivered. Hospitals are acutely understaffed, especially with respect to nursing staff and doctors. Doctors are usually too busy running their own private practices, therefore leave very little time for public patients (Rozario 1995). These problems are common knowledge and well documented in the health-related research of NGOs and academics. At present some drastic health reform is being undertaken in Bangladesh in an effort to make the government more responsible for the health care of its citizens. In this reform funding is being diverted from the NGO sector to the government (Thornton *et al.* 2000). However, the measures adopted so far by the Bangladeshi government, through the influence of numerous donor agencies, fall short of real insight into the Bangladeshi social structure. Thus, the prospect of this present reform radically transforming the health care system in Bangladesh is remote. So, under these conditions, most genuine migrants are understandably reluctant to return to Bangladesh.

Of the positive outcomes that were listed about their return, the respondents focused mainly on issues to do with family reunion and a sense of belonging to one's own culture and country. However, the majority of these respondents were students while abroad, often on their own or with only their spouse. In contrast, a genuine migrant often has the opportunity to sponsor their relatives. Especially in the US, once members of a family migrate, they can gradually sponsor relatives, which then deals with the problem of separation from their loved ones. In addition, they deal with the problem of identity by socialising almost exclusively with other Bangladeshis.

Return Migrants and Social Transformation

Returned migrants have much potential to contribute to the development of Bangladesh, but their contribution is not always positive. More importantly it is of little or no use trying to encourage migrants to return to the country under the present circumstances. Below are concrete examples of both negative and positive contributions return migrants can make to the country. However, circumstances were different immediately after the liberation of Bangladesh when a significant number of migrants returned to actively take part in the 'development' of the country.

The following example shows that there is not necessarily a positive association between overseas skills and development. This is the case of a young businessman who was educated in the UK from an early age, including his early schooling. A few years after his graduation he returned to Bangladesh and married the daughter of an industrialist. Initially he worked with his father-in-law in the latter's business but then he established his own business of mediating between the garments industrialists in Bangladesh and foreign importers of garments. At a very young age he has become a very wealthy man as his profits are huge.

His contribution to the country seems to be little or nothing. Perhaps from a purely economic point of view one can argue that he is a productive businessman and must be generating some employment through his business. Also it can perhaps be argued that he was able to use his links with foreign importers for the benefit of garments factory owners, although he was making substantial profits himself.

From a more sociological/anthropological point of view one could also argue that he is not using his skills to do anything special for the country as such, but to make a profit for himself. For instance, he is complacent about the fact that while he is making huge profits, the garment workers are being paid virtually nothing and working under horrific conditions, where workers are denied even their basic rights. He does not care about the problems of such 'low class' people. He has not even left the comfort of his house in an upper class area of Dhaka so as to avoid traffic congestion and pollution. His assistants deal with garment factory owners.

These contrasting view points raise the question of 'what is development'? From the capitalist point of view, it is pure economic growth, but from a sociological point of view, that businessman is not making a genuine contribution to the development of the country.

In contrast, the following stories are more positive in terms of the returnees' contribution to development. Most of the well-known and large indigenous NGOs in Bangladesh were founded back in the 1970s by return migrants. For example, professor Mohammad Yunus, the founder of Grameen Bank, obtained his Ph.D. from the US. Grameen Bank is now well known internationally, so much so that it is now being presented as the model to be replicated everywhere in the world. Indeed over 60 countries have adopted Grameen Bank's model of microcredit for the poor. While I have some reservation about the way Grameen Bank is being seen as 'the solution' to the poverty of the world, there is no doubt that Professor Yunus' idea of taking microcredit to the village poor was novel, and his model of microcredit has benefited over two million people in Bangladesh, and elsewhere.

Again, the founder of Gonoshastha Kendra (The People's Health Centre), Dr Zafrullah Chowdhury, obtained his degree from the UK. The founder of BRAC (Bangladesh Rural Advancement Committee), the largest indigenous NGO in the southern region, was also educated abroad. The chief manager of the Research Branch of BRAC, Mr Mustaque Chowdhury, and many other researchers from his section obtained their degrees from a foreign university. There are many other indigenous NGOs including some founded by women (like Proshikha, Nijera Kori, Naripokko, UBINIG) which are now operating in Bangladesh and many of the prominent staff in these NGOs probably are also return migrants. In many respects, all these NGOs and the Grameen Bank were revolutionary in their approaches to development, especially in relation to rural areas and to women in particular. Unfortunately, the results of the NGO programmes these days are rather mixed, and for various reasons complex.

While in some respects NGOs' new and revoluntary approach to 'development' can be explained by their links with or direct participation in the liberation war of Bangladesh, inspired by socialist ideals of the then Awami League Party and its leader Sheikh Mujibur Rahman, the ideas and skills they derived from their overseas training have also played an important role in their novel initiatives.

Further examples are more recent returnees from the UK, Australia and the US, who have returned to the country after doing their Ph.D.s. They are very committed to their teaching, research and most of all to their students. They supply them with recent journal articles or book chapters, not available in Bangladesh, and some are engaged in translating some foreign texts into Bengali. They are all doing whatever they can to maintain a reasonable educational atmosphere for their students. This is very difficult given the politicised nature of the education system at universities in Bangladesh these days.

The female teachers have been integrally involved in a recent female students' campaign against a series of rape incidents at the campus of Jahangir Nagar University. Their motivation to assist the female students with the campaign has nothing to do with their overseas obtained education as such, however, it was clear that some of the strategies adopted by the campaign had parallels with women's movements in the UK, Australia and the US.

From these concrete examples, it is clear that return migrants should be encouraged to return to Bangladesh as they have much potential to contribute to the development of the country. But the question is how? The situation of Bangladesh is such that returnees are most reluctant to return, as discussed. Those who have returned, even many of those who returned in the early 1970s, have returned largely because they had no option of remaining overseas as permanent residents. They went abroad on a student visa or temporary work permit and therefore had to return.

There are no government policies or strategies to actively encourage or provide incentives for skilled migrants to return to the country. Indeed there is little perception that there may be a need for this. For the last three decades the explicit policy has been to encourage and facilitate international migration, although largely contract labour migration.

Not only are there no any incentive programmes for return migrants, the government officials are uncooperative with Bangladeshi expatriate employees, who may be funded by some international organisations.

The general social and political malaise makes people self-centred and relatively unconcerned with the welfare of the society at large, with no interest in the wider agenda or the future of the country.

Impact of Government Incentive/Recruitment Programmes

In only very rare cases, respondents said they had incentives from the government to return to the country. Most respondents returned either because they had a job to return to or because of a government directive (bond signature) but there were no real incentives as such. No one was aware of any special incentive programmes of the Bangladeshi government to facilitate the return of skilled migrants. Typical responses as to suggestions for policies included: offering returnees attractive salary packages; improving work conditions; improving law and order; providing information; providing job security and social security and relaxing the age bar in government positions. These show the concerns they have about these issues.

FUTURE TRENDS AND HOW TO MAXIMISE THE POSITIVE IMPACTS OF RETURN MIGRATION

Before considering how to maximise the positive impacts of return migration, the issue of concern with Bangladesh is how to both discourage emigration and encourage return migration. There is a desperate urge to emigrate out of Bangladesh and no incentive to return on the part of most middle class people.

A Bangladehi friend living in Australia made this remark about a fellow Bangladeshi who did not emigrate out of Bangladesh: 'He cannot be much good, anyone worth anything does not continue to live in Bangladesh, they go abroad.' This friend was perhaps exaggerating somewhat, but not much in the case of the younger generation.

The only way to address this problem is to begin to address some of the root causes of emigration from Bangladesh in the first place. The outflow of trained personnel from developing countries, popularly referred to as the 'brain drain', has had detrimental effects on the development of these countries. The United Nations Conference on Science and Technology for Development back in 1979 recommended that:

Developing countries should formulate policies for the establishment of a scientific and technological manpower capacity. Such policies should *inter alia*, ... (e) Make a thorough evaluation, at the national level, of the 'brain drain' problem, including the migration of skilled manpower, with a view to identifying measures for tackling the problem and reversing the exodus of the scientific and technological manpower (Pires 1992, p. 355).

However, there is yet no real plan or programmes in Bangladesh, such as the Return and Reintegration of Qualified Nationals that was created by IOM back in the 1970s, initially for Latin American countries. In recent years many such programmes have been relatively successfully established in other countries, China and Taiwan, for example.

Perhaps the problems of Bangladesh are considered insurmountable by international bodies and therefore no direct attention has been given to the formulation of any policies to find a solution to the country's brain drain problem.

As we have seen from the respondents' comments, they had no assistance or incentives from the government or anyone else while returning to the country. There is no doubt that returnees would welcome any assistance they can get in returning, and adjusting to Bangladesh. But from the point of view of their contribution to the country's development, the international bodies, together with the Bangladeshi government, have to find ways in which their skills and training can be put to effective use.

Many statements have been made about the importance of international cooperation at numerous meetings and symposiums concerning international migration and development. Yet, as Stephen Castles has pointed out, there is an inherent interest conflict between sending countries and receiving countries. The former want access to the labour market of richer countries, adequate pay, conditions and protection for their citizens, and long-term benefits through remittances, training and orderly return. All too often, the latter just want cheap, flexible labour and care little about the human rights and social well being of the migrants (Castles 1999, p. 16).

However, Castles goes on to argue that if they combine to take a longer term view, both types of country could have an interest in orderly migration and regulated conditions for migrants, combined with strategies that would support the sustainable development of the sending country. If migration helps contribute to more productive economies and more prosperous societies, that is likely to benefit everybody through greater international trade and security, as well as through social and cultural interaction (Castles 1999, p.16.).

While Castles makes an important point about the potential outcome of cooperative efforts for the developing economies, it is difficult to imagine that the developed nations, lacking the necessary political will, will cooperate. As Appleyard argues, although the general background described so far has been well-known for years, there has been a 'dearth of systematic thinking at the international level on the linkage between large-scale migration, population increase, racial inequality and global insecurity' (Appleyard 1992a, p. 23).

For Appleyard, the four essential aspects of a development package that would address the issues of both the income and demographic differentials between the developing and developed countries are trade, debt relief, investment and effective aid. The burden of accumulated foreign debt in developing countries is probably one of the most fundamental obstacles to human development (Appleyard 1992a, p. 24). Recent widespread public support and pressure on the relevant governments and organisations including the World Bank, International Monetory Fund (IMF), etc. both in the developing and the developed countries in favour of debt relief has indeed been impressive. However, it is all too noticeable that even such powerful public pressure has failed to move the relevant bodies to take steps to remedy the situation which would begin to make a difference to the developing countries. Despite much noise about substantial debt relief for many of the developing countries, so far little or nothing has actually happened.

The usual kinds of exploitative relations/conditions continue to feature in both trade and investment relations, which are integrally related to debt problems in the first place, between richer and poorer nations. This also has implications for the relations between the lower and upper classes within individual nations in both parts of the world. Genuine cooperative aid and development assistance with a view not only to enhance economic growth, but also for the redistribution of wealth (both internationally, and internally within the developing nations) does have a role to play. However, with all of these, lack of political will is the fundamental obstacle both at the international level and within individual developing countries.

It is clear that the dysfunctional nature of Bangladeshi social structure that has been discussed can only be tackled effectively if genuine political effort is made both by international bodies as well as by the Bangladeshi government and its people internally. The structural problems of Bangladesh which motivate people to emigrate out of the country and which work as disincentives for existing migrants to return to the country are linked to the international relations of production, that is the modern economy, and the recent reform measures undertaken by the IMF, World Bank etc. in the form of 'Structural Adjustment' and related development policies.

To encourage skilled migrants to return to the country, there is a need to address these structural problems that are internal to Bangladesh, as well as external factors, including the role of the donor agencies in Bangladesh. The state, i.e. the government, has to be more accountable and functional, so that the law and order of the country can be restored, security of the public can be ensured, and the problem of corruption and the system of bribery can be dealt with. It is also very important that employees are paid a much higher salary to enable them to have a decent standard of living, work professionally, improve the quality of education and health systems and address environmental and pollution problems. Many of these problems can only be tackled through a change in the political will of the elite in the country and of international bodies like the IMF, World Bank and World Health Organisation (WHO).

Bangladesh was not always in such a state of affairs. As part of Greater India less than a century ago, what is now Bangladesh was considered full of promise in terms of its fertile soil, rich fisheries and a healthy population. Throughout history the people of East Bengal, now Bangladesh, had been more politically involved and committed to the welfare of the region. Indeed as recently as 1971 through the war of liberation, Bangladeshis displayed resilience and political commitment, either with direct participation in the war or through protests in other forms.

Why do the Bangladeshi middle class and the elite seem to lack commitment to do any 'good' for the country today? What has happened to the kind of commitment Bangladeshis showed when they were fighting against their common enemy, the then West Pakistan?

Understanding the range of commitments, obligations and behavioural motivations of Bangladeshis, we have to understand the social context. As Wood points out, we need to contextualise their behaviour to Bangladeshi society's 'highly imperfect, socially embedded markets, overall extreme scarcity of resources, a dysfunctional and imperfectly marketised state and a correspondingly high reliance upon personal social resources' (Wood 1999, p. 3).

This dysfunctional nature of Bangladeshi society can be linked back to the history of liberation. Unfortunately, since the liberation of Bangladesh, political loyalty, rather than meritocracy, has become the basis of recruitment to the civil service (Wood 1999). This started with the special favouritism that was shown by the Awami League to the so-called Freedom Fighters. Although the initial step in this regard by Sheikh Mujibur Rahman might have been innocent, since this period the whole system has been contaminated and has continued in the same pattern. The politicisation of university campuses also goes back to this period. Most of the senior cadres in the civil service gained their position in this way and their relative incompetence might also be explained by this. The tradition of corruption and the bribe system is also linked to these relatively weak civil service cadres.

Inside Bangladesh, a political climate has to be facilitated whereby the poor and women can raise their 'voice' when they are not getting their due share in the economy, legal field or in politics. But more importantly, the middle class Bangladeshis must come around to see that their interests lie in joining the hands of the poor. A collective voice, mass movements, and solidarity between the poor and the middle class against the dysfunctional system are necessary. Until and unless effective voices are raised nothing will change, not even with the intervention of donors with the Bangladeshi government. The government has to be accountable to the people, and a collective voice between the middle class and the poor is the only way. No one will listen to the poor, and it is a mistake to assume that the situation of the poor can only be improved at the expense of the middle class. This does not have to be the case (Wood 1999).

The middle class has a critical role to play. Unless they begin to protest, there is no prospect for any real change. People have become accustomed to living with such problems. The middle to upper middle classes, understandably, have better networks at different government or commercial levels, and somehow they try to survive. They have an on-going struggle as they try to manage within the dominant mode of survival with the system of corruption, bribery, relatively low salary, anxiety about the family's security, human rights issues, the local *mastans* and dysfunctional health and education systems. But the poor have no leverage at the government or commerical level, and they suffer all the time without a break.

The international bodies and donor agencies also must play their part in this. Firstly, by addressing some of the international structural issues, putting pressure on an appropriate power-base (IMF, World Bank) to change things in relation to trade, debt relief, investment and aid as they affect Bangladesh. Secondly, they can facilitate internally in the creation of a 'collective voice' of the people so as to make the government and elite in the society gradually more accountable for everything: public funds, legal structure, market situation, education and health system and so on.

This process is clearly going to be slow, but some work has already begun. We have to ensure that existing genuine efforts do not go astray. There are individuals in different sections of society who can be used as 'change agents'. These potential 'change agents' are those who are not committed to the present dysfunctional system and are looking for a better way. In some ways returnees are in a good position to take up this role. At the same time, the potential emigrants can also be recruited as 'change agents'. The returnees have experienced life elsewhere and know what changes they desire to make the country more 'liveable' for themselves and their families.

There are others who are already engaged within the country, working for some real change. The NGO sector is a good example, although there are also many problems here. Since the early 1970s numerous NGOs have been flourishing in Bangladesh. Some of them have now grown very big in terms of their coverage of the rural population and have become very well known internationally. Others remain small, while many new NGOs have also started up over the last three decades. Bangladesh now has over 2500 NGOs.

Of these, some of the earliest ones were indigenous and founded by return Bangladeshi migrants. These founders were inspired by the socialist philosophies, the doctrines of the then Awami League. These NGOs include BRAC, the largest NGO in the southern hemisphere, Proshikha, Gonoshastha Kendra (People's Health Centre), Nijera Kori and a few others. All these NGOs had shared a stated commitment to social mobilisation and conscientisation (facilitating the collective 'voice' of the poor). There is no doubt that they have some real achievements to their credit. There are many instances in which groups associated with these NGOs have benefited from their training in conscientisation. Landless men and women have worked together to resist unfair wages and oppressive behaviour in the Integrated Rural Works Programme and Food for Work Programmes. Women's groups have organised successfully to protest against having to give bribes to authorities and so on. However, these success stories are few. In any case, there were other structural limitations, including those imposed by foreign donors and the absence of an appropriate political apparatus (Rozario 1997).

Over the last decade or so social mobilizaton programmes of these NGOs have been undermined, among other factors, because of the increasing emphasis on microcredit by the donor agencies. As Rogaly has pointed out, the single-track allocation of resources 'earmarked for the very poorest people' to microcredit has meant and will mean that there is no intervention in health and education or other development issues such as social mobilization (Rogaly 1996, p. 101). There are many other problems associated with this blue-print approach to anti-poverty agendas through microcredit, but for the moment the point is that there is a need to redress this situation, especially in relation to social mobilisation programmes. This is because such social mobilization programmes, that is an organised voice, are essential to make political leaders and government officials accountable to their citizens, middle class or lower class, men or women.

Ain 0 Shalish Kendra (Legal Aid Centre) which was founded more recently is another radical NGO involved in delivering legal aid services to the poor. They have also been involved in pushing the government to introduce various new laws in relation to oppressive gender relations. In recent years, some independent research institutes have been initiated locally. These are involved in an advocacy role to bring in positive changes in the society. Any attempt to bring in more sustained changes can tap into the existing efforts by these 'change agents' but returnees can no doubt also play a crucial role in this.

Because Bangladesh is still heavily reliant on external development assistance, the donor community also has a critical role to play in bringing positive changes to the Bangladeshi social structure. Although, in theory, foreign donors are not supposed to involve themselves with 'politics', in practice it is never the case. It is well known that aid is never free from strings. It is also well known that 'donor funds are partially responsible for the scale of corruption, rent-seeking and inequalities in the society' (Wood 1999, p. 11).

Clearly, there are obstacles and problems which, at present, effectively discourage skilled Bangladeshis from returning to Bangladesh and which make it difficult for those few who do return to make an effective contribution. These need to be addressed in a systematic and concerted manner. The following recommendations suggest a possible line of approach and outline some of the issues that need to be considered.

CONCLUSION AND POLICY SUGGESTIONS

1. At present, there appears to be no effective programme in place in Bangladesh to encourage genuine migrants to return permanently or for substantial periods of time.[3] The first step would be to institute such a programme, and to give it enough funding and enough political support to enable it to address some of the problems that have been discussed. Given the dysfunctional nature of the government of Bangladesh, this would require intervention and assistance from international bodies. 'Change agents', including potential returnees, should be consulted in the establishment of the programme as well as relevant government officials.

2. An initial approach might start with a number of returnees within a single industry (or perhaps a group of related industries) in a single district. Individual returnees working in isolation are likely to meet high levels of resistance and resentment from established staff, especially if they are provided with special salaries and conditions (see the case study of Mr Ahmed). A group of people who could provide mutual support and who could coordinate their interventions would be likely to be more effective than individuals scattered in different industries and contexts.

    Appropriate models which can be adapted for the Bangladeshi context may already be available in the experience of return migration in other countries, such as Taiwan or China. Once an effective programme has been set up in a single area, it can be tried out in another context. A similar approach may be practicable in the case of the Bangladeshi civil service itself.

3. As suggested by many of the respondents, Bangladeshi expatriates or other foreign experts could be brought in to initiate training institutes in special fields where there is a felt need in the country (e.g. IT). These experts could be brought in for a specified period to train people locally. A special scholarship system could be established to fund students to access these training programmes.

   Such programmes could provide an effective alternative for meritorious students to travel abroad for higher studies. At present, very substantial resources are directed towards funding the education of Bangladeshi students overseas, from public funds, donors, and of course the families of the students themselves. If a significant proportion of the resources were directed into setting up an effective alternative within Bangladesh, this would both reduce the high loss rate of skilled Bangladeshis through overseas education, and also bring back substantial numbers of overseas Bangladeshis to teach in these programmes, either on medium-length contracts or permanently. In order to ensure that the qualifications obtained were recognised internationally, these programmes might be set up, initially at least, as colleges attached to appropriate overseas universities.

4. Returnees, whether in industry and government, or in education, need to be paid a salary commensurate with what they would get overseas. They also have to be ensured good health and education facilities for themselves and their children. Where (as in most cases) appropriate schooling is not already available, special school facilities may need to be constructed on the International School model. Special health complexes could be constructed, equipped with modern technology and internationally competent staff at all levels. Here, again, concentrating on one or two localities might make such an approach more practicable.

   These then could be used as models to be emulated and the facilities expanded to be available to non-returnees. However, efforts would need to be made to ensure that the existing Bangladeshi culture of corruption, bribery, unprofessionalism, etc. would not contaminate the new programmes. Unless the class issue is effectively addressed, it will still be the very rich and upper middle classes who will monopolise such measures, regardless of need.

5. If the returned migrants are to act as 'change agents', then mechanisms would also need to be devised so that the personnel involved in these new programmes have an effective voice in Bangladeshi society. At present, real criticism of the dysfunctional Bangladeshi system is either stifled, or

diverted into the largely irrelevant contestation between the two major political parties and their associated interest groups. There are high levels of dissatisfaction with the present state of the country, but with no real focus around which this dissatisfaction can cohere, most people among the middle class understandably choose either to extract as much as they can from the system or to seek overseas migration.

Returnees have, in most cases, direct experience of more effective and functional modes of government, and are in a good position to make relevant and informed criticisms. If ways can be found to set up linkages between these people and the more critical voices in the NGO sector, along with other relevant actors, this could help constitute an effective 'collective voice' for those elements of the middle class who are prepared to push for change. If this can be achieved, then the seed for real change could take root and continue to grow.

6. Donor agencies have a critical role to play in ensuring that returned migrants act as effective change agents (see point 5). They need to fund selectively to groups, NGOs and individuals to facilitate this programme. Social mobilisation programmes have been undermined in recent years because of the exaggerated emphasis on microcredit as the primary way of ameliorating poverty. Microcredit can be a useful tool, but it is now clear that it cannot substitute for an effective poverty-reduction strategy, if only because most of the obstacles are social, not financial. Funding should be used selectively to encourage those elements that are working effectively to challenge the social barriers that prevent the poor from accessing the facilities they need and from taking a full part in the governance of their society.

7. International bodies like IOM, WHO and the World Bank also have a critical role to play in order to ensure they facilitate, rather than prevent the development of a 'collective voice' of critique. There have been recent statements from such agencies calling for reform of the structure of governance and for the institution of genuine democracy. Most major international organisations, however, remain divided on such issues, and there is a real risk that a 'collective voice' of critique might be perceived as a threat to IMF, World Bank or global capitalist interests. It needs to be stressed that effective integration of Bangladesh into the evolving global society can only be achieved as a result of structural reform of Bangladeshi society in the direction of greater participation, reform of corruption and mismanagement and the adequate provision of social services such as health and education.

8. The skilled migrants who choose to remain overseas have made a significant contribution to the developed societies where they now live. It would be desirable for developed countries which receive skilled migrants to

recognise the debt they owe to the developing countries which spent their resources in training these skilled migrants in the first place, and to find some way to repay this debt. This could be in the form of appropriate aid to address some of the structural problems and obstacles that stand in the way of potential returnees returning to their countries.

9. Last but not least, there is a need to address the gender dimension by ensuring that a substantial proportion of returned skilled migrants are female, and that their specific concerns are highlighted, both in the planning and management of any programmes for returned migrants, and in the mechanisms which are created to express the collective voice of the returned migrant group.

NOTES

1   The analysis and conclusion was done by Dr Santi Rozario who also directed and conducted the field research. Dr John Gow was responsible for the statistical analysis and the tables, especially 'Overview of Sample'. We also acknowledge the contribution of the three research assistants who have conducted most of the interviews: Ms Hasina Ahmed, Dr Naseem Hussain and Ms Puspa Rodrigues.

2   'From 1976 to 1983, the country earned over $US2 bn. from them, their proportion of the GNP rising from 0.7 per cent. In 1976, to 4.1 per cent in 1981' (Gardner 1995:2). Most Bangladeshi remittances in the 1980s came from the Middle East: 78.12 per cent in 1983, the rest being from Britain.

3   The UNDP TOKTEN (Transfer of Knowledge Through Expatriate Nationals) programme, which covers 25 developing countries including Bangladesh, is for short-term consultancies only (two to eight weeks). We included a question about TOKTEN in the interview schedule, but few of our interviewees had even heard of it.

4. China: Government Policies and Emerging Trends of Reversal of the Brain Drain

Luo Keren, Fei Guo and Huang Ping

BACKGROUND

China is the most populous country in the world, with a total population of 1.27 billion in the mainland in 2000. In 1953, when China conducted its first census after the founding of the People's Republic, the total population of the mainland was 594 million. By the time of the third census in 1982, the total population had increased to more than 1 billion (State Statistical Office 2001). The last two decades of the twentieth century saw a remarkable slow down in terms of natural population increase. This is partially a result of the widely recognised family planning programme, which aims to encourage couples to have fewer children, ideally only one child.

There are 56 ethnic groups in China with the majority being Han. The proportion of the Han population in 2000 was about 91.59 per cent of the total population: 55 ethnic minorities comprise only 8.41 per cent of its total population. In the past five decades, the proportion of the ethnic minority population has increased slightly.

China's population is relatively young compared with many developed countries. The proportion of young people (0–14) is 22.89 per cent of its total population while the older population comprises 6.96 per cent of its total population. Although the population aging problem has not been serious so far, it is predicted that in the decades to come China will face serious problems with aging. The family planning programme, which encouraged couples to have one child has had an impact on the population structure.

In the past decades, Chinese education attainment levels have seen a remarkable increase. Among the population aged six years and above, the illiteracy rate has dropped from 33 per cent in 1964 to 6.7 per cent in 2000. The proportion of university-educated people has increased from 416 per 100 000 people in 1953 to 3611 per 100 000 people in 2000. It is claimed that this is because of compulsory education up to junior high school level. However, some studies and reports show that in recent years school drop-out rates have increased, especially among migrant children who do not have equal access to local schools in the cities (Guo 2001).

In 2000, about 64 per cent of the total population lived in the countryside while 36 per cent lived in cities and towns. The proportion of the urban population has increased considerably in recent decades. In 1982, the proportion of the urban population was 20 per cent while in 1953 this figure was only 13 per cent. The increasing level of urbanisation has been a direct result of a gradual relaxation of the policy restriction over people's spatial mobility. The household registration system, or *hukou*, which divides the entire Chinese population into agricultural and non-agricultural population since late 1950s has been very effective in the pre-reform era in restricting people's spatial movement. Non-agricultural residents enjoyed a much better life than agricultural residents. They had access to government subsidised foodstuffs and daily necessities, better education opportunities and better employment opportunities. The change from agricultural to non-agricultural status was strictly controlled, therefore migration from the countryside to cities and towns was restricted.

After the implementation of economic reform policies in the late 1970s, and especially in the early 1980s, Chinese people have gradually gained more freedom in terms of spatial movement. The market-oriented economic system has freed a significant number of rural surplus labourers, and at the same time, many cities started to provide job opportunities for migrants from the countryside. By the late 1990s, it was estimated that the total migrant population (both permanent and temporary) ranged from 50 to 80 million (Solinger 1999).

A BRIEF REVIEW OF INTERNATIONAL MIGRATION AND GOVERNMENT POLICY

Since the late 1970s, the Chinese government has allowed students and scholars to study overseas in the hope that they would return to modernise the country. Since then more than 320 000 students have gone overseas to study, nearly half to the US. In the same period, only 110 000 have returned (Larmer 2000). Most of those who returned were officially sponsored, either on state scholarships or under institute sponsorship. Many of these students and scholars were obligated to return under the agreement of their official sponsorship. The Tiananmen Incident in 1989 almost stopped the flow of returning overseas Chinese students, as a number of countries either granted the students permanent resident status or extended their stay. China's official media agency, the *Xinhua News Agency*, made a similar estimation, claiming that among the 300 000 students and scholars overseas, only one third of them had returned (*Xinhua News Agency* 1999). Most of these overseas students were China's brightest, especially in the science and engineering disciplines. Therefore China suffered a serious 'brain drain' problem, especially in higher education and research institutions. However, in recent years, it has been observed that an increasing number of students have returned to China. In 1998, it was reported that 7379 students came back, which was a sharp increase, compared with 1593 returnees in 1990 (Larmer 2000). *Xinhua* claimed that about 80 per cent of Chinese students overseas intended to return to their homeland to start a career (*Xinhua News Agency* 1999).

A report in the *Far Eastern Economic Review* (Wilhelm and Biers 2000) provides a number of stories of the successful return of overseas professional Chinese who have found their fortune and success in China, and this has made them feel that there is 'no place like home'. Another report in *Newsweek International* (Larmer 2000) also suggests that there is an increasing number of western-educated highly-qualified overseas Chinese who have returned to China. They often work in law firms and multinational companies and/or establish their own firms. Zweig (1997) conducted a study on the views of mainland Chinese in the US about returning to China and found that the majority of Chinese did not intend to return. Economic factors, such as better income and housing in the US, as well as professional concerns, such as lack of career mobility and poor work environment in China, were important. Only 9 per cent of respondents indicated an intention to return but Zweig predicted that if China's economy continues to grow, significant numbers of Chinese would return in the future.

So far, most studies on return migration to China have focused on trends and the number of returnees, contributing factors in decision-making and attitudes about return. Most studies have been conducted in countries outside China. Studies on impacts of return migration on Chinese society, community and institutions, as well as returnees' family have been limited. Except for some journalist reports, very few studies have actually been carried out in China on people who have already returned.

China may wish to duplicate Taiwan's experience in reversing its brain drain. Like China in the 1970s and 1980s, Taiwan's intellectual brain drain was from the 1950s to the 1980s. It is reported that from 1950 to 1980, 80 000 university graduates left Taiwan to study abroad. Among those students who went during the 1960s, only about 5 per cent returned (Zweig 1997). However, in the 1980s, Taiwan's socio-economic systems entered the so-called post-industrial development and a large number of overseas students and scholars returned to Taiwan.

Emigrants from China in recent times were mainly students and scholars who went to the US, European countries, Japan, Australia and New Zealand. There is a recent trend of independent emigration to countries like Australia and Canada, but the number of emigrants has been relatively small compared to the students and scholars. According to statistics released by the Ministry of Education, since 1978 only about 110 000 people have returned out of the total 320 000 Chinese overseas students and scholars, including those who were sponsored by official programmes. If the figures included those students who were self-sponsored, the return rate would be even smaller. UNESCO estimated that there were 713 200 Chinese studying abroad from 1978 to 1998 (Li and Lui 1999). At the same time, the average return rate of Chinese studying abroad was about 33.3 per cent, among which 83 per cent were state-sponsored students and scholars, 56.5 per cent were institution-sponsored and only 3.9 per cent were self-sponsored. Among those who went to the US to study (53.3 per cent of the total), the return rate was only 18.8 per cent (Cheng 1999). Table 4.1 lists the number of officially-sponsored overseas students and scholars, and returnees, by receiving country from 1978 to 1998.

The Chinese government has taken steps to reduce the impact of the 'brain drain'. It is stipulated that those studying abroad and covering their own expenses, must serve in China for a certain period of time or pay back part of their education fee. Those sponsored by the state or by institutes must sign an agreement before leaving the country.

In spite of strict restrictions on leaving the country, the Chinese government has made efforts to adopt a positive attitude towards the return of its overseas students, scholars and other skilled labour, who are labelled 'overseas talents'. The Central Government has also carried out a series of reforms of the relevant policies and regulations. In 1990, many departments under the State Council released documents to stimulate the return of skilled Chinese educated overseas. In 1992, the state council issued *A Circular on Studying Abroad*, in which many restraints on exit-entry by those studying abroad and their families were eliminated, and sending institutions and Chinese embassies overseas were asked to provide assistance to overseas students and scholars. This document was the first to provide a more relaxed environment for those studying abroad. Local authorities, at various levels, also adopted similar policies for their administrative territories. In 1993, the Central Government introduced a policy of 'supporting studying abroad, encouraging return and securing free movement'. As a result, the late 1990s started to see an increasing number of returnees from overseas.

Table 4.1 Estimated number of officially-sponsored overseas Chinese students and returnees, 1978–98

Receiving country	Overseas students	Returnees	Stayers	Return rate (%)
US	160 000	30 000	130 000	18.8
Japan	50 000	25 000	25 000	50.0
Canada	20 000	10 000	10 000	50.0
Germany	20 000	10 000	10 000	50.0
UK	16 000	10 000	6 000	62.5
France	11 000	6 000	4 000	63.5
Australia	10 000	4 000	4 000	60.0
Others	13 000	4 000	110 000	15.4
Total	300 000	111 000	200 000	33.3

Source: Li and Lui (1999)

Table 4.2 provides information on the proportion of returnees in China's three most developed cities, Beijing, Shanghai and Shenzhen. Since the mid-1990s, Chinese governments at various levels have implemented a series of programmes to attract 'overseas talent' to return to China to take up positions and manage research projects or invest in private business or joint ventures. A number of 'science parks', 'special development zones' and 'high-tech zones' have been established in the capital city, Beijing, and most provincial cities. For example, in 1999 the Beijing government issued a provisional regulation of encouraging overseas Chinese students and scholars to work in Beijing, particularly to work in the Zhong Guan Cun Science Park, located in Beijing's north-west suburb. According to this regulation, returnees are entitled to a number of benefits, including simplified application and registration proce-dures for setting up a business venture; waiver of business taxes in high-tech areas; eligibility to apply for special research funding and low interest loans to establish private business; eligibility to import some tax-free equipment, material and other necessary goods for research and establishing business, and eligibility to import some tax-free durable goods for personal use (*Shenzhou Xueren 1999*). Returnees with scientific and technological projects or pro-grammes are warmly welcomed in Beijing to develop and produce new and high-tech products. Table 4.2 shows that Beijing ranks first in the number of returned students and scholars. Beijing had 60 per cent of all return doctoral degree holders who were employed in science parks.

Table 4.2 Information on the number and characteristics of returned overseas students/scholars in Beijing, 1999, Shanghai and Shenzhen, 1997

Factor	Beijing	Shanghai	Shenzhen
Total returnees	20 000	17 000	676
Returnees from developed countries	-	>70%	>80%
No. of 'science parks for returned scholars'	2	5	None
Proportion of China's doctoral degree holders in its 'science parks'	60%	18%	13%
Master's degree holders in 'science parks for returned scholars'	30%	53%	23%
Enterprises in 'science parks for returned scholars'	48	674	-

Source: Data collected by Luo Keren from interviews with Scientific and Technological Cadre Bureau of Beijing, the Overseas Scholars' Affairs Office, Shanghai, and Shenzhen Bureau of Personnel in 1999.

The rapid economic development and social change in Shanghai and gradual improvement in policies and service for returnees has brought about a 'return wave' in recent years. Among all returnees, there are two groups of people who are targeted by policies, doctoral degree holders in all disciplines, particularly in science and technology, and entrepreneurs. Shanghai has taken the following measures to attract overseas talent:

- establishing special offices to strengthen coordination and management;
- setting up networks between home institutions and overseas organisations;
- outlining the main policy 'welcome back';
- making various sorts of assistance available for returnees;
- improving complementary service;
- helping establish projects and investments in 'science parks'.

Considering that Shanghai's total population is about one per cent of the total population in China, the number and proportion of overseas students and scholars from Shanghai is very high. It has constituted about one quarter of total overseas Chinese students and scholars since the 1980s. At the same time, Shanghai has also seen a great number of returnees, about 17 000 people, which accounts for one sixth of total returnees in China. It is clear that Shanghai has become a most attractive city for returnees.

MAJOR CHARACTERISTICS OF THE SAMPLE OF RETURNEES

Shanghai has become the top city in China for returnees and was chosen to carry out the survey. In total, there were 185 respondents. The sample consists of a high proportion of males (81.8 per cent), which may reflect the pattern of returnees in general. Attempts were made to interview as many female returnees as possible, but it was very hard to find sufficient number of female returnees. There is a tendency that if a decision to return is made, normally it is the husband who returns, while the wife stays overseas. All respondents interviewed obtained an advanced degree overseas, among them 68.1 per cent having a Ph.D. On average, they had worked overseas for a few years after completing their education. The average age of the sample was 39.79, with the youngest 26 years old and oldest 57 years old. Most of the returnees were between 35–44 years old (56.2 per cent) and 35–39 years old (24.9 per cent). The majority of the respondents were married (85.6 per cent). Almost half of the respondents were professionals, while about 30 per cent were in management positions. More than 80 per cent of the respondents were in the service sector, which includes information system services, banking and financial services and other conventional services.

Almost all our respondents were equipped with higher degrees and western working experience and many of them were in senior management positions or were business owners themselves (33.5 per cent). About 43.5 per cent of the respondents were in teaching and research positions in various universities and research institutions. Private and joint-venture as well as university and research institutions were the major sectors that attracted overseas skilled returnees. This pattern directly reflects government policies which encourage the return of overseas talents in these areas (Tables 4.3 and 4.4).

Table 4.3 Returnees by occupation

Occupation	Number	%
Manager/entrepreneur	57	33.5
Professor	23	13.5
Researcher	22	12.9
Associate professor	20	11.8
Associate researcher	9	5.3
Other professions	39	23.0
Total	170	100.0

Note: Not stated = 15

PROCESS OF RETURN MIGRATION

Researchers in some western countries, including Australia, have indicated that people who plan to return to their home countries are those who have obtained residence status overseas and who are able to take advantage of both sides. However, the survey in Shanghai found that only 27.6 per cent of respondents had obtained, and still kept, permanent residential status of other countries or held foreign citizenship. Among permanent returnees (78.4 per cent of total returnees), only a small proportion (9.0 per cent) still owned property overseas. Among temporary returnees (15.9 per cent of total returnees), about 71 per cent still owned property overseas. Among intermittent returnees (4 per cent of total returnees), about 57 per cent still kept their property overseas. It seems that those who planned to return to China on a permanent basis, did not or could not, purchase property overseas. Those who returned to China on a temporary basis tended to have property overseas.

The sample includes returnees from 28 different countries. The first eight most popular countries were the US, Japan, Britain, France, Canada, Germany, Australia and Russia. About 72.4 per cent had working experience overseas, with those who came from the US and Japan having a higher proportion (81 per cent and 80 per cent respectively). A noticeable proportion of respondents went overseas before the late 1980s, with a peak period around 1989 (13 per cent of total respondents). The average number of years of working overseas was 4.36, with the longest being 14 years.

Table 4.4 Major characteristics of the Shanghai sample, China

Characteristics	Number	%
Total	185	100
Age		
Less than 35	35	18.9
35 to 44	104	56.2
45 and over	46	24.9
Sex		
Male	150	81.1
Female	35	18.9
Marital status		
Married	155	85.6
Single	14	7.7
Widowed/Separated/Divorced	12	6.6
Highest overseas education level		
Doctorate	111	68.1
Master's	38	23.3
Bachelor's	11	6.7
Vocational certificate	3	1.8
High school	0	0
Present occupation		
Manager/entrepreneur	56	30.3
Professional	92	49.7
Other	37	20.0
Industry		
Agriculture	9	5.0
Manufacturing	26	14.4
Service sector	145	80.6

The period of stay in China, by education level, indicates that higher degree holders tended to have a longer plan of stay. About 75.9 per cent of doctoral degree holders claim they plan to stay in China on a long term basis, compared to 65.7 per cent for Master's degree holders and 27.3 per cent for Bachelor's degree holders. This may reflect government policies that are more beneficial to higher degree holders, especially those with doctoral degrees. A large proportion of returnees from Britain claimed that they plan to stay in China on a long term or permanent basis, while more returnees from Canada and Australia reported that they were here on a temporary basis. This is certainly a reflection of the differences in immigration policies in these countries. Obtaining permanent resident status in the UK is much harder than in Australia and Canada, therefore returnees from Britain tended to plan their stay in China on a permanent basis.

Table 4.5 shows that more than half of the respondents claimed that their return was on a permanent basis. Only a small proportion of the respondents reported that they had returned to China on a temporary basis. A larger proportion of those who have worked overseas for less than two years came back on a permanent basis while a smaller proportion of those who have worked overseas for more than two years came back on a permanent basis. It seems that longer working experiences effect returnees' basis of return.

Table 4.5 Anticipated length of return

Length of return	Years of overseas working experience			Total
	Less than 2 years %	3 to 5 years %	More than 5 years %	%
Permanent	81.6	63.4	46.9	66.4
Temporary	14.3	14.6	12.5	13.9
Intermittent	4.1	22.0	40.6	19.7
Total	100.0	100.0	100.0	100.0

Table 4.6 lists the major reasons for return. This shows that government policies have played an important role in attracting returnees from overseas. More than one quarter of the returnees claimed that they returned in response to government policies or programmes. About 20 per cent of returnees were motivated by the better opportunities in Shanghai, which may have also resulted from policies and programmes. Other major reasons, such as being close to family members and friends, also seemed important.

The number of enterprises in 'Science Parks for Returned Scholars' reached more than 600 in 1997. It is believed that the number has grown much higher in the past two years, particularly following China's accession to the World Trade Organisation (WTO). The government policies and general social, economic and political environments have played an essential role in attracting people from overseas.

Table 4.6 Major reasons for return

Reason	Number	%
Favourable government policies	82	29.5
Better job opportunities	57	20.5
To be close to family members	38	13.7
To be close to friends	33	11.9
Better business opportunities	33	11.9
Other reasons	35	12.5
Total	278	100

Table 4.7 lists the percentage distribution of returnees by age group and with whom they returned. More than half of the respondents reported that they returned on their own, while around 42 per cent of the respondents have returned with a spouse or the whole family. Compared with the information in Table 4.5 which shows that the proportion of return on a permanent basis is more than 60 per cent, it may indicate that some returnees have determined to stay in China for a long period of time in spite of the fact that their spouse may have decided to stay overseas. It may also suggest that some returnees are single people. Without further information, this finding is not conclusive.

Table 4.7 Return with family members by age group

Returning Unit	Less than 35 years %	35 to 44 years %	45 years and above %	Total %
Return by oneself	67.6	50.5	55.6	54.9
Return with spouse	5.9	11.7	17.8	12.1
Return with whole family	20.6	35.0	26.7	30.2
Others	5.8	2.9	0.0	2.7

Table 4.8 presents the most important assistance received by returnees upon their return. This is a self-reported question, and the answer could be in more than one category. In this table, only the more important assistance is listed. Over half of the returnees got a housing allowance, which is one of the most important factors assisting returnees in having a smooth transition. Normally housing allowance is awarded upon their return as a one-off cash payment or as a subsidised apartment/house allocation. The sample included a noticeable proportion of university teaching and research staff, who normally received some housing allowance in the form of subsidised housing allocation. They reported that the most important assistance they received also included help with finding a job and with their children's education. About 52.1 per cent of the returnees had obtained job offers from their employers before return (not shown on the table).

Table 4.8 Most important assistance from government programmes or employers, in facilitating their return

Type of assistance	Number	%
Housing allowance	69	53.1
Finding employment	17	13.1
Settlement arrangement	16	12.3
Children's education	14	10.8
Spouse's job	5	3.8
Other assistance	9	7.0
Total	95	100.0

Note: Not stated = 90

Many respondents have closely followed what has been happening in China in terms of government regulations and general social and economic environment. They have various information sources. About 64 per cent of our respondents reported that they searched for information about the prospective job market in China before they made a decision, and about 20 per cent of them collected their information by visiting China before they made a decision to return. If possible, they would secure a job offer before they actually moved back. A large proportion of our respondents were able to find employment before they returned.

The Chinese government has actively promoted its incentive programmes to attract more qualified 'overseas talent' in recent years. Various levels of government have organised 'recruitment fairs' or 'recruitment trips' to some major cities overseas, including cities in the US, Europe and Australia. Many overseas diplomatic mission offices also play a role as recruiter to promote the government's incentive programmes. They display brochures and pamphlets in their offices and also distribute information through various channels. Table 4.9 shows that about half of the respondents reported that they were aware of the government's incentive programmes. Those who had worked overseas for more than five years were more likely to be informed of government programmes than those who had worked overseas for less than five years. It may suggest that the longer they worked overseas, the more chance they would have in being informed about the programmes.

Table 4.9 Awareness of incentive programmes and receipt of assistance

Awareness & Assistance	Years of overseas working experience			Total
	Less than 2 years	3 to 5 years	More than 5 years	
	%	%	%	%
Aware of incentive programme	40.9	44.4	67.7	49.5
Not aware of incentive programme	59.1	55.6	32.3	50.5
Received assistance	56.1	61.3	70.8	61.5
Did not receive assistance	43.9	38.7	29.2	38.5

The government incentive programmes often include various assistance to returnees, such as housing allocation, academic title or position, a certain level of salary or allowances as well as assistance towards children's education. The results show that more than half of the returnees in the study reported that they had received assistance from either the government or their employers. Those who had worked overseas for more than five years were more likely to receive assistance than those who had worked overseas for less than five years. Those who had worked overseas for less than two years were least likely to receive any assistance. This finding suggests that the years people spend overseas may have certain effects on their qualification, and therefore on their bargaining power with prospective employers.

The study shows that only half of the respondents had detailed knowledge about particular government policies. Many of them couldn't describe what the preferential policies were that would benefit returnees. Government overseas missions and organisations could have played a better role in informing overseas students and scholars of recent changes in policies. Returnees from the seven major countries (France, Japan, Canada, US, Germany, Russia and UK), where there are large numbers of overseas Chinese students, reported that only half of them knew the contents of some government policies; the rest were not aware of the specific contents of government policies. The seemingly contradictory finding – on one hand, many people returned to China in response to government policies, and on the other hand, many of them were ignorant of the specific contents of the policies – may indicate that the specification of government policies and the general improvement of the social and economic environment of society have all played some roles in attracting overseas returnees. Although some people were unable to say exactly what the government policies were, they had an impression that the overall social and political environment had changed in favour of those who had obtained overseas qualifications and who were willing to come back.

Table 4.10 shows that about one half of the respondents claimed that they made their decision to return in less than six months. Those who had worked overseas for more than five years took longer to make the decision, while those who had worked overseas for less than two years tended to take a much shorter time to make their decision. This result, of course, is affected by returnees' time spent overseas. It seems to reflect certain patterns of decision-making process among returnees.

Like migration, return migration is a family matter and decision-making is expected to be made through mutual understanding with other family members, especially partners. More than half of returnees were supported by their partners when they made the decision to return to China. Another 30 per cent had a neutral opinion from their partners. Ten per cent of partners did not support their decision to return. This finding suggests that the majority of returnees' decision of return was supported by their partners. As we know from the previous section on demographic profile, the returnees were predominantly males.

Government policies that encourage the return of highly qualified 'overseas talent' have played an important role. Many returnees returned to China in response to government policies. Many have received actual assistance from the state or their employers. The study also shows that the decision to return seems to be jointly made by the returnees and their partners. The time returnees have worked overseas affected their awareness of government incentive policies and also affected whether they were able to receive any assistance from government or their employers. It can be assumed from this that as long as policies are in favour of returned 'overseas talent' and there are opportunities available for returnees, China will see a continued reversal of the 'brain drain' in the future.

Table 4.10 Time to make decision and partner's reaction to return

Decision-making	Years of overseas working experience			Total
	Less than 2 years %	3 to 5 years %	More than 5 years %	%
Time to make the decision				
Less than 6 months	66.0	47.1	30.3	50.0
6 to 12 months	14.6	23.5	12.1	16.7
1 to 2 years	12.8	20.6	18.2	16.7
Over 2 years	6.4	8.8	39.4	16.7
Partner's reaction				
Supportive	66.7	47.2	60.0	58.6
Not supportive	8.9	13.9	10.0	10.8
Neutral	24.4	38.9	30.0	30.6

IMPACT OF RETURN MIGRATION

Most returnees made their decision to return based on careful study and comparison between their home and host countries. They normally had high expectations, such as of better job/business opportunities before their return. Income is certainly a consideration, but it was rarely claimed by most respondents. The results from the survey show that returnees in enterprises (managers and business owners) generally had a higher income level than their domestic counterparts, while professionals in research institutes and universities normally had more or less an average level income. During the interviews, complaints were often voiced by professionals about a sharp decline in their real income after they returned from overseas. Few of them were really satisfied with their current economic status but seemed happy about their job status at their institutes. Housing assistance which many of them received from their employers was an important factor which ensured their better-than-average living standard in Shanghai.

Income, Living Conditions and Satisfaction

A large proportion of returnees (35.2 per cent) reported that their income decreased, 21.0 per cent of the returnees' income didn't change much, 13.6 per cent claimed that they had a higher income than before their return, and a very small number of returnees (1.1 per cent) claimed they made an extremely good living in Shanghai after returning. The respondents in the survey tended to compare their income or living standard with that before their return. Many of them (39 per cent) never compared themselves with the local co-workers in terms of their income or living standard. Among those who compared their own income with their local counterparts, about half felt that their income level was more or less the same as their co-workers who had never studied or worked overseas. Around one third said that they earned a more than average income compared with their local co-workers. Only 4 per cent reported that they earned a much higher income compared with locals and 15.5 per cent of returnees stated that their income was lower than their co-workers.

When asked whether they were satisfied with their position in their work place, few were satisfied. Among senior professionals, only 28.8 per cent felt satisfied. For associate professionals, only 18.8 per cent were happy about their current position. People in management viewed their job more positively, and 47 per cent of enterprise managers were satisfied with their jobs.

In addition to income, we used means of transport to indicate their economic well-being. Among all respondents, about 33.3 per cent went to work by bike, 23.3 per cent by vehicle provided by their work place, 12.8 per cent by private car, 4.4 per cent by taxi and 3.3 per cent by motorbike. Among those who went to work by car, 87.0 per cent of them owned their own car. Despite the low level of satisfaction among returnees, the results show that the majority of returnees (79.1 per cent) didn't have problems in adapting to the daily life in China; only 20.9 per cent had difficulties in re-adjusting. Those over 40 years old experienced difficulties. It is probably true that middle-aged people had higher expectations before returning than their younger counterparts. Family responsibility may also be a factor contributing to their difficulties.

Observations and interviews in Australia among potential returnees to China showed that those who intended to return wanted to 'play a big role' in the work places in China and held high expectations about their return. However, this study shows that among those who had already returned, for many people the level of satisfaction was not as high as they would have liked. The primary motivation for return was to 'give full play to their professional knowledge and skills'. Most of them paid special attention to whether the job in China fitted their education and training background. In addition, although many people claimed that they did not like to compare their income level with their local co-workers, most of them were concerned about how their colleagues or co-workers viewed them. Respect and responsibility were the two major concerns of returnees.

Working Conditions

About half of the sample worked at research institutes and universities, about 32 per cent in the commercial or services sector, 11 per cent in the industrial sector, 6.6 per cent in the medical sector, 1.6 per cent in government organisations and about 1.1 per cent in NGOs. Not surprisingly, more than half of doctoral degree holders were in research institutes and universities.

Table 4.11 shows the percentage distribution of returnees' employment status and whether they have a managerial position if they are employed. Men and women in the sample do not show any significant difference in terms of their employment status. Overall around 72 per cent of the respondents were employed and around 25 per cent were running their own business, either as an employer or self-employed. However, there is a gender difference in terms of job position. Although around half of the total respondents claimed that they were doing managers' jobs, the male proportion in managerial jobs was considerably higher than that of women. China is a traditional society in which men are considered the leaders of society and major breadwinners in the family. Although our respondents came from overseas and most of them had earned at least a Master's degree, the gender difference in terms of managerial position was still noticeable.

Table 4.11 Percentage distribution of employment status and position by gender

Employment	Male %	Female %	Total %
Employment status			
Employee	72.5	73.5	72.7
Employer	21.0	20.6	20.9
Self employed	5.8	2.9	5.2
Other	0.7	2.9	1.2
Managerial position			
Yes	50.5	38.5	48.1
No	49.5	61.5	51.9

The results from Table 4.12 suggest that among those who had received assistance from government or other sources, the majority (62 per cent) had received research funds. A further 13.4 per cent had received support for purchasing research equipment or establishing some facility for work. Around 8.5 per cent received a bank loan, which normally were low-interest or no-interest loans. Among other types of supports and assistance, some people had received donations from private enterprises or were offered preferential conditions when establishing an enterprise themselves.

Table 4.12 Most important assistance/support facilitating work from government and other sources

Type of assistance/support	Number	%
Research funds	88	62.0
Facility or equipment	19	13.4
Loan or finance	12	8.5
Other types	23	16.2
Total	142	100.0

Table 4.13 shows that many of the respondents were able to access the latest information and material in their fields by using the internet (37 per cent) and professional periodicals (20 per cent). A considerable proportion of returnees (26 per cent) claimed they obtained the latest information in their field by visiting overseas or through overseas connections. Returnees' work places – mostly research institutes or universities – also have some information available.

Only a small proportion (3 per cent) relied on libraries for information. This is a common problem in many cities in China as library collections are often out-of-date or inconvenient to access. It is understandable that returnees who experienced convenient access to libraries or labs overseas would like to make good use of their overseas visits for obtaining the latest information in their fields. Most of the returnees had established connections with their overseas colleagues and friends. By having access to the latest information and material through overseas visits, many returnees could have a direct or indirect impact on their work place, co-workers and their fields of expertise.

Table 4.13 Most important channels of acquiring information, material and equipment

Channel	Number	%
Internet	37	36.6
Periodicals	20	19.8
Overseas visits/connections	26	25.7
Private connections in China	3	3.0
Library	3	3.0
Work place	11	10.9
Other	1	1.0
Total	101	100.0

Table 4.14 provides the percentage distribution of job satisfaction by age group and years of overseas working experience. A greater proportion of people who worked overseas for less than two years felt satisfied with their current job, while a smaller proportion (53.3 per cent) of those who worked overseas for five years or more showed less job satisfaction. Those who have worked overseas for a longer period of time have a higher expectation about their jobs back in China, or they were more used to working environments in the West. If their current jobs do not meet their expectations, they may be more likely to feel dissatisfied. Similarly, the results suggest that younger people are more likely to feel dissatisfied than older returnees. People younger than 35 years of age may face more challenges, such as having a lower position in an institute or enterprise and therefore they may have less access to other opportunities. Around half of the respondents aged 45 and above felt satisfied with their current position. The age difference in job satisfaction may also be affected by returnees' qualifications. Younger people may not have obtained high enough credentials for a better position back in China.

Table 4.14 Job satisfaction by age group and years of overseas working experience

	Satisfied with job %	Not satisfied with job %	Total %
Years of overseas working experience			
Less than 2 years	79.1	20.9	100.0
3 to 5 years	66.7	33.3	100.0
More than 5 years	53.3	46.7	100.0
Age group			
Less than 35 years	75.8	24.2	100.0
35 to 44 years	62.9	37.1	100.0
45 years and above	58.3	41.7	100.0

Impact on Society

Almost all respondents considered that what they had learned and gained overseas was important for their current career development, running a business or taking up a position in research institutes or universities. The majority (82 per cent) of respondents claimed that their knowledge and skills gained overseas were important to their current work. About 11 per cent of returnees claimed that the business network they established overseas helped their business in China. Some (5.8 per cent) appreciated that the capital or savings they had accumulated overseas helped their establishment in China.

As part of their incentive policies, governments at various levels have attempted to relax regulations on returnees' overseas trips, either for family or business reasons. Our findings showed that the majority (63.7 per cent) of returnees enjoyed the freedom of being able to go overseas while a noticeable proportion (36.3 per cent) of returnees still considered it inconvenient to go overseas due to complicated approval procedures or lack of funding for their trips.

The survey used self-evaluation techniques to calculate the impact of returnees on the community and society. The overall impression was positive. About 60.6 per cent regarded themselves as carriers of advanced techniques and managerial skills that had made a contribution to Chinese society. About 26.7 per cent expressed that they have made a positive impact on social transformation in terms of transmitting western culture, ideals, values, as well as international business practices and rules. However, 10.0 per cent considered that their influence was not strong enough at this stage. The results indicated that those with higher degree (Ph.D.) tended to be less involved in decision-making, probably because they were in research institutes and universities, where conducting research and teaching was relatively independent work.

More than half (52.2 per cent) of the returnees had remitted to members of their families regularly when staying abroad. When they came back they also brought back money for settlement and investment. Among all returnees, about 43.1 per cent came back with between US$10 000 and 50 000, 31.2 per cent with over US$50 000 and 25.7 per cent with less than US$10 000. The top items of consumption for the returnees were housing, durable appliances, support for members of families and investing in business and stock markets. Although direct investment by returnees using their own savings was less important than buying a house or durable appliances, it is believed that once they settled, they would actively participate in business investments or the stock market.

Most returnees kept in touch with overseas colleagues, friends and family members. E-mail was the most popular means of communication. To keep up-to-date, 87 per cent read foreign periodicals regularly, among which 46.6 per cent read professional periodicals, 27.0 per cent read monographs and 25.7 per cent read popular and entertainment magazines. For those who didn't read foreign periodicals regularly, 40.0 per cent explained they didn't have time to read while 13.3 per cent claimed they could not afford to buy foreign periodicals.

Table 4.15 shows a list of reported contributions made by returnees to their work places. The most important contribution was personnel training, which included students in research institutes and universities. Improving profit profiles of their work place and making scientific inventions were also considered as important contributions. However, quite a small proportion (10 per cent) of respondents claimed that establishing international linkages was their important contribution. This is probably because international linkages were considered as an indirect contribution to their work place, while other contributions such as improving profits were regarded as direct contributions. Only a very small proportion (3 per cent) reported that they contributed to their work place through decision-making. This is probably related to high expectations before return and low level satisfaction after return. Not 'playing a big role' was probably an important factor in making respondents dissatisfied.

Table 4.15 Contributions to the work places by returnees

Type of contribution	Number	%
Personnel training	110	37.0
Improvements in profits	60	20.2
Scientific and technology intervention	50	16.8
Involvement in decision-making	46	15.5
Establishment of international links	10	3.4
Improvement in management	3	1.0
Other	18	6.1
Total	297	100.0

There is an emerging trend of return of skilled and business migrants to China. Government policies that encouraged return of 'overseas talent' have shown some results, particularly in research and higher education areas. Returnees played an important role in transferring to China what they learned and gained overseas. Many of them were placed in an important position either in enterprises or research institutes. With China's entry to the WTO, we would expect to see more returnees from overseas to take advantage of rapid economic development. However, the more worrying problem that this study was unable to address was the impact of the return on the stability of family relationships. The study has shown that a significant proportion of married people returned to China alone and left their family members overseas. The potential impact of return migration on marriage and related issues needs to be addressed if a follow-up study is possible in the future.

CONCLUSION

China's policy makers recognised the seriousness of its brain drain problem in the past two or three decades. They have realised that it was impossible to reverse the out-flow of skilled and highly educated people, especially in today's increasingly globalised world. Instead of imposing strict restrictions on emigration, they started to apply a more practical approach that encouraged the return of 'overseas talent'. As we can see from this study, these policies, and the positive environment associated with the policies, have had some impact on the pattern of return migration of skilled and business people. Although many of these returnees may not be able to utilise particular policies, they may be influenced by the positive gestures of government policies. The results also suggest that returnees have started to play a noticeable role in transferring to China what they learned and gained overseas. Many of them are placed in important positions either in enterprises or research institutes, and many are playing a role in decision-making or providing advice for decision-makers. We would expect to see greater impacts of returnees on decision-making in institutions and organisations, as well as in policy making in general in the future.

China's brain drain problem is similar to that which has occurred in other developing countries, including Taiwan in the 1960s and 1970s. China learned from Taiwan's experience on reversing the brain drain. The model of 'science and technology parks' was directly copied from Taiwan and other south-east Asian countries. It seems true that 'science and technology parks' in many major Chinese cities have played an important role in attracting returnees from overseas. Like welcoming foreign capital and investment in the 1980s, China now opens its arms to welcome its highly qualified 'overseas talent' who are equipped with western education and working experience, sometimes with capital as well. More overseas Chinese will be attracted by the improving working and living conditions in China.

Problems associated with the return include re-adjusting to life in China, children's education, corruption and an inefficient bureaucratic system. Although these problems will not be solved immediately, many respondents hope that working and living conditions will improve.

After joining the WTO, China's social and economic environment is expected to improve further and more people from overseas are expected to return. Cities such as Shanghai, Beijing, and other coastal cities will become more attractive to highly educated overseas returnees. However, China is worried that competition for highly qualified human resources will be intensified and more returnees will be employed by multinational companies or joint-ventures – as the income differences between foreign companies and domestic enterprises are quite significant. Thus, one 'brain drain' (to overseas) problem is being solved while another 'brain drain' problem may occur within China.

As this study was conducted two years before China joined the WTO, it was unable to capture this trend. It is believed, however, that government policies and regulations have played an important role in directing the flows of return migration. This study has shown that a large number of returnees were employed by universities and research institutes – reflecting the government's incentive programmes in research and education sectors. It is hoped that future policy changes will also play a significant and positive role in guiding the distribution of returnees between multinationals and domestic enterprises.

This study raises a question as to whether overseas returnees contribute to increasing inequality in China. The results clearly suggest that returnees who are employed by universities or research institutes earn more or less the same income as their domestic co-workers. Only those who are employed by foreign enterprises or have their own business enjoy a much higher income level. In terms of income, it seems that most of the returnees are not in the highest income brackets in China. However, on the other hand, many returnees are 'rich' in terms of resource channels and opportunities. The financial assistance and subsidies they receive upon their return, from their employers or government programmes, are much more generous than their domestic counterparts receive in income. Many of them are granted special conditions even before signing their employment contracts, such as paid overseas visits and holiday and opportunities for attending overseas conferences.

The special treatment that returnees enjoy may create tensions between returnees and their local counterparts. The popular nickname for overseas returnees, 'sea turtles', reflects some resistance from the locally educated people who, on the other hand, are called 'land tortoises'. In public debates and the media, the terms 'sea turtles' and 'land tortoises' are frequently used to distinguish the place where a person received his/her formal education. This, in turn, is seen as distinguishing their views on certain issues. Although not necessarily richer than others in terms of income, overseas returnees have certainly received much attention and have evolved into a special category in Chinese society. This seems inevitable and is probably the only way that a significant number of returnees can be encouraged to come back home.

5. Taiwan: Significance, Characteristics and Policies on Return Skilled Migration

Ching-lung Tsay

BACKGROUND

In the past half century, the Taiwan economy grew rapidly from a very low level. The average annual growth rate of real GDP was 8.7 per cent in 1951–69, 10.0 and 8.2 per cent in the 1970s and 1980s, respectively, and 6.4 per cent in 1990–2000. In terms of per capita GNP, the figure was around US$200 in the early 1950s and did not reach US$500 until 1972. It went over US$2000 in 1980, reached $8000 in 1990 and $14 000 in 2000.

The number of students going abroad was also closely related to government policy and regulations. Before 1987, Taiwan was under martial law and international migration was under strict control. As a result, students needed to apply for permission to study abroad. A key consideration in the control over student migration was the concern over the 'brain drain'. There was a strong fear that the better educated would leave Taiwan and only a small proportion of them would return. As primary and secondary schools were mainly provided by the government, it was believed that student migration represented a loss of human capital investment. For political and economic reasons, a student needed a permit from the authority to receive further schooling in a foreign country.

The major government policies and regulations over student migration can be classified into the following four periods (Tsay and Tai 2001):

- the Tightly Controlled Period (before 1962) – only those students who passed the required government tests were permitted to go abroad;
- the Relaxed Period (1962–75) – students were not required to take the tests if they wanted to study abroad on their own financial support;
- the Screening System Period (1976–89) – students (with own support)

needed only to be screened by reviewing their relevant documents such as admission to an advanced institution and permission to enter a foreign country. The long lasting practice of granting permission for overseas education to those who passed the written tests was terminated in 1976;

- the Open-door Period (after 1989) – after Martial Law was lifted in 1987, control over international migration was completely removed in July 1989. From then on, access to foreign education was available to any one who could afford it. The government no longer imposes any regulations or requirements on students intending to be further trained outside Taiwan.

While the income level was low and the migration control was tight, there were only a few hundred students going abroad for advanced studies each year in the 1950s. As shown in Table 5.1, the number increased to a few thousand in the following decade when the restrictions on studying overseas were relaxed. As per capita GNP was under $350 in the 1960s, only very wealthy families could afford to send their young people to study abroad. Consequently, the figures for 1950–59 and 1960–69 were 4515 and 21 248 respectively. The majority of them went to study in the US on scholarships. In the 1970s, the total number reached 31 365. As per capita income went over US$2000 in 1980, the number of students going abroad was between 5400 and 9200 in each year of the 1980s and totalled 64 216 for the decade. In this period, especially after 1985, an increasing proportion of Taiwanese college students went abroad for advanced training on family support. In fact, the control over student immigration had loosened in the late years of the Screening System Period (1976–89). The number of people going to study abroad increased from 6000 to 9000 in 1985–89, while the per capita GNP doubled (from $3291 to $7626).

After the Open-door Period started in July 1989, the size of the student migration rose to over 11 000 in 1990. It surged to 29 000 in the next year and then stayed between 24 000 and 27 000 in most years of the 1990s. The unusually high number observed in 1991 clearly represents the acceleration effect created by the liberalisation of student migration in 1989. The significant increase in the volume of students going abroad reflects the combined effects of both economic development and changes in government policy.

Table 5.1 Number of students going to study abroad, number of highly educated returnees, and number of locally trained masters and doctorates, 1970–98

Year	A Going abroad	B Return	C Locally trained	D Total supply	B as % of A	B as % of D
1950–59	4 515	400	-	na	8.9	-
1960–69	21 248	1 172	-	na	5.5	-
1970–79	31 365	5 166	11 290	16 456	16.5	31.4
1980–84	28 321	5 269	13 229	18 498	18.6	28.5
1985–89	35 895	9 611	24 648	34 259	26.8	28.1
1990–95	135 064	30 238	62 430	92 668	22.4	32.6
1996–98	80 766	7 627	46 254	53 881	9.4	14.2
1970–95	230 645	50 284	111 597	161 881	21.8	31.1
1950–98	337 174	59 483	157 851*	215 762*	17.6	26.8*
1950–98#	337 174	67 170	157 851*	215 762*	19.9	30.4*

Notes: * For 1970–98 only.
\# Adjusted by doubling the number of returnees in 1996–98.
Sources: National Youth Commission and 1999 Education Statistics of Taiwan.

RETURN MIGRATION

While Taiwan was concerned about the 'brain drain' in the 1950–80 period, the government was keen on encouraging and facilitating the return of Taiwanese 'brains' abroad, especially those in the US. The major purpose was to have them involved in national development and construction projects, industrial upgrading and the improvement in higher education and research. Tsay and Tai (2001) examined government policy and related programmes by dividing them into three stages:

- In the first stage (1950–55), the Ministry of Education started a small programme to target the highly educated in the US by contacting them and providing them with services in job-matching and some financial assistance for the cost of return. As the number of returning students was not large, this stage was more experimental in nature;

• In the second stage (1955–71), the government set up an ad hoc cabinet-level committee to promote and facilitate the return of the foreign trained. As the ratio of students going abroad to returnees stayed at a low level (less than 10 per cent in the 1950s and 1960s), this programme was strengthened in 1969. A service centre was created to actively encourage the return migration of those with a masters or doctorate degree or those with special talent;

• In the third stage (after 1971), the National Youth Commission (NYC) took over the major responsibility for facilitating return migration of the highly educated as well as assisting them with job placement or business creation. Besides the NYC, there were several other government agencies which were active in recruiting the highly educated from overseas. They include the National Science Council and the Ministries of Education and Economic Affairs. All the organisations involved had specific programmes and funds to attract the highly educated to return to work in the fields of their concerns.

The NYC kept records of return migrants with masters and doctorate degrees or equivalent. Tsay and Tai (2001) argue that this data source is more suitable than others, such as the population census, for the study of return migration of the highly educated. Table 5.1 shows that the total number of returnees in 1950–98 was close to 70 000. In the 1950s and 1960s, the figure was only 400 and 1172, respectively. As a result, the ratio of returnees to students going abroad was 8.9 per cent and 5.5 per cent, respectively. For 1970–79, the total number of returnees jumped to 5166 when government policy and measures became more active and aggressive. The resulting go–return ratio was 16.5 per cent.

A significant 'reversal of the brain drain' did not become evident until the 1980s. The annual inflow of highly educated return migrants went over 1000 in 1982 and doubled by 1988. For 1980–89, the total volume was almost 15 000. The yearly size of return migration continued to increase from 2863 in 1990 to its peak of 6510 in 1994. The total number for 1990–95 was 30 238. As a result, the go–return ratio for 1980–95 was about 23 per cent, with a high ratio of 26.8 per cent in the 1985–89 period. The figure was much higher than what was observed for the earlier three decades. While the ratio does not mean exactly that one out of every four or five persons who went to study abroad returned to Taiwan, it does suggest an increasing trend towards 'brain drain reversal'.

Before 1995, all highly educated (with master's or doctorate degrees) return migrants registered with the NYC were reimbursed with a grant to cover their airfare and travel expenses. This programme was terminated in 1996, however, and the NSC records indicate a remarkable decline in the size of the return migration from 6272 in 1995 to 2760 in 1996. The number further declined to 2341 in 1998. For each year in 1996–98, it is suspected that the actual volume of return migration is double the registered one. Taking this fact into account, the estimated number of returnees in 1950–98 is 67 170, which is about 20 per cent of the volume of students going abroad (Table 5.1). On average, there is one case of return migration in every five cases of student migration.

Table 5.1 shows the importance of the returnees in the total supply of the highly educated between 1970–98. Between 1970–79 and 1980–89, the number of locally trained master's and doctorates increased from 11 000 to 38 000. It further surged to 109 000 for 1990–98. As a result, the share of the returnees in the total stock of returnees and locally trained was 31, 28 and 32 per cent in the 1970s, 1980s and 1990s, respectively. Overall, the returnees account for about 30 per cent of the total supply of the highly educated in 1970–98. The proportion was especially high (35 per cent) in 1992–94 when the number of returnees increased sharply.

It is evident that returned 'talent' has played an important role in the supply of skilled labour and professionals in post-World War II Taiwan. These returnees are believed to have made significant contributions to economic growth and educational development. The next section examines data on the characteristics of Taiwan's highly educated returnees and this is followed by a history of the policies that have emerged to encourage return migration. Given the relative success of Taiwan in this domain, this analysis may provide valuable insights for other regions of the world as well as providing a backdrop for the sample survey results.

CHARACTERISTICS OF RETURN MIGRANTS

Sending children to study abroad was very expensive for most families in Taiwan, especially in the earlier years when the income level was low. In a culture that puts heavier weight on men than women and within a context of limited economic sources, more male students than females went abroad (Tsay 1987). The available data indicate that the proportion of female students going overseas for education was 28 per cent in the 1950s, 32 per cent in 1960s and 39 per cent in 1970–89 (Tsay and Tai 2001). The uneven distribution of students going abroad by gender has certainly exerted some impact on the sex composition of the highly educated returnees. As shown in Table 5.2, the proportion of females among returnees was 22 and 17 per cent in the 1950s and 1960s, respectively. Afterwards, it increased to 22 per cent in the 1970s, 35 per cent in the 1980s and 43 per cent between 1990–94.

Table 5.2 Distribution of highly educated returnees by gender, 1950–94

Year	Number	Male %	Female %
1950–54	76	76.3	23.7
1955–59	323	78.8	21.2
1960–64	353	78.7	21.3
1965–69	819	87.5	12.5
1970–74	2 055	78.4	21.6
1975–79	2 973	77.2	22.8
1985–89	9 611	65.4	34.6
1990–94	23 966	57.0	43.0
Total	40 176	62.9	37.1

Note: The highly educated returnees refer to those with advanced degrees (mostly doctorates and masters) and who registered their returns to Taiwan with the National Youth Commission (to receive the reimbursement of airfare).

Source: National Youth Commission.

The distribution of returnees by highest degree received abroad, from 1976 to 1998, is presented in Table 5.3. As the size of return migration grew, there was a declining trend in the share accounted for by doctorate degrees. The proportion was 28 per cent in 1976–79, 16 per cent for 1980–95 and 13 per cent for 1996–98. In the same timeframe, the proportion of master's increased from 58 to 87 per cent. In the early years, some of the returnees did not earn their degrees in a foreign country but they went out for specific research projects or training programmes. The percentage of this group was 14 per cent in 1976–79 and 6 per cent in 1980–84, but it has become negligible since the late 1980s.

The increasing dominance of returnees at the master's level reflects changes in the market demand for the highly educated in Taiwan. It also reveals the fact that more and more students went out on family support after the income level improved in the mid-1980s. For self-supported students, it is economically reasonable to obtain a Master's degree quickly and return to work in Taiwan. A Ph.D., which takes much more time and effort to obtain, is not necessary except for academic jobs or senior research and management positions in industry.

Return Migration in the Asia Pacific

Table 5.3 Distribution of highly educated returnees by degree received, 1976–98

Year	Total No.	Doctor %	Master %	Research %
1976–79	2 404	27.8	58.3	13.9
1980–84	5 269	14.3	79.5	6.2
1985–89	9 611	17.3	80.3	2.4
1990–95	30 238	16.1	83.2	0.7
1996–98	7 627	12.7	87.3	0.0
Total	55 149	16.5	81.4	2.1

Source: National Youth Commission.

As Table 5.4 shows, in 1976–79 about a half (52 per cent) specialised in science and technology and the other half in social sciences and humanities. The share of the science and technology category dropped to around 40 per cent in the 1980s and then 34 per cent or lower in the 1990s. In the same time, the proportion of social sciences and humanities increased to about two thirds. Within the science and technology group, the percentage of engineering increased while other areas declined or stayed unchanged. For the set of social sciences and humanities, significant increase in the share was observed for business–economics. On the other hand, the sub-groups of liberal arts and social sciences lost their relative importance. In summary, changes in the composition of returnees by area of specialisation are characterised by the increasing importance of engineers and business professionals among the total returnees. This finding reflects the process of Taiwan's economic development in the past few decades.

With regard to the country in which the returnees studied, Table 5.4 reveals the dominance of the US in terms of market share. For the period 1976–97, 84 per cent of returnees studied in the US while the share for Japan and UK was 6 per cent and 4 per cent, respectively. Except for the first three years, the share of the US was between 75 and 90 per cent in almost every year. Japan was rather important at the beginning, accounting for 22 per cent of the total returnees in 1976–79. Its share declined rapidly to below 10 per cent in the 1980s and then 5 per cent in the 1990s. On the other hand, the share of the UK has increased significantly in recent years to about 10 per cent in 1996–97.

Table 5.4 Distribution of highly educated returnees by area of specialisation, 1976–98 (%)

Year	Total	Sciences & technologies	Social sciences & humanities
1976–79	2 404	51.8	48.2
1980–84	5 269	43.0	57.0
1985–89	9 611	39.5	60.5
1990–95	30 238	34.5	65.8
1996–98	7 627	31.3	68.7
Total	55 149	36.5	63.5

Source: National Youth Commission.

Table 5.5 provides information on the composition of the highly educated returnees by their work place type in Taiwan. When the number was small in the 1970s, about a half of the returnees worked in universities or research institutions. However, the proportion in higher education dropped dramatically from 49 per cent in 1971–74 to 15 per cent in 1990–95. The share of research institutes declined only slightly from 7.0 to 5.7 per cent. There are also clear changes in other types of work places. The category of returnees in their own business accounted for only 13 per cent in 1971–74 but this proportion increased to 28 per cent in 1993 and 65 per cent or more for later years. For 1990–95 as a whole, the corresponding figure was 51 per cent. A somewhat similar pattern of change was also found for the group of returnees working for private firms. Its share increased from 6 per cent in 1971–74 to a peak of 26 per cent in 1980–82, and then reduced to 20 per cent in 1990–95. The two categories of returnees working for government agencies and public firms have lost their relative importance. Between 1971–75 and 1990–95, the proportion of the former group shrank from 11 to 5 per cent, while the corresponding figures for the latter group were 14 and 3 per cent.

The pattern of changes in the composition of returnees by type of work places is even more remarkable when the data for 1996–98 are in the comparisons. As shown in Table 5.5, returnees in their own business accounted for 84 per cent of the total number in 1996–98, while those working for private firms was 11.7 per cent. By comparison, the share of returnees engaged in university teaching and research was only 3.0 per cent, and the percentage in government agencies and public firms was negligible. It is clear that in the late 1990s the relative importance of the group running their own enterprises has continued to increase, while the proportions working for universities, research institutions, government agencies and public firms has further decreased.

Table 5.5 Composition of highly educated returnees by type of work place

Year	Total No.	Research Inst %	Unis & Cols %	Gov't Agencies %	Public Firms %	Private Firms %	Own Business %
1971–74	1 786	7.0	49.2	11.4	13.8	5.9	12.7
1975–79	2 973	6.3	41.4	10.6	8.7	9.9	21.3
1986	1 583	10.9	29.4	12.1	7.7	20.7	19.2
1990–95	30 238	5.7	15.1	5.3	3.4	20.1	55.7
1996–98	7 778	0.5	2.5	1.4	0.0	11.7	84.2

Source: National Youth Commission and 1999 Education Statistics of Taiwan.

This, however, needs to be viewed with caution as the estimate of returnees for 1996–98 is probably low, due to incomplete registration. For those in their own business, the government assistance for setting up enterprises was still a strong incentive for them to register their return with the government agency in charge (NYC). However, returnees in other types of work places might have lost the major incentive to report to the NYC since the programme of reimbursing airfares was terminated in 1996. To the extent that this possible bias exists, the 1996–98 figures have exaggerated the relative weight of the group owning their own business and suppressed that of the rest.

As indicated earlier, about two-thirds of total returnees between 1950–98 came back in 1990–98 and 22 per cent came in 1980–89. Furthermore, the registration data for the years before 1975 and after 1995 are either not available by characteristic or are incomplete in coverage. Table 5.6 compares the compositional differences in key characteristics of the returnees in 1975–79, 1980–89 and 1990–95. The three time intervals represent the period before the development of high-tech industries, the period of high-tech development, and the post-development period, respectively. The purpose of the comparisons is to reveal the relationship between the development of high-tech industries and the characteristics of the highly educated returnees from abroad.

Table 5.6 Selected characteristics of returnees

Characteristics	Categories	1975–79	1989–89	1990–95
A. Gender	Male	77.2	65.3	57.0§
	Female	22.8	34.7	43.0§
B. Degree	Doctor	27.8*	16.2	16.1
	Master	58.3*	80.0	83.2
	Research	13.9*	3.8	0.7
C. Area of Speciality	Engineering	46.6*	61.5	69.8
	Sciences	35.7*	25.5	17.8
	Medical Science	7.4*	8.2	7.2
	Agriculture	10.3*	4.8	5.1
	Sub-total	51.8*	40.7	34.2
	Education	7.0*	13.0	13.2
	Liberal Arts	38.6*	22.7	17.2
	Business & Economics	37.7*	55.1	64.5
	Social Sciences	16.7*	9.1	5.0
Sub-total		48.2*	59.3	65.8
	Japan	21.7*	7.5	3.6
	US	61.4*	84.3	87.7
	UK	3.4*	1.3	3.9
	Other	13.5*	7.0	4.8
Type of work place	Research Institute	6.3	9.1#	5.7
	Uni & College	41.4	26.3#	5.3
	Gov Agency	10.4	12.3#	5.3
	Public Firms	8.7	10.4#	3.4
	Private Firms	9.9	23.7#	20.1
	Own Business	21.3	18.1#	50.5

Notes: * 1976–79 only. # 1980–1982 and 1986 only. §1990–94 only.

In terms of gender structure, the proportion of females increased from 23 to 35 and then 43 per cent in the three stages. In the post-development period, however, the relative importance of females was smaller than that of males by 14 percentage points. The composition by degree indicated a decline of doc-torates from 28 per cent in 1975–79 to 16 per cent in the years after 1980. Table 5.6 further reveals that the majority of returnees had gone to the US for advanced training, accounting for 84–88 per cent in the years after 1980. While Japan was important in the early years, its share dropped from 22 per cent in 1975–79 to 8 and then 4 per cent in the next two periods.

Data on area of specialisation reveal that among the disciplines of sciences and technology, the share of engineering has increased continuously while that of sciences and agriculture decreased. In the social sciences and humani-ties, the relative weight of business and economics surged substantially but that of liberal arts and social sciences lost. It is clear that fields directly related to industrial development, such as engineering and business management, have become more popular among returnees. For the type of work place, the figures show that in 1975–79 more returnees worked in educational-research institutions and other government related organisations than in private or own firms. However, the situation has completely reversed in the 1990s. Half of the returnees were running their own business and 20 per cent were working for private firms. The share for university teaching and research was only one fifth.

The analysis has pointed to the increasing importance of returnees working for the private sector or owning their own business. As shown in Table 5.7, the records of the NYC revealed that the annual number of returnees was around 600 to 700 in the 1980s. It surged rapidly to 1500 in 1990, over 50 000 in 1993 and 55 000 in 1995. The total volume for 1983–95 was 26 917, while the estimated size for 1983–99 was 45 929 (having adjusted for the under-registra-tion in 1996–99).

A similar pattern of increase has also been observed for the number of the highly educated returnees from abroad who were employed in the Hsin-Chu Science-based Industrial Park (HCSBIP). In the early years after the establish-ment of the HCSBIP by the National Science Council (NSC) in 1980, there were less than 100 returnees working in the park. Table 5.7 indicates that the number did not reach 1000 until 1993. After that, it climbed rapidly to 3000 in 1998 and 5000 in the year 2000. The proportion of returnees in the total number of employees of the industrial park was below one per cent in the 1980s. It increased from 4.9 per cent in 1995, and then declined slightly before reaching the 2000 level of 5.2 per cent. In other words, there is at least one returnee in every 20 persons who are currently working in the HCSBIP.

The last column of Table 5.7 shows the share of the HCSBIP in absorbing the return flows of the highly educated to Taiwan. In the few years after its estab-lishment in 1980, the industrial part accounted for 5 per cent or less of return migrants. It then increased from 7 per cent in 1986 to 29 per cent in 1990, and

38 per cent in 1995. From then, the proportion is about 50 per cent or higher in 1996–99. As indicated earlier, the data on the highly educated returnees need to be adjusted for the bias due to under-registration with the NYC (see previous section). To the extent that the adjustment is insufficient, the figures in the last column of Table 5.7 for 1996–99 are exaggerated. Based on the increasing trend in 1983–1995, a reasonable estimate is that about a half of the total returnees working for the private industries are currently working in the HCSBIP.

Column 2 of Table 5.7 shows annual flows of returnees registered with the NYC, while the data in the third and fourth columns are stocks of returnees employed to work in the industrial park and the total employees in the HCSBIP, respectively. This inconsistency in the nature of the data used could have also caused some upward bias for the percentages presented in the last column of Table 5.7, especially for the recent years. While these deficiencies should be kept in mind, they are certainly not serious enough to deny the dominant role of the HCSBIP in absorbing highly educated returnees to Taiwan.

POLICY AND STRATEGIES

From the 1950s to the 1980s, the Taiwan government was seriously concerned about the phenomenon of the 'brain drain' and its adverse effects. On the one hand, student migration was under state control but this was substantially relaxed in the 1980s. On the other hand, the authority took an aggressive policy towards attempting to reverse the 'brain drain'. Various measures have been implemented to induce highly trained manpower to return from abroad and to work in Taiwan (see Appendix 1 for a complete list). The official policy has been:

- to improve and strengthen the institutions of higher learning and scientific research in Taiwan, with inputs from the highly educated returnees.
- to encourage Taiwan's 'brains' abroad (especially in the US) to move back and to contribute their knowledge and skills to the national development plans and construction projects.

As early as 1950, the Ministry of Education began with a small-scale experimental programme of contacting the highly educated in the US and providing assistance to facilitate their return. An ad hoc cabinet-level committee was set up in 1955 to take responsibility for promoting and facilitating return migration while a service centre was created by the committee in 1969. When the ad hoc committee was abolished in 1971, the responsibility was transferred to the NYC, another cabinet-level agency set up in 1966. Since then, the NYC has played a key role of recruiting the highly educated from abroad.

Table 5.7 Total returnees working for industries in Taiwan, number employed in Hsin-Chu Science-based Industrial Park (HCSBIP), and total employees in the Industrial Park, 1983–2000

Year	Returnees Working for Industries in Taiwan	Returnees Employed in HCSBIP	Number of Employees in HCSBIP	Returnees as a proportion of HCSBIP employees (%)	Returnees in HCSBIP as a prop of total in Taiwan (%)
1983	605	27	3583	0.8	4.5
1985	720	39	6670	0.6	5.4
1987	605	92	12 201	0.8	15.2
1989	605	223	19 071	1.2	36.9
1991	1 695	622	23 297	2.7	36.7
1993	5 272	1 040	28 416	3.7	19.7
1995	5 490	2 080	42 257	4.9	37.9
1983–1995	26 917	6 979	247 747	2.8	25.9
1996	2 620	2 563	54 806	4.7	-
	(5 240)*				(48.9)*
1997	2 581	2 859	68 410	4.2	-
	(5 162)*				(55.4)*
1998	2 260	3 057	72 623	4.2	-
	(4 520)*				(67.6)*
1999	2 045	3 265	82 822	3.9	-
	(4 090)*				(79.8)*
2000	-	5 025	96 110	5.2	-
	(-)				(-)
1983–2000	36 423#	23 748	622 518	3.8	51.4#
	(45 929)*#				(40.8)*#

Notes: *: Adjusted for under-registration (see text for details)   #: For 1983–99 only.

There are 19 programmes under seven organisations including the NYC, Ministry of Education, Ministry of Economic Affairs, National Science Council (NSC), Academia Sinica, the Industrial and Technology Research Institute (ITRI), and the Science and Technology Advisory Group for the Cabinet. For each specific programme, the particulars cover the application procedure, the qualifications for application, the items of assistance, and the timeframe of programme implementation.

The six programmes under the NYC are rather general in inducing Taiwanese students and scholars abroad to return and work in Taiwan. Except Programme 1-C, all the programmes of the NYC are still effective. In the 1990s, the programmes expanded to cover all the people who received master's or doctorate degrees either in a foreign country or in Taiwan. In this sense, the major function of the NYC has changed from assisting the recruitment of the highly educated from abroad to providing employment services to all graduates of doctorate and master's programmes both in Taiwan and abroad. This adjustment is appropriate as the share of returnees in the total supply of highly educated manpower in Taiwan reached one third in 1990–95 (Table 5.1). There has been less reason to argue for a special kind of assistance and services exclusively for those receiving master's or doctorate degrees in a foreign country.

Even though the NYC no longer limits its service to returnees, it is worthwhile to review its role in recruiting the highly educated from abroad. The major types of assistance and services provided by the NYC include the following:

- travel subsidy;
- job placement;
- business investment assistance;
- visiting professors and experts;
- programmes to step up recruitment;
- national development conferences;
- links with overseas professionals.

Travel Subsidy

The provision of travel subsidy started in the early 1950s with the experimental programme under the Ministry of Education. From the early 1970s to the end of 1995, all the returnees were entitled to a reimbursement of airfare and travel allowance from the NYC if they had registered their return with it. The very basic item of assistance in almost all the programmes is the provision of travel expenses. In some programmes recruiting senior experts, the assistance even covers the family relocation costs and the air tickets for a spouse and up to two non-adult children.

The NYC programme of reimbursing airfares to the returnees was terminated at the end of 1995. As a result, the number of registered returnees dropped by over 50 per cent in 1996 and continued to decline slightly in the following two years.

Job Placement

One of the major mandates and functions of the NYC is to facilitate the recruitment of Taiwanese scholars from overseas. The commission renders assistance to both the scholars overseas looking for employment in Taiwan and the domestic employers seeking highly educated personnel from abroad. The services include the following:

Recommendation
The NYC refers the applicants to the potential organisations of employment based upon their preference and area of speciality. These organisations include government agencies, government and private universities and colleges, state enterprises and private corporations.

An information clearinghouse
Each month, the NYC compiles information on the returned scholars looking for employment and distributes the data through a newsletter, free of charge, to over 2500 potential employers. Likewise, the NYC compiles and publishes a bulletin on 'master or higher degree holders wanted' and distributes it overseas. Such information is also announced in international editions of several Taiwan-based newspapers, to publicise job opportunities in Taiwan.

The computerised job information system
Since 1983, the data on educational and career backgrounds of all returning students have been computerised. In 1986, the NYC added information on 3000 leading private enterprises; government agencies; state enterprises; universities; colleges and research institutions into the system. This measure has been a successful and useful tool for returning scholars to locate and contact the potential employers.

'The scientist pool'
Before a returning scientist can find a suitable permanent job, he or she is given a one-year research appointment. Since 1979, 50 such temporary appointments have been made each year. The number increased to 75 in 1986, and then to 100 in 1989. Funding for the programme is provided by the National Science Council to encourage the return of highly trained scholars and supporting them before permanent jobs are available.

Business Investment Assistance

Overseas professionals in science, technology and engineering are encouraged to establish their own businesses in Taiwan and to transfer new technology to the island. For this reason, the NYC provides assistance in obtaining loans, production sites and facilities. If a loan is approved by the Commission, it is passed on to a relevant bank with the recommendation. The funds are provided by special funds and banks, and other financial organisations. An individual may apply for a business-funding loan for an amount of up to NT$1 000 000. That amount includes NT$400 000 in credit loans.

Visiting Professors and Experts

Many scholars, scientists and specialists might not want to migrate back to Taiwan permanently, while their expertise and knowledge could be highly valuable to Taiwan. To deal with this problem, the Taiwanese authorities have adopted special measures (including a comparative salary) to induce them to teach or work in Taiwan for a short period of time. Under the National Science Council and the Ministry of Education, more than 3700 senior scientists and experts and 2500 well-established scholars have returned to work in Taiwan as 'Visiting Professors' or 'Visiting Research Professors'.

Programmes to Step Up Recruitment

The government, in 1983, set up a programme to step up the recruitment of high-tech experts abroad because of the shortage in high-level manpower needed for national development. The programme has been implemented through long-term and short-term efforts from both the government and private sectors. The major aim was to attract and to hire overseas experts who have considerable experiences and who already had significant achievements in their professions to begin their 'second careers' in Taiwan. This approach is different from other measures which are mainly targeting new master and doctoral degree-holders abroad. The government efforts to enlist such well-experienced experts include the following.

Competitive salaries
The recruits are offered almost the same pay they receive abroad. When the formal salary is low, they are given allowances for research or housing to narrow the pay gap between Taiwan and abroad.

Good working conditions
The working environment, in terms of teaching and research facilities, is improved wherever possible to meet the needs of the returnees.

Housing facilities
Those who return to engage in teaching or research or work in the Hsin-Chu Science-Based Industrial Park are provided with free housing. Alternatively, they are given financial assistance if they choose to purchase their own housing units.

Adequate schooling for children
Assistance in children's schooling is provided, including bilingual schools.

National Development Conferences

A National Development Conference has been held in Taipei 14 times since 1972 and more than 3000 overseas scholars and professionals have participated in it at the government's expense. The conference holds panel discussions for government officials, scholars and professionals at home. Topics include economic development; science and technology development; social welfare; politics; culture and education. This highly successful public relations operation is a way of finding out what Taiwan's scholars and experts abroad are thinking.

Links with Overseas Professionals

Since 1975, the NYC has collected and established files of overseas Taiwanese scholars and professionals. This information is passed on to domestic academic and research organisations and industries to facilitate them in the recruitment of high-level scientists and specialists. Beyond this, the NYC has also assisted Taiwan's overseas scholars to organise more than 20 professional societies and to hold academic conferences annually with an aim to promote scholarly exchanges and mutual cooperation between Taiwanese scholars abroad and at home. The NYC also sends officials, scholars and professionals from Taiwan to attend these conferences. The meetings provide opportunities for the exchange of knowledge and technical information, the technology transfer to Taiwan and the recruitment of Taiwanese experts from abroad.

On account of Taiwan's long history of experience with the 'brain drain' and its relative success in reversing it to some extent, the following survey results will provide up-to-date data on the current situation.

SURVEY OF RETURN MIGRANTS

The survey that was undertaken in 2000 included 114 respondents. 61.4 per cent were males and 38.6 per cent were females. This combination is very close to the gender distribution of the highly educated return migrants working for industries as revealed by the registration data of NYC (61 per cent male and 39 per cent female). As expected, the proportion of males is higher among the older respondents (aged 35 and over) than among the younger ones under 35 (Table 5.8). The mean age of all the cases is 34.3, with a range from 25 to 50. On average, males are almost four years older than their female counterparts. For males, the age group with the biggest share is 30–34 (43 per cent), followed by the group of 35–39 (36 per cent). For females, the biggest share is found for ages 25–29, followed by the 30–34 age category.

Table 5.8 Respondents by age and sex

Age	Total		Male		Female	
	No.	%	No.	%	No.	%
25–29	23	20.2	4	5.7	19	43.2
30–34	44	38.6	30	42.9	14	31.8
35–39	31	27.2	25	35.7	6	13.6
40–50	16	14.0	11	15.7	5	11.4
Total	114	100.0	70	100.0	44	100.0
Total under 35	67	58.8	34	48.6	33	75.0
Total over 35	47	41.2	36	51.4	11	25.0

In terms of ethnic groups, over 70 per cent of the respondents were native Taiwanese (Fou-kenese and Hakanese) and the rest were 'Mainlanders'. There is not much variation in the ethnic composition across gender and age groups. The distribution by marital status differed between the two sexes. The married proportion was much higher among males than females. This fact held true for both the younger and older groups, especially the former.

The human capital possessed by the respondents is shown in Table 5.9. In terms of the highest degree received, the proportion having a doctorate degree was 21 and 2 per cent for men and women, respectively. The share of Master's degree or lower was higher among females. The higher level of educational attainment for males remains unchanged when age was controlled. According to Table 5.9, men also gained more work experience and had higher positions in the host country. The mean years of work experience for males was double that for females. A higher percentage of men had professional or technical positions, as compared to women (81 per cent compared to 36 per cent).

Table 5.9 Human capital of return migrants

Degree & experience	Males		Females	
	No.	%	No.	%
Highest degree obtained overseas				
Total	77	100.0	45	100.0
Bachelor	7	9.1	7	15.6
Master's	54	70.1	37	82.2
Ph.D.	16	20.8	1	2.2
Work experience overseas				
Total	78	100.0	45	100.0
No	52	66.7	32	71.1
Yes	26	33.4	13	28.9
Less than 5 years	18	23.1	12	26.7
More than 5 years	8	10.3	1	2.2
Employment overseas				
Total	26	100.0	11	100.0
Professional/ Technical	21	80.8	4	36.4
Administration	5	19.2	7	63.6

The characteristics of the job at the time of interview are presented in Table 5.10. Half of the respondents worked for integrated circuits companies, followed by telecommunications (20 per cent) and then electronics (15 per cent). In terms of speciality, the respondents were almost equally distributed in the technical, business and research and development departments. The positional distribution showed a concentration of managers (34 per cent), followed by professionals and technicians (19 per cent each). There were also some in sales and administration (11 per cent each).

Table 5.10 Job characteristics of respondents

Characteristics	No.	%
Industry	123	100.0
Integrated Circuits	63	51.2
Computers & Peripherals	5	4.1
Telecommunications	25	20.3
Opt electronics	19	15.4
Precision Machinery	2	1.6
Software design and Service	7	5.7
Other	2	1.6
Department	121	100.0
Technical Dept	35	28.9
R & D	29	24.0
Business Dept	33	27.3
Human Resources	5	4.1
Finance	5	4.1
Other	14	11.6
Position	118	100.0
Professional	22	18.6
Technical	23	19.5
Administration	14	11.9
Manager	40	33.9
Researcher/Teacher	1	0.8
Sales person	13	11.0
Other	5	4.2

About two thirds of respondents returned to Taiwan in 1995 or later, regardless of sex. At least a half of them (51.4 per cent) gave their main motivation for returning related to family factors. The second most common reason given was 'mental factor' and the third was 'job factor'.

According to Table 5.11, the majority of respondents did not have a pre-arranged job before return. About two thirds of them used normal channels to seek their job or spent more than a month finding a job. Only a third of respondents were aware of government programmes for facilitating return migration. However, almost 40 per cent of them did receive benefits provided by government projects. The table shows some differences between men and women. Men generally had a higher tendency to arrange a job before returning, had more information on government policies and benefited more from government policies.

Table 5.11 Job-finding method and information channel of return migration

Factor	Males		Females	
	No.	%	No.	%
Method of job finding				
Job arranged before return	21	28.0	4	9.3
Sought after return	54	72.0	39	90.7
Time spent finding job				
Under 1 month	34	63.0	24	63.2
Over 1 month	20	37.0	14	36.8
Information on gov policy				
Yes	25	33.3	11	25.6
No	50	66.7	32	74.4
Benefited from gov policies				
Yes	10	38.5	2	15.4
No	16	61.5	11	84.6

Table 5.12 provides the results of wage and income comparisons between the last work in the host country and the first job in Taiwan. Around 80 per cent of the respondents indicated that their wage in Taiwan was lower than overseas, by well over 100 per cent. The average disparity was well over 100 per cent.

Table 5.12 Wages and income in last employment overseas and first work in Taiwan

Factor	Males		Females	
	No.	%	No.	%
Wages				
Taiwan higher	2	2.6	1	2.3
Taiwan lower	64	83.1	33	75.0
No difference	5	6.5	4	9.1
No idea	6	7.8	6	13.6
Income				
Taiwan higher	10	13.0	4	9.3
Taiwan lower	39	50.6	16	37.2
No difference	18	23.4	15	34.9
No idea	10	13.0	8	18.6
Total	77	100.0	44	100.0

Incomes as a whole, as opposed to wages, include other benefits – such as housing, superannuation, subsidies, etc. On this basis, income in Taiwan was lower. Nevertheless, the average income was still only half what they had earned overseas.

With regard to job satisfaction in Taiwan, more than a half of the respondents were satisfied: 76.9 per cent of males and 55.3 per cent of females. But one fifth of males and 34.2 per cent of females answered 'no idea' to this question. At the same time, 61.5 of males and 67.4 per cent of females mentioned the possibility of moving abroad again in the future. This is particularly evident among males in the older age group (77.1 per cent) and females in the younger group (75.0 per cent).

DISCUSSION

To understand the possible impacts of skilled returnees on the development of high technology industries, in-depth interviews were conducted with the human resources managers of eight companies in such high tech industries as integrated circuits and semiconductors. The firms were characterised by a high degree of involvement from highly educated returnees. Four of the corporations had their boards chaired by returnees and/or their operation team dominated by returnees. In the other four companies, the proportion of returnees on the total payroll was as high as 10 per cent, double the average. It is believed that their reactions and comments on the relationship between the 'brain drain reversal' and high tech development are rather typical and deserve due attention.

The results of the interviews can be summarised in the following four points. First, highly educated returnees can be subdivided into those with experiences from abroad and those without. The group having work experience overseas have been the major contributor to economic development in general, and the development of high-tech industries in particular. The recent returnees, most of them with a master's degree and no work experience abroad, are not much different from the Taiwan trained in terms of work performance. Thus, most companies do not seem to have any strong preference for hiring recent returnees.

Second, highly educated returnees can be categorised into the old, middle and young generations. The old generation is composed of mostly business owners and the managerial class, with grown up children. Their motivation for returning to Taiwan included the intention to make good use of their expertise and experience. Additionally, the family consideration was crucial as most of them had elderly parents staying in Taiwan. For the middle generation, the major consideration was better job opportunities and higher income. As most of the young generation have not had work experience abroad, they returned to Taiwan for employment. They compete with the Taiwan-trained master's degree holders for jobs.

Third, government programmes for recruiting the highly educated from abroad are mostly outdated now and need to be modified. In the future, the government should compete internationally for the labour force required for the new high-tech industries. Regulations and requirements should be relaxed in terms of visa, work permits and residence rights for experts from China and other countries. Without an inflow of foreign talent, it will be difficult for Taiwan to compete in the international market in the future.

Fourth, to attract highly skilled migrants it is important to improve the infrastructure such as transportation and traffic, environment and life style and education and culture. Good living conditions are the key to having high-tech experts from all over the world to come to work in Taiwan.

CONCLUSION

The Taiwan case study provides an example of an economy that has seen great benefits from attracting back skilled Taiwanese. This flow of people, even though it amounted to only 20 per cent of the outflow, has been a vital resource. They have been encouraged to return by a wide range of incentives and policies and the growth in the Taiwanese economy.

More importantly, the bridges that have been established between overseas sites, such as Silicon Valley and Taiwan, have enabled flows of capital, skills and technology. 'A closely knit community of Taiwanese returnees and US-based engineers and entrepreneurs...has become the bridge between Silicon Valley and Hsinchu' (Saxenian 2001, p. 223). These bridges are now well established and are incorporated into wider transnational communities of Taiwanese. Social networks were often converted into business and more formal networks of Taiwanese. 'This transnational community has accelerated the upgrading of Taiwan's technological infrastructure by transferring technical know-how and organizational models, as well as by forging closer ties with Silicon Valley' (Saxenian 2001, p. 223). Taiwan offers world class manufacturing, flexible development and integration and access to key customers and markets in China and Southeast Asia for companies based in the US – where the bulk of the new product design in leading-edge technologies is carried out.

This type of integrated or symbiotic relationship is unique to Taiwan among our four case studies. It has taken 40 to 50 years to develop and has largely come about because of the foresight in policy development and the close relationship that has existed between the US and Taiwan over the past 50 years. This relationship is poised to become even closer as Taiwan is in a unique position, in terms of providing easier access to the Chinese market. The role of permanent and temporary returnees has already been established and will continue to evolve and incorporate a wider range of host countries. Australia (as Chapter 2 showed), Japan, the UK, Canada and others are all in a good position now to take advantage of the skills and networks of the Taiwanese who have migrated to their shores.

6. Vietnam: Emergence of Return Skilled Migration

Dang Nguyen Anh

BACKGROUND

As of 1 April 1999, the population of Vietnam was 76 327 173 persons with 16 661 366 households. Males accounted for 49 per cent of the total population. Due to a low rate of international migration, natural increase is the direct cause of increasing population density in Vietnam. The population density increased from 194 persons/km^2 in 1989 to 231 persons/km^2 in 1999 in Vietnam – making it one of the countries with the highest population density in the region. It ranks third in Southeast Asia behind Singapore and the Philippines, and is classified as third among 42 countries in Asia and the Pacific. Many provinces in this region such as Ha Tay, Hung Yen, Nam Dinh and Thai Binh have population densities over 1000 persons/km^2. Vietnam is one of the countries with the lowest amount of arable land per head (0.1 ha), a level close to the limit that enables national food security.

The population is unevenly distributed among the regions. The Mekong River Delta has the largest population (16.1 million people or 21 per cent of the total), followed by the Red River Delta with 14.8 million people (19.4 per cent of the total). Although both regions contain 40 per cent of the country's population, they cover less than 16 per cent of the land area. Table 6.1 shows that the Red River Delta has the highest population density of the country (1180 persons/km^2). By contrast, the Central Highlands, Northwest and Northeast are regions with proportionately large land areas and small population sizes. These three regions account for 45 per cent of the total land but have only one-fifth of the total population.

Table 6.1 Population, area and population density by geographic region, Vietnam 1999

Region	Population size No.	Population %	Density person/km²	Area km²
Red River Delta	14 799 691	19.4	1180	12 542
Northeast	10 860 804	14.2	162	67 042
Northwest	2 226 372	2.9	62	35 909
North Central	10 007 669	13.1	196	51 060
Central Coast	6 528 081	8.6	195	33 477
Central Highlands	3 061 901	4.0	67	45 700
Southeast	12 707 950	16.7	285	44 589
Mekong River Delta	16 130 675	21.1	408	39 536
Total	76 323 143	100.0	231	329 855

Source: Central Census Steering Committee (CCSC) 2000.

Even within each of the geographic regions, population distribution is widely varied. The areas of high densities are also the populous regions characterised by higher levels of urbanisation. Hanoi has the highest population density of 2909 persons/km² and Ho Chi Minh City of 2407 persons/km². At the other end of the scale, the Mekong River Delta, the most populous region, has a fairly even population distribution. The population densities of the Mekong Delta provinces ranged from 300 to 700 persons/km². It may be said that the population distribution among geographic regions in Vietnam has been and will be a challenge to the country's sustainable development.

The sex ratio of Vietnam's population is less than 100 and is lower than that of the international standard. It is because a higher proportion of the male population died during the wars against invaders from 1940 to 1975. However, the male ratio is higher than the female ratio among the population born after the wars, so the sex ratio of Vietnam's population is gradually increasing. The sex ratio in 1979 was 94.2 and it increased to 96.7 in 1999 (96.7 male/100 female).

Over the last 10 years, the average GDP was 8 per cent per annum; the living standard of the population has improved and the inflation rate has been reduced. The population's demand for food, foodstuffs and consumer goods has been satisfied and exports have grown quickly.

Table 6.2 shows that the structure of economic sectors changed from 1989–99. In 1989, more than 50 per cent of the total human resources worked in the collective sector. The state sector accounted for one third, and other economic sectors accounted for two thirds. In 1999, the number of people working in the collective sector reduced by 50 per cent, and accounted for only 27 per cent of the total workforce. The workforce of the state sector reduced to the same rate and was only 10 per cent of the total workforce. The number of working people in the other economic sectors increased to 63 per cent in 1999.

Table 6.2 Employed population by economic sector

Economic sector	1979 %	1989 %	1999 %
State	17	15	10
Collective	51	55	27
Other economic sectors	32	30	63

Source: CCSC 2000.

The state and collective sectors accounted for 37 per cent of the employed population in 1999. The private sector accounted for 61 per cent of the total workforce and had the maximum increase since 1989. Other economic sectors, including the private capital sector, the joint venture sector and 100 per cent foreign investment sector, have a small portion of the total workforce, but this portion has increased considerably since 1989 (CCSC 2000).

Unemployed people account for 4 per cent of the total workforce. The un-employment rate of the urban areas is three times higher than that of rural areas. The unemployment rate for ages 15–19 is approximately 11 per cent. This rate gradually reduces with increasing age, except for the ages over 50.

Over the last 10 years, education and training activities in Vietnam have expanded and produced an increasing percentage of grade pupils and voca-tional education people and graduates. The literacy rate of Vietnam has im-proved considerably over the last 10 years. The literacy rate among the popu-lation over 10 was about 88.2 per cent in 1989 and this has increased to 91 per cent in 1999. In 1989, the male literacy rate was 9 per cent higher than the female literacy rate but the difference was only 6 per cent in 1999. The literacy rate in urban areas is higher than that of rural areas – the rates are 95 per cent and 90 per cent respectively. The male literacy rate is 4 per cent higher than the female literacy rate in urban areas, while in rural areas the difference is 7 per cent (CCSC 2000).

In urban areas, 53 per cent of grade pupils graduate from primary schools while the corresponding percentage in the rural area is less than 40 per cent. The education difference between the urban and rural areas is more defined in the last grades of primary and secondary schools: 20 per cent of grade pupils in urban areas are in secondary school and this percentage is twice that of rural areas. The census shows that 94 per cent of urban citizens have graduated from grade schools while the percentage in rural areas was only 89 per cent.

SURVEY RESULTS

Table 6.3 shows the characteristics of the sample of 100 skilled return migrants. Young and middle-aged people made up the majority of skilled return migrants. The percentage of the age group under 35 is highest (42 per cent), more than twice as high as the percentage of the age group over 45 (19 per cent). This was an advantage for information collection because young people are very enthusiastic and capable of providing details on their personal information, qualifications and their business in the past.

All survey interviewees were skilled return migrants, 60 per cent of who currently had professional jobs. The percentage of management and business people was half of the above-mentioned people (31 per cent). 76 per cent of interviewees worked in the service sector (education, health, scientific research), 18 per cent of interviewees were involved in industries and construction and the remainder worked in the other sectors. The percentage of the survey interviewees working in the agricultural sector was lowest (1 per cent).

The results show that 59.8 per cent of the sample had obtained a Bachelor's degree before going abroad and 23.7 per cent had gained a secondary education. The percentages gaining a Master's, Ph.D. or intermediate level were much lower. However, there was a big difference between the highest qualifications obtained in Vietnam and overseas. For instance, the percentage obtaining a Master's degree in Vietnam was 8 per cent while 14 per cent gained their degree overseas. Thus most had a first degree from Vietnam and undertook postgraduate study overseas. Relative to the other three case studies, the Vietnamese sample was less highly qualified – an indication of Vietnam's relative economic position and history of disruption due to wars.

The majority of interviewees (72 per cent) were married. The percentage of married men is lower than the percentage of married women. It shows that generally in society the marriage age for women is lower than the marriage age for men. Among the interviewees the percentage of divorced or separated people is very small.

Table 6.3 Characteristics of interviewees

Characteristics	%
Age	
Up to 35 years	42.0
35 to 45 years	39.0
Over 45 years	19.0
Sex	
Male	50.0
Female	50.0
City	
Hanoi	50.0
Ho Chi Minh City	50.0
Occupation	
Management, Business	31.0
Professional, Technical	61.0
Others	8.0
Industry	
Agriculture	1.0
Industry, capital construction	18.0
Services (Health, Education, Science)	76.0
Others	5.0
Highest degree obtained in Vietnam	
Secondary education	23.7
Intermediate level/Vocational	3.1
Bachelor's	59.8
Master's	8.2
Ph.D.	5.2

Table 6.3 Characteristics of interviewees (continued)

Characteristics	%
Highest degree obtained overseas	
Secondary education	15.1
Intermediate level/Vocational	48.8
Bachelor's	20.9
Master's	14.0
Ph.D.	1.2
Marital status	
Never married	24.0
Currently married	72.0
Separated, Divorced	2.0
Widowed	2.0

EMIGRATION AND PROCESSES OF RETURN

As Table 6.4 shows, the major reason for going abroad was to study and almost 80 per cent of the sample gave this as their reason. A small portion of interviewees (7.1 per cent of total sample) said that the purpose of going abroad was to be reunited with their family or they were forced to go as refugees after the Vietnam war ended in 1995.

Table 6.4 Interviewees' reasons for going abroad by main characteristics

Characteristic	Study	Business	Join Family	Refugee	Visiting Scholar	Other
	%	%	%	%	%	%
Year of departure						
Before 1995	77.1	2.1	2.1	10.4	2.1	6.3
After 1995	78.0	-	2.0	-	16.0	4.0
Sex						
Male	81.6	-	2.0	4.1	8.2	4.1
Female	73.5	2.0	2.0	6.1	10.2	6.1
Qualifications obtained in Vietnam						
Secondary	73.9	-	-	17.4	4.3	4.3
Vocational training	-	33.3	-	-	-	66.7
Bachelor's	86.0	-	3.5	1.8	7.0	1.8
Master's	85.7	-	-	-	14.3	-
Ph.D.	40.0	-	-	-	60.0	-
Age						
Up to 35 years	75.6	2.4	2.4	-	9.8	9.8
35 to 45 years	92.3	-	-	2.6	5.1	-
Over 45 years	50.0	-	5.6	22.2	16.7	5.6
City						
Hanoi	90.0	-	-	-	8.0	2.0
Ho Chi Minh City	64.0	2.0	4.0	12.0	10.0	8.0
Average	77.6	1.0	2.0	5.1	9.2	5.1

There was a difference in the reasons for going abroad between men and women. The percentage of men going abroad for the purpose of education was higher (81.6 per cent) than for women (73.5 per cent). Almost all interviewees with a Vietnamese Bachelor's or Master's degree went abroad for higher education (86 per cent). No interviewee with an intermediate level education or secondary education went abroad for education. This group of people went abroad for business or other purposes. About 74 per cent of interviewees with an intermediate level education from Vietnam continued their education abroad, with the percentage being highest among people who migrated overseas permanently. 60 per cent of interviewees with Vietnamese Ph.D.s went abroad for study tours. Their main aim was to exchange experiences and to expand their international relations.

It is clear that the middle-aged group largely went overseas for higher education purposes: 92.3 per cent went for this reason compared to 75.6 per cent for the younger group and 50.0 per cent of the over 45-year-olds.

Analysing the relations between the place of residence and the migration purpose for each period, the survey shows that before 1995 all the interviewees in Hanoi went abroad for education, while the percentage in Ho Chi Minh City was only 57.7 per cent. After 1995, the percentage in Ho Chi Minh City increased but was still lower than that in Hanoi.

More than a half of the interviewees (57.1 per cent) studied or did business in Europe, while 27.1 per cent went to the Asia Pacific region and 10 per cent went to Northern America. Only 1 per cent went to the Middle East before 1995.

Sixty per cent of people who departed for study or business purposes, both before and after 1995, went to Europe. Before 1995 the percentage of interviewees going to Eastern Europe was the same as the percentage that went to the rest of Europe. However, after 1995 the percentage of interviewees that went to Western Europe and Northern America was very high (31.4 per cent), while the percentage of interviewees going to former Eastern European countries was 5.9 per cent. The results show the change in the foreign relations policies of Vietnam's Communist Party and the Government's guideline: 'Vietnam would like to make friend with all the countries'.

Results in Table 6.5 show that almost 15 per cent of interviewees went to North America (Canada and the US) before 1995. The percentage of interviewees going to Asia Pacific countries was 27.1 per cent before 1995 and 34 per cent after 1995. This shows the integration of Vietnam into the region and new policies of Australia, New Zealand and Singapore. With the extension of programmes and projects granting scholarships to Vietnamese students, many people have gone to these countries for work, training and research.

Table 6.5 Destination by year of departure

Year of departure	Europe %	North America %	Middle East %	Asia Pacific %
Before 1995	56.3	14.6	2.1	27.1
After 1995	58.0	8.0	-	34.0
Average	57.1	11.2	1.0	30.6

Table 6.6 shows that the average duration time of interviewees in foreign countries was 38 months (more than three years). The reason for going abroad influenced their time overseas. Refugees had the longest time overseas (127 months), while the group 'other' had the shortest stay overseas (12 months). The group migrating for education had an average stay of 34 months.

There was no big difference in length of overseas stay between men and women. Analysis of the difference in ages has pointed out that older people stayed overseas longer compared with the younger people. This is because older people left for foreign countries in the 70s and 80s. They have returned to their home country in recent years.

The difference in overseas stay between the Hanoi group and the Ho Chi Minh City group is very clear. The average overseas duration of interviewees from Hanoi was 32 months and was much lower than the group from Ho Chi Minh City (more than 45 months). The group of people going abroad after 1995 had an average stay overseas of 10 months while the group that went before 1995 had an average time of five years. These differences reflect the impact of the war that ended in 1975 and the fact that many refugees fled from Ho Chi Minh City (Saigon) in the South.

Table 6.6 Average overseas duration by characteristics of interviewees

Characteristic	Overseas duration (months)
Reason for moving	
Study	34
Business	32
Join family	48
Refugee	127
Visiting scholar	29
Other	12
Gender	
Male	38
Female	38
Age Group	
Up to 35 years	15
35 to 45 years	43
Over 45 years	80
City	
Hanoi	32
Ho Chi Minh city	45
Year when moved overseas	
Before 1995	68
After 1995	10
Average	38

Preparation for Return

In every case, careful preparation was considered important for a successful return. This preparation was evaluated using two criteria: the information source before return and the desires of returning migrants before they actually returned.

Table 6.7 shows that 68 per cent of interviewees had gathered information about Vietnam before returning. Conversely, this means that a large portion (32 per cent) had not collected information before returning. The proportion gathering information increased with age. Sixty-four per cent of people under 35 years had looked for information before returning, while the percentage among older groups was 66.7 per cent and 78.9 per cent. For short-term migrants (less than one year), the percentage of people over 45 years who gathered information was higher than for other groups (71 per cent compared with 66.7 per cent and 65 per cent).

Analysis of information sources shows that the group over 45 years relied less on friends and relatives than the other two age groups. Almost all the group of 35–45 years and 77.8 per cent of the group under 35 years had received information from friends, family and mass media. Not many young people got information from domestic organisations. The information obtained during vacations in Vietnam was limited for under 35 year olds and over 45 year olds, as the possibility for vacations in Vietnam was limited.

The results show that there was a difference between men and women in gathering information before returning: 80 per cent of men looked for information on the country, while only 50 per cent of women did. However, for the group who lived more than three years overseas, the percentage of women that gathered information was higher than for men (79 per cent and 61 per cent). Women relied more heavily on information from friends and relatives (82.1 per cent), while 60.7 per cent got information from mass media and 17.9 per cent from domestic organisations. On the other hand, 70 per cent of men got information from mass media, 37.5 per cent from domestic organisations and 35 per cent from vacations in Vietnam.

Overseas duration clearly influenced the amount of information gathered before returning. Over 70 per cent of people who lived abroad for three years had gathered information before returning while the percentage of the two other groups is smaller. The longer someone had been away, the more important it was to check on the current situation in Vietnam. Lastly, the time of returning also influenced the propensity to gather information before returning. The percentage of returned migrants after 1995 gathering information was higher than for those who returned before 1995. Friends, family and mass media were the main sources of information.

Table 6.7 Information collection of interviewees before return

Types	Gathered info %	Relatives & friends %	Mass media %	Domestic organs %	Vacation %	Other source %
Age						
Up to 35 years	64.3	77.8	63.0	22.2	22.2	7.4
35 to 45 years	66.7	88.5	80.8	38.5	53.8	7.7
Over 45 years	78.9	40.0	46.7	26.7	6.7	13.3
Gender						
Male	80.0	67.5	70.0	37.5	35.0	7.5
Female	56.0	82.1	60.7	17.9	25.0	10.7
Overseas duration						
Less than 1 year	66.7	75.0	62.5	37.5	20.8	8.3
1-3 years	67.6	68.0	72.0	32.0	40.0	12.0
More than 3 years	70.4	78.9	63.2	15.8	31.6	5.3
Years of return						
Before 1995	65.4	88.2	41.2	29.4	29.4	-
After 1995	68.9	68.6	74.5	29.4	31.4	11.8
Average	68.0	50.0	45.0	20.0	21.0	6.0

Note: More than one source of information could be given so the percentages in each row total more than 100 per cent.

Understanding of Government Policies and Promises of Employment

Although the above results show that a large percentage of skilled return migrants found out about the country's situation before returning, it seems that they received little information about the incentive policies of the government. Only 21 per cent of interviewees knew about these policies. The fact that almost 80 per cent of the sample went overseas for education, many sponsored by the state, makes them quite a different group to the other samples in this study. That is, there were fewer returning permanent emigrants. Age and longer overseas stay both influenced knowledge about the state's incentive policies. The highest percentage (26 per cent) of migrants obtaining this information was the group of over three years' stay overseas. Surprisingly, people who returned after 1995 had less knowledge of the state's incentive policies than those who returned before 1995.

Regarding the promise of employment, the survey's result showed that only a small portion (28 per cent) of returned migrants had the promise of employment before returning. It is not a high percentage but many returned migrants had stable jobs before departing, so their return to their former organisations was anticipated.

The research results do not show any differences by sex or age in the promise of employment. However, unlike understanding of the state's policies, the percentage with promised employment reduced with increased length of stay overseas. This means that a longer period overseas for students and business migrants (unless permitted by local organisations) is considered as a violation of regulations, and in many cases, they did not return to work for their former organisations. In some cases, the regular staff status was cancelled by local organisations. For migrants who returned before 1995, the percentage with promised employment was higher.

These results are indicative of policy changes in recent years. The entry of skilled return migrants has required only the completion of paper procedures and it is not necessary to have employment. Formerly, employment was set up for skilled returning migrants before or after their return but now the number of skilled emigrants and returning migrants is increasing, so they have to arrange their own jobs after they return. The labour market has become more open and many more jobs are filled on a competitive basis, especially in joint ventures and private Vietnamese-owned firms.

A significant proportion, 62 per cent of interviewees, had received state support after their return. From the data obtained, it is evident that the main forms of support were expenses for travelling, employment and housing. In all kinds of support, migrants who returned before 1995 had received more state support than those who returned after 1995.

Aspirations before Returning

Table 6.8 shows that for 58 per cent the greatest desire on returning was to be able to use their knowledge gained overseas. The second desire was to gain family acceptance (48 per cent). Third, 45 per cent hoped that their knowledge and experience obtained overseas would be useful for the country. It is interesting that there is a difference in the sentiment and thinking between men and women. Men wanted to be able to use their knowledge and experience in their jobs while women were more concerned about gaining family acceptance.

Table 6.8 Aspirations before returning

Types		Job or business opports.	Benefit from gov't policies	Utilise overseas learning	Family accept.	O/S exper. and know. useful	No positive expects.	Other
		%	%	%	%	%	%	%
Sex								
	Male	18.0	6.0	68.0	44.0	56.0	2.0	-
	Female	18.0	6.0	48.0	52.0	34.0	2.0	6.0
Overseas duration								
	Less than 1 year	16.7	5.6	75.0	50.0	47.2	-	-
	1–3 year	18.9	5.4	56.8	48.6	54.1	-	2.7
	More than 3 year	18.5	7.4	37.0	44.4	29.6	7.4	7.4
Age								
	Up to 35 years	19.0	9.5	59.5	52.4	40.5	-	2.4
	35 to 45 years	25.6	5.1	66.7	41.0	53.8	2.6	2.6
	Over 45 years	-	-	36.8	52.6	36.8	5.3	5.3
Average		18.0	6.0	58.0	48.0	45.0	2.0	3.0

Note: More than one aspiration could be given so the total for each row does not equal 100 per cent.

Those who stayed overseas for more than three years had quite different aspirations to those who had been away for a short period. The most important aspiration for those who were away for more than three years was family accept-ance but only 44 per cent of interviewees selected this. Their desire to use their overseas knowledge and to serve the country were also less important: 37 per cent and 30 per cent, respectively. For interviewees over 45 years, family ac-ceptance played a very important role. For interviewees aged 35–45 years, job-related factors were their most important aspirations. The majority of these people (66.7 per cent) wanted to apply their knowledge in their jobs after they returned.

Factors Affecting the Decision to Return

The majority of interviewees (87 per cent) had returned permanently while the remaining 13 per cent were moving regularly or staying only temporarily in Vietnam – including for vacation. Table 6.9 shows a difference in year of depar-ture and of return. The percentage of people who returned permanently was higher for the group who migrated before 1995 than for the group who left Vietnam after 1995. Temporary movement was more common among the post-1995 departures and intermittent movement was similar across the two groups.

Age is also a factor with both the younger and older age groups showing less tendency to return permanently. The over 45-year-olds had the greatest ten-dency to return on a temporary and intermittent basis.

Table 6.9 Return migration types by basic characteristics

Characteristic	Permanent %	Temporary %	Intermittent %
Age			
Up to 35 years	81.0	14.3	4.8
35 to 45 years	100.0	-	-
Over 45 years	73.7	15.8	10.5
City			
Hanoi	90.0	8.0	2.0
Ho Chi Minh City	84.0	10.0	6.0
Year of departure			
Before 1995	96.2	3.8	-
After 1995	83.8	10.8	5.4
Year of return			
Before 1995	89.8	6.1	4.1
After 1995	84.3	11.8	3.9
Average	87.0	9.0	4.0

Nearly 70 per cent of interviewees made their decision to return by themselves. The percentage of return decisions made by women themselves was higher than for men (74 per cent and 60 per cent, respectively). Conversely 32 per cent of male returnees had their decision made by 'others' – more than three times higher than for women. Perhaps this is related to the fact that a higher proportion of males (81.6 per cent) went overseas to study than did females (73.5 per cent) but this does not explain all of the differences. The percentage of women who made a decision together with a partner or boyfriend was double that of men.

The longer the overseas period of stay, the higher the tendency to make the decision alone – 74 per cent of those who had been away for more than three years made the decision by themselves. On the other hand, short-term migrants did not follow this pattern. More than 30 per cent of them had followed the decision made by others, even if 63 per cent of them made their decision to return by themselves.

The decision of skilled migrants to return to Vietnam was most strongly influenced by the family factor (Table 6.10). But 'no choice' was the second most important factor. Other factors include: influence of friends, families, job opportunities and the state's incentive policies.

However, there was a difference in the relative influence of these factors between men and women. The major reason for returning for women was the family while the major reason for men was 'no choice' and 'other' reasons. The group of more than three years' overseas duration was most strongly influenced by the family factor while the group of one to three years' overseas duration was less influenced by this factor. Only 18 per cent of the group of more than three years' duration returned because they had no other choice while the percentage of the group of less than one year was 44 per cent. The group of more than three years' duration was less influenced by the state's policies, but more by job opportunities in Vietnam.

Table 6.10 Return decision by factors of influence

Types	Gov't policy %	Friends & Family %	Job opps. %	Bus opps. %	Family %	Job diffs. %	No choice %	Other %
Sex								
Male	12.0	12.0	12.0	2.0	24.0	4.0	36.0	30.0
Female	10.0	22.0	20.0	6.0	36.0	-	22.0	18.0
Overseas duration								
Less than 1 year	13.9	11.1	13.9	5.6	30.6	2.8	44.4	16.7
1–3 years	10.8	21.6	13.5	2.7	24.3	-	21.6	29.7
More than 3 years	7.4	18.5	22.2	3.7	37.0	3.7	18.5	25.9
Marital status								
Single	4.2	25.0	8.3	-	25.0	-	41.7	20.8
Married	13.9	15.3	18.1	4.2	30.6	2.8	26.4	25.0
Average	11.0	17.0	16.0	4.0	30.0	2.0	29.0	24.0

The group of widowed, divorced and separated people was not mentioned in Table 6.10 because they made up a very small number. The results showed that unmarried people returned because they had no other choice (42 per cent), and married people were influenced more by family factors (31 per cent).

OUTCOMES AFTER RETURNING

Employment Conditions

Three sectors that have absorbed many skilled return migrants are universities and research institutions (42 per cent), business and service organisations (20 per cent) and state administration organisations (13 per cent). Other sectors such as NGOs, international organisations and production units account for a small portion.

The survey results show that 41 per cent of skilled return migrants were in management positions in their organisations – either as a team or group leader or a department head or director. The highest percentage was in the group 45 years and over, followed by the group of less than 35 years and lastly the group of between 35–45 years. The percentage of women in management positions was higher than for men, which is interesting.

The percentage of the group with less than one year overseas in management positions is higher than for the groups with longer duration overseas. This practice shows that many people, before moving, had management positions that they kept after a short overseas stay. The percentage of people returning after 1995 in management jobs is higher than for those returning before 1995. It could be that return migrants before 1995 did not return to their former appointed positions.

It is difficult to gather information on income but the survey asked about income when they lived abroad compared with present income and income relative to their colleagues' income. In general, more than half the returnees (55 per cent) admitted that their incomes decreased in comparison with their incomes abroad – 35 per cent said that their incomes were much lower than they earned abroad. This fact is easily understood: returnees mainly come back from developed countries, where their incomes were higher than in Vietnam. Only 21 per cent of respondents said that their present incomes were higher than their incomes abroad and 22 per cent thought their incomes were equivalent. Table 6.11 shows the effect of age: income increases with age, as the seniority system is still an important component of the Vietnamese model.

Table 6.11 Respondents' income compared with their income abroad

Characteristic	Much lower %	Lower %	Same %	Higher %	Much higher %
Sex					
Male	36.0	16.0	30.0	16.0	2.0
Female	34.0	28.0	14.0	20.0	4.0
Time living abroad					
Under 1 year	36.1	22.2	19.4	16.7	5.6
From 1–3 years	35.1	24.3	18.9	18.9	2.7
Over 3 years	33.3	18.5	29.6	18.5	-
Time of returning					
Before 1995	30.8	19.2	19.2	23.1	7.7
After 1995	36.5	23.0	23.0	16.2	1.4
Average	35.0	22.0	22.0	18.0	3.0

Timing of return migration also played an important role in the income of skilled returnees. In general, people who returned before 1995 earned more than people who returned after 1995. This is interesting given the results on employment status above. Recent returnees may have had to deal with many things to reintegrate into the business environment (setting up new business relationships, adapting to present conditions) and so they may not have had enough time to accumulate and increase their incomes.

In comparison with their colleagues' incomes, more than half of the skilled returnees (53 per cent) said their incomes were equivalent. At present, the Vietnamese government applies a system of uniform wages for all people of the same level (university, MBA, doctorate degree, etc.). For those working in state-owned enterprises for the first time, they receive a starting salary at the first level. Many returnees expressed concern about this salary system. Many cities and provincial authorities are pioneering ways of attracting highly-skilled workers and talent by offering accommodation support, allowances, etc. However, these measures are unlikely to be successful due to the lack of resources and poor implementation in practice.

Table 6.12 shows that the salaries of men and women are unequal, especially in non-state owned organisations. Whereas 24 per cent of men reported lower or much lower incomes than their colleagues, 36 per cent of women were in these categories.

Table 6.12 Returnees' income compared with colleagues' income

Characteristic	Much lower %	Lower %	Same %	Higher %	Much higher %
Sex					
Male	12.0	12.0	58.0	14.0	4.0
Female	2.0	34.0	48.0	16.0	-
Time living abroad					
Under 1 year	2.8	16.7	66.7	11.1	2.8
From 1–3 years	10.8	18.9	54.1	16.2	-
Over 3 years	7.4	37.0	33.3	18.5	3.7
Time of returning					
Before 1995	11.5	26.9	42.3	19.2	-
After 1995	5.4	21.6	56.8	13.5	2.7
Age					
Up to 35 years	38.1	26.2	21.4	14.3	-
35 to 45 years	41.0	23.1	17.9	12.8	5.1
Over 45 years	15.8	10.5	31.6	36.8	5.3
Average	7.0	23.0	53.0	15.0	2.0

More than 75 per cent of interviewees were satisfied with their current jobs. The 35–45 year age group had the highest percentage (87 per cent), followed by the group over 45 years (75 per cent), and the group of under 35-year-olds had the lowest percentage (67 per cent). There was no difference between men and women in employment satisfaction. Those who returned before 1995 were more satisfied with their job than those who returned after 1995 (85 per cent and 74 per cent respectively)

The most important factor in employment dissatisfaction for 46 per cent of skilled return migrants was working conditions. The suitability of the job was considered the second most important factor. Overall, 36 per cent of interviewees said that they had suffered in their job. Many complained about material working conditions.

Material living conditions and information-update conditions in Vietnam are worse than overseas. (Female, 26 years, research officer)

Working method in Vietnam is different with overseas. Working speed is low. Personal possibility is not high. Material conditions is not good, lacking of internet, materials, newspapers. (Male, 40 years, manager of research department)

Material conditions are far away to apply the obtained knowledge. A lot of issues in Vietnam's laws and policies should be changed. (Male, 41 years, teacher)

In practice, personal relationships in jobs also reduce effectiveness. The working relationship is described as 'apply–give' relations and this mechanism delays working speed and has limited effectiveness. Another waste of human resources is the use of professional people in different fields. Administrative work takes a lot of time. This restrains professional workers and wastes human resources. The survey's results show that 35 per cent of interviewees either regularly or occasionally had to carry out administration work. Some opinions given were:

Working method in Vietnam is not clear and low effective. Administration and foreign relations take a lot of time. (Male, 46 years, freelance consultant)

Unprofessional skills of colleagues and in the state organs. Complicated social relations, the work is not difficult, but there are not fixed and clear standards. (Female, 40 years, research officer)

Nowadays, the use of professional manpower in the wrong way wastes a lot. (Female, 41 years, research officer)

There is no mechanism to employ the right persons for the right jobs. There is no criterion for evaluation on works as the evaluation is based on employers' feelings. (Female, 49 years, project manager)

The oldest age group rarely suffered difficulties compared with the younger people. Older people are more familiar with working in Vietnam. The younger people had less experience with working in Vietnam before moving abroad or are more frustrated with the Vietnamese way of working. Fewer men (28 per cent) than women (44 per cent) had faced difficulties in their job. This result could reflect either better preparation by men (80 per cent had obtained information before return compared with 50 per cent of women) and/or better treatment of men in the work place.

Length of overseas stay and year of return also influenced the propensity for work obstacles. The group with less than one year's overseas stay experienced fewer difficulties than the rest. It could be that one year's duration overseas is not long enough to adapt to another system and it is also does not allow for too much change to have taken place in Vietnam. The analysis of the year of return shows that the percentage of returned migrants before 1995 who faced difficulties was higher than for those who returned after 1995 (46 per cent and 32 per cent respectively). This means that living standards, working conditions and means in Vietnam have been improved since the mid-1990s.

Overall, 80 per cent of interviewees said that they had not faced any of these problems after returning. All of them had grown up, lived and worked in Vietnam for a long time, so readjustment was not a problem. However, 20 per cent of interviewees had experienced difficulties in adjusting. The following are some opinions of this group:

> First month I feel as stranger to slow and fond life in Vietnam, but then I am familiar with that. (Female, 24 years, business owner)
> Problems are resolved based on personal relations, not based on regulations and principles. (Female, 41 years, research officer)
> Many reasons, wasting time in the office: talking, tea drinks, eating, offering. At home I see that the children are very hard learning, parent feel very tired. (Male, 42 years, research officer)

All interviewees confirmed that they had received support from colleagues in Vietnam to shorten the time of their integration and to increase their work effectiveness. Almost all return skilled migrants confirmed that colleagues expected them to provide new ideas or execution methods.

Possibility of Using Outside Information

The degree to which information flows are interrupted, after return, is a major concern of this research. Table 6.13 shows that 90 per cent of interviewees said that they could get documentation or publications in foreign languages and 60 per cent could use the internet. Access to up-to-date information is crucial for remaining in the global information network.

On the other hand, many people faced difficulties in accessing foreign TV – only 28 per cent of interviewees could view foreign TV programmes. In Vietnam, watching foreign TV programmes is only possible through a parabolic antenna system but this is not easy as it requires permission from authorities. Furthermore, not all families have the finances to pay to install this type of antenna. Cable TV is a new service but it is not well developed, even in big cities, due to the high cost.

Table 6.13 shows that people between 35 and 45 years read more foreign language publications but watched least TV. Not unexpectedly, usage of the internet decreases with age: the group under 35 years of age had the highest usage (76 per cent) while the over 45-year-olds had the lowest use (37 per cent). Other than for the internet, men accessed more mass media than women. People who returned after 1995 used foreign language documents and the internet most while those who returned before 1995 watched overseas TV and listened to the radio more.

Table 6.13 Access to different information sources

Characteristic	Read foreign language publications	Watch overseas TV	Listen to overseas radio	Use internet
	%	%	%	%
Age				
Up to 35 years	83.3	31.0	21.4	76.2
35 to 45 years	94.9	23.1	5.1	60.5
Over 45 years	84.2	31.6	21.1	36.8
Sex				
Male	92.0	28.0	16.0	57.1
Female	84.0	28.0	14.0	68.0
Time of returning				
Before 1995	84.6	46.2	23.1	40.0
After 1995	89.2	21.6	12.2	70.3
Average	88.0	28.0	15.0	62.0

Relationships with Colleagues Overseas

Continued relationship with friends and colleagues overseas helps returnees to keep up-to-date with information and maintain their professional skills. Most skilled returnees maintained their relationships with the places where they worked and studied. E-mail is fast and low-cost and most returnees (81 per cent) used it to communicate. Mail was used to communicate by 56 per cent while phone and fax were only used by 35 per cent of returnees. The content of information exchanged was both professional and personal. Some comments were:

> I pay much attention to business, exchange views on mutual concerns, gather necessary information for business. Besides, I maintain relationship of sentiment, asking after health and exchange mail in the occasion of new year, season's greeting, birthday of friends and teachers. (Man, 28 years)
> We usually send mail to ask and inform each other of health and present business. (Male, 42 years, researcher)
> I communicate with friends, professors, researchers to exchange of business and family life. (Male, 40 years, editor)
> They are my abroad partners, I sometime send greeting card in the occasion of new year or company establishment. (Male, 50 years, deputy director)

PRESENT LIVING STANDARDS

Accommodation and Transport

The quality of accommodation is one indicator of the success of returning. Returnees had an average of 1.14 children and 2.54 bedrooms: 69 per cent of returnees had a house and 24 per cent were in living quarters. So, in the nuclear family model, the available bedrooms met the demands of couples with two children. In this way, the accommodation conditions of skilled returnees were significantly better than for the average population.

Almost all respondents (86 per cent) used a motorbike. In Vietnam, the motorbike market has flourished recently and owning a motorbike is not as difficult as in the 1990s. In addition, car ownership was increasing: a 1998 living standard survey showed that 0.23 per cent of households had a private car (in 1995 it was 0.15 per cent). In this survey 5 per cent of skilled returnees owned a car so they were well above the average.

Adaptability to Domestic Living Conditions

Adaptability to present living conditions is an important part of reintegration: 70 per cent of interviewees did not face any significant difficulties in adapting to the domestic living conditions but 29 per cent said they had definite difficulties in reintegration, especially with respect to climate and polluted foodstuffs.

> I am ill because of humid and polluted climate, moreover, I feel that water is not clean and foodstuffs is not hygiene, so many poisoning food cases occur. (Male, 30 years, hotel manager)
> Besides of objective conditions, facilities in home, social safety, relationships in family and office are obstacles in reintegration progress of skilled returnees...In addition, relationships in the family, neighborhood. office are complicated. (Female, 39 years, deputy manager)

It appears that women adapted less easily than men: 38 per cent of woman faced difficulties compared with 20 per cent of men (see Table 6.14). Moreover, as would be expected, the longer the time spent abroad, the greater problems in adapting. Only 8 per cent of people who lived less than one year abroad faced difficulties adapting on their return whereas 51.9 per cent of returnees who lived abroad for over three years had difficulties.

Table 6.14 Difficulty in adaptability and satisfaction with present living conditions

Characteristic	Difficulty in adapting to present living conditions		Satisfaction with present life		
	Yes	No	Yes	No	Do not know
	%	%	%	%	%
Sex					
Male	20.0	80.0	70.0	20.0	10.0
Female	38.0	62.0	64.0	22.0	14.0
Time living abroad					
Under 1 year	8.3	91.7	61.1	30.6	8.3
From 1–3 years	32.4	67.6	70.3	16.2	13.5
Over 3 years	51.9	48.1	70.4	14.8	14.8
Time of returning					
Before 1995	26.9	73.1	61.5	23.1	15.4
After 1995	29.7	70.3	68.9	20.3	10.8
Average	29.0	71.0	67.0	21.0	12.0

Two thirds of the sample were satisfied with life in Vietnam – more men than women, more who had been away a long time and more of those who returned after 1995. As mentioned above, men had less difficulty than women in the reintegration progress. Similarly, returnees who lived less than one year abroad (61 per cent) were satisfied with living conditions. Returnees who lived more than one year abroad were at 70 per cent. People who returned after 1995 expressed more satisfaction with present living conditions than others who returned before 1995.

Though there were a lot of different opinions, most returnees thought that their decision to return had been right and reasonable. The main reason that pushed them to return was that they wanted to apply the knowledge learnt abroad and to make a contribution to their country. All of them affirmed that they had met a lot of difficulties when they returned; however, they overcame them and had adjusted to their new life.

Some comments were:

> Thanks to Vietnamese government's scholarship, I would like to devote myself to my country without any hesitancy. (Male, 41 years, businessman)
> I wish to contribute much to my country and receive high appreciation from my boss. (Female, 40 years, editor)
> Return is a right decision in spite of many obstacles, however, I think I should make a little contribution to my country. (Male, 40 years, overseas Vietnamese)
> Firstly, I regretted to return, then I feel comfortable when I am used to present life. (Female, 25 years, staff)

ECONOMIC IMPACT OF SKILLED RETURNEES

Knowledge and Professional Skills

Almost all returnees valued what they had learnt overseas: skills, knowledge, experiences and new ideas. Nearly 90 per cent of respondents stated that they were very useful to their present business. Men valued the usefulness of accumulated knowledge more than women (96 per cent and 84 per cent respectively) as did those who had lived abroad for less than one year. Most people living abroad for under one year obviously went to exchange experiences and gain professional skills. They assimilated knowledge rapidly and quickly applied it to their businesses when they returned. So, knowledge application was effective. People who returned after 1995 applied their knowledge better. Most people confirmed that new knowledge and ideas were readily received in Vietnam and were useful for returnees. Vietnam has just opened its doors to western countries and a lot of advanced knowledge is re-applied.

> The field I trained abroad links to my business, thinking method I learn abroad is useful to my present business. (Female, 38 years, lecturer)
> Despite 1 year course, it provided me with a general approach to the theme I am studying. I can apply directly or indirectly into my business and it gave a good result. (Male, 25 years, researcher)
> What I have learnt abroad, are new methods and professional skills which are not taught in Vietnam education system. (Female, 42 years, lecturer)
> New ideas help me to apply theory into fact more detail. (Male, 29 years, researcher)
> Knowledge, experience I absorbed abroad play an important role in enriching my understanding effectively, objectively and properly. (Male, 45 years, Research manager)
> I learnt responsible spirit to business. At the same time, I also learnt discipline, manner, seriously working style. (Female, 34 years, researcher)
> Abroad working style is really industrial, high pressure and knowing effectively working organisation. I am always proud of that. (Male, 25 years, businessman)

Increased foreign language skills were also considered important. In a business environment a foreign language, especially English, is considered very valuable.

I am very pleased to answer and speak directly to foreigner without an interpreter as before. (Female, 38 years, lecturer)

Knowing a foreign language basically makes me comprehend the lifestyle, working manner and business culture of our partner. Moreover, it makes our business more successful. (Male, 28 years, businessman)

Effect on Decision-making in Work Places

About 50 per cent of the sample had had no impact on decision-making because they were not in a position to do so. For example, 'I am normal staff without any title', said one skilled returnee. Some of them said they did not give any of their own opinions as they were 'staff'. Complexity in status is an obstacle for skilled returnees to overcome if they are to contribute knowledge, experience and ideas into their work situation. It is unfortunate that most of them were state cadres working in state-owned agencies and organisations where selection and promotion do not place priority on professional skills.

In state-owned organs, ministerial leader does not care for expert's ideas. (Male, 46 years, independent consultant expert)

I am an ordinary employee in a institute. Additionally, I have not received any support from leaders so I have no rights to decide. (Male, 40 years, researcher)

In this ministry, a lot of people are more important than I. (Female, 46 years, staff, Ministry of Planning and Investment)

Because I have no power in organisation, I only deal with assigned duty. (Female, 32 years, doctor, National University)

So, even though new knowledge and experiences were gained overseas, and seen as valuable, only 53.5 per cent of returnees were able to impact on decision-making in their place of employment. Skilled returnees were unable to change many working styles in the system, especially regulations. They suffered from bureaucratic working styles in state-owned agencies. Management mechanisms and leaders' opinions did not recognise the valuable role of skilled professionals. Thus, there is an urgent demand for macro changes in guidelines and management mechanisms in state agencies.

Remittances

Most of the respondents were sent overseas by their organisations to study, research or exchange professional skills. Only 51 per cent of skilled returnees remitted money and goods to their family at home while they were studying and working abroad. The main reason for this low remittance rate was that low scholarships did not cover minimal expenditure and many could not find even part-time jobs. They spent a great deal of time on their work or study overseas, and families placed no demands on them for remittances.

Most returnees (77 per cent) accumulated less than US$10 000 while they were overseas, 18.6 per cent saved US$10 000–50 000 and 4.3 per cent over US$50 000. On their return most of the money was spent on the family's demands: such as building or repairing their accommodation (43.5 per cent); buying home appliances (38 per cent); luxury goods (20.7 per cent) and supporting other members in the family (39.1 per cent). A small amount of money was invested in business and real estate (8.7 per cent), and virtually nothing in the stock market (1.1 per cent).

SOCIAL IMPACT OF SKILLED RETURNEES

One of the aims of this project was to understand the adaptability and reintegration of skilled migrants when they returned home. First, over 50 per cent acknowledged that they were more responsible for their family and relatives after they returned than they had been before. The same proportion realised that the role of the family was more important in life. Despite a slight difference in opinions of males and females, women attached more importance to family and relations than men (55.1 per cent compared to 51 per cent). Duration of living abroad had a certain impact on change in conception of migrants. Long-term migrants (over three years) experienced the greatest change in perception. Relatives and family had become more important to older people.

A longer time abroad and age also led to increasing realisation of the value of the family. Returnees changed their outlook on family and relations in various ways – such as visiting and helping when relatives were in difficulty. Other returnees, inclined to a spiritual life, attached importance to their duty to relatives. They felt pride in their family and relations when they went abroad. Coming into contact with the western 'individualism-inclined' lifestyle enabled migrants to appreciate the cultural traditions and lifestyle in their homeland. Only when they went away from their homeland, did they realise the meaning of mutual help among relatives. Many came to think that family and relations were indispensable to life.

The following opinions were recorded in interviews:

> Distance makes people close up and spares time for them to think about their responsibility. (Male, 29, researcher)
> I have a deeper affection for my family and relation when being away from home. (Male, 48, company director)
> I have to strive for perfection to help relatives not only in terms of finance, but also ways of settling life. (Female, 42, researcher)

After years of living in foreign countries and then returning home, migrants reintegrated into the community and had certain effects on the community and society: 55.2 per cent of interviewees felt that they had had an impact on their community. Double the number of males to females felt this (73.5 per cent compared to 36.2 per cent). The impacts, however, lessened with time living aboard. Migrants assessed their impact on community and society in different ways. Most people who were involved in research and teaching assumed that what they were doing affected the community and society.

> My research partly contributes to finding out better solutions to coastal resource management and community development. (Female, 26, researcher)
> A returnee like me has a great and direct impact on students' conception. (Male, 28, teacher)
> I hope I can help the community to have a better understanding of the world through my existing and future research'. (Male, 28, researcher)
> Knowledge which I receive and projects which I participate have made contribution to the community and society. However, it takes time to see changes. (Female 42, researcher)

Impacts on community and society can also be found in daily activities in the community. 'Being a highly conscious citizen, I always take part in activities which help to deal with issues in my community such as mobilising capital to build children's playing grounds and settling environmental problems' (Female, 36, researcher).

Nearly half of the interviewees (45 per cent) did not see their effects on the community and society. They said: 'I am now an ordinary citizen' in a large society and just like 'a grain of sand cannot change deserts' (Male, 33, receptionist).

ATTITUDES TO POLICIES

In the era of globalisation, Vietnam has paid attention to the development of a knowledge-based economy. Skilled returnees are regarded as part of Vietnam's valuable and necessary human resources in the processes of industrialisation and modernisation. The return of skilled workers depends on the country's policies on recruiting and using that talent.

Before returning, only 21.6 per cent of migrants knew about Vietnam's programmes, regulations or policies for assisting and promoting their return. Of these, 61.9 per cent received direct assistance in terms of housing (9.5 per cent), travel costs (23.8 per cent), employment (14.3 per cent) and other forms. Many cities and provinces have regulations on housing and financial assistance to skilled local people or returnees. For example, provinces such as Da Nang and Binh Duong issue incentive policies that consist of land grants, house construction and life settlement.

Besides positive aspects, these policies have shortcomings when focusing on luring 'grey matter of the province', but not 'grey matter for the province'. Aside from policies, initial macro-economic policies have helped to change the country's current status: 'In general, Vietnam has yet to encourage talents to return home. However, the development of the multi-sector economy has become a motive for some talents to return home' (Female, 42, researcher). Many people think that returning home is synonymous with responsibility for contribution to the homeland: 'Difficulties in the country help many people to understand their homeland more comprehensively, and foster their affection for it and its people' (Female, 50, vice director). This reflects opinions of many Vietnamese people living in Australia. Elderly people tend to return home in order to die in their birthplace, whereas the younger generation look forward to economic opportunities in the homeland.

At the micro-level, return migrants want state policies to focus on favourable and stable working conditions. By favourable, they mean that they should be given positions and work that suit the knowledge they have gained during their training and work overseas. They want the government to issue regulations and policies on appropriate work assignments and treatment that are commensurate with their skills. Some comments that indicate this are:

> To tap the internal force, it is necessary to have policies on maximally utilizing knowledge and promoting skilled returnees to worthy posts. (Male, 45, department deputy head)
> Policy makers have to understand returnees well to bring into play their talent, and create working motives with incentives and encouragement. (Male, 27, researcher)
> Individuals who return home after studying abroad are in dire need of being assigned to important work and positions. Have to rightly use their ability and degree. Empower them to hold the initiative in work. (Female, 40, editor)

Along with the desire for taking on the right work, skilled migrants want the state to issue more incentive policies on salary. Most of them go abroad for study to enrich their professional knowledge, and then return home, longing for a better future that uses this knowledge. For this reason, they hope to be well treated at work.

> Good working conditions and satisfactory salary are two current basic policy solutions. (Female, 44, researcher)
> Skilled returnees need the same salary or at least 80 per cent of the salary of labourers in foreign countries in the same post. (Male, 36, specialist)
> It is necessary to have more concrete incentive policies targeting those who have worked in foreign countries, and rightly assess their contribution to the country. (Female, 34, worker)

From a macro aspect, most skilled returnees want the government to have a sound recruiting policy which assigns the right post to the right person and neither wastes nor discriminates in the utilisation of talents. Apart from laws, regulations and policies, the state needs to closely monitor their implementation. At present, the privatisation of state-owned enterprises is a solution to raise production, trading and capital mobilisation and develop individuals' abilities and talents. This should help returnees.

Returnees hope that state policies will be clearer and more concrete in the future. Discrimination-free policies must be returnee-centred, publicised and well implemented. Unfortunately, the existing management mechanisms, cumbersome administrative procedures and bureaucratic working procedures result in ineffectiveness and a waste of human resources. Some of the comments were:

> Renovate working style in state agencies first, and then respect talents. (Male, 46, independent consulting expert)
> Administrative procedures should be simplified. The right work for the right person. No discrimination between overseas Vietnamese and local people. (Male, 41, employee)
> Better propagation of economic policies and simplifying business procedures. Existing policies are not clear, specific and consistent. (Male, 68, entrepreneur)

In addition to direct measures, indirect policies also are useful in propagating and calling for skilled workers to serve their homeland. Most of the opinions show that attracting talent in foreign countries has not been soundly recognised in current policies.

> It is necessary to provoke the national spirit as well as give better treatment to overseas Vietnamese. (Male, 29, researcher)
> The government should bring about policies on propagating and educating national traditions to raise the community spirit and national pride of Vietnamese people working and studying abroad. At the same time, it should issue clearer incentives which will encourage them to devote themselves to the cause of industrialisation and modernisation. (Female, 50, vice-director)

CONCLUSION AND POLICY SUGGESTIONS

In a globalising world, migration from Vietnam to other countries will increase along with its economic development. Of the migrants, a large proportion will be those with 'grey matter' who want to seek a suitable job or study in foreign countries. A large number of policies on raising the quality of Vietnam's human resources to meet the requirements of a knowledge-based economy, have been issued and implemented. From 2000, for example, the Vietnamese government is to send students to study abroad with expenditure from the state budget. The expenditure for the first year of this programme is estimated at VND100 billion (US$7 million). Many international organisations, universities and enterprises also financially assist their young cadres in training abroad.

Vietnam is unique among the case studies in that there is a fair level of compulsion or obligation for people, whose period abroad has been funded by the state or their organisation, to return. The greatest passion once they returned was to utilise their acquired knowledge and experience to serve their country. Skilled returnees mostly worked in universities, research bodies and state-owned enterprises and about half hold managerial posts. Some worked for non-governmental organisations and international organisations, after some years of working in state agencies. The main reasons for moving out of the state sector were that salaries were too low, their work was not challenging enough and there were shortcomings in the working environment.

Skilled returnees, especially scientific researchers, have serious work habits and new methods. They are characterised by dynamism, a strong sense of responsibility in work and good command of foreign languages were often mentioned. But salaries are low, not all returnees were highly appreciated in the work place and only 53.5 per cent participated in decision-making. The remainder had no decision-making powers due to their low position and social status in their work place.

The living conditions of returnees were somewhat better than for the rest of the population. The economic and social impact of returnees are potentially high, given the level of commitment to re-building Vietnam. But the working relations and systems for promotion provide barriers.

Skilled manpower plays an essential role in the process of industrialisation and modernisation. In reality, Vietnam has yet to issue open policies and mechanisms to tap human resources. The fact that the salary scale is based on seniority and managerial post, instead of professional skill, diminishes the creative dynamism of experts and wastes skilled resources. Some provinces and cities have introduced policies to try and lure local talents. However, such measures are exploratory and lack adequate investment. A system of uniform policies should be perfected to attract skilled persons and returnees. A developing country like Vietnam is in dire need of many qualified scientists who are able to grasp the world's advanced science and technology. For this reason, it is necessary to offer them preferential treatment in order to be able to attract them home.

Policy Suggestions

1. Raising the quality of human resources to serve industrialisation and modernisation and building the infrastructure of a knowledge-based economy should be the focus of the national development strategy. Apart from issuing macro policies prioritising education, training, technology and science, the government should strengthen and respect talents in every field. Specifically, it should bring forward preferential policies on housing, income and employment to attract talented people back to the country.

2. The state should issue policies on propagating national traditions, and enhancing community awareness and national pride. Concrete policies on encouraging talents to return home are also needed.

3. The existing minimum salary is a formality and does not stimulate enthusiasm and creative dynamism among workers. Salary reforms will encourage not only skilled labourers in foreign countries to return home but also domestic workers to work more effectively.

4. The number of salary levels in a pay-scale should be lowered. The fact that pay-scales have too many levels and the difference between salary coefficients is minor does not stimulate the enthusiasm and creativeness of employees. Starting salaries imposed on university graduates, master's and doctorate degree holders should be made clear.

5. It is advisable to create jobs that are suitable to professional skills of employees to further develop their talent, and to pay them an attractive salary so that they work with ease. It also necessary to assign important tasks and high-ranking posts to skilled returnees, create a serious working environment, have incentive policies and stimulate high-quality research products.

6. Technical conditions, especially information provision (internet, foreign publications) should be upgraded. A fair working environment needs to be established for employees regardless of where they trained.

7. Taking advantage of the greater mobility of capital over labour, adequate programmes and strategies on human capital development and utilisation should be put in place, to provide alternatives to labour emigration, particularly of highly skilled workers.

8. Specific attention should be given to ensure that overseas Vietnamese (*Viet Kieu*) who settle in many countries around the world have equal treatment and chances to open a business. Given the current crisis in North America and ASEAN countries, Vietnam may become an attractive destination for businessmen and professionals to return to.

7. Socioeconomic Impacts of Return Migration: Developing a Comparative Framework

John Gow and Robyn Iredale

INTRODUCTION

This book presents a series of case studies on the experience and impact of return migration in the four study countries as well as a study of potential return migrants using Australia as a host country. This chapter develops a framework for comparative analysis of these impacts and experiences in order to outline both their specificity to the particular countries and some salient features in common. It is through consideration of both commonalities and differences that broader implications can be considered in relation to skilled migration policy.

Before these matters can be considered further, however, it is necessary to consider the extent to which the data generated by this study can be used to substantiate such a comparative analysis. In particular there are two methodological issues that need to be considered, inconsistencies in the sampling procedures and questions asked in the four case studies. Although at the beginning of the project a common questionnaire was developed for implementation in all four cases, a subsequent range of logistical matters ensured that the final data gathering was not consistent with this original intention. In particular:

- The original questionnaire was administered, coded and entered prior to and during the development of the coding scheme and as a result many of the questionnaire items were coded in such a way as to be inconsistent with the surveys that followed the specifications in the coding manual. In many cases these inconsistencies were such that they could not be remedied through subsequent recoding;

- The questionnaire that was administered in Taiwan was shorter and completely different from those administered in the other cases;
- In the absence of baseline data on the numbers and gender composition of skilled return migrants in the four regions it was not possible to determine the sampling rates represented by the sampling quotas in the four countries;
- Although an original methodological intention of the study was to have the sample population balanced with respect to gender through quota sampling of 50 per cent male and female, this was only achieved in Vietnam. In Bangladesh, despite considerable efforts to recruit women to the study, only about one quarter of the sample was female. In Taiwan the proportion of women in the sample was just over one third while in China the proportion was less than 20 per cent;
- Sample sizes ranged from 100 (Vietnam) to 185 (China).

This places some limitations of the way the quantitative data in particular can be used. The most notable limitations are:

- **Comparative:** Given the differences in the questions asked, sampling frameworks and coding, countries cannot be directly compared statistically.
- **Inferential:** Given the sample size, the capacity of the data sets to generate inferential statistics at a level of confidence of 95 per cent or better is limited. This is particularly the case when using either age or gender as an independent variable since the sample populations were predominantly young and, as already discussed, male.

Hence the arguments presented in this chapter are rather more tentative than they might otherwise be and, where possible, triangulated with evidence from open-ended questions and the broader discussion in the case study chapters. Where direct comparative forms of data presentation are used in the body of this report they will compare Bangladesh and Vietnam since this is directly available from the data files. Where possible, relevant related evidence will be drawn from the other two case studies.

THE SOCIO-ECONOMIC CONTEXT

Although it may be difficult to specify the impact of return migrants on receiving countries in terms of economic transformation and growth in a direct sense, a range of indicators from the study strongly suggests that return migrants are strategically located within the leading socio-economic sectors. They are young, predominantly under the age of 45, and highly educated as indicated in Table 7.1. Except for Vietnam, where the largest proportion of returnees in the study came back with technical or vocational qualifications, the largest single group came back with postgraduate qualifications.

Table 7.1 Education levels of respondents

	Bangladesh %	China %	Taiwan %	Vietnam %
High school	(a)	(a)	(a)	15.1
Vocational school	4.7	1.8	(a)	48.8
Bachelor's degree	14.1	6.7	11.5	20.9
Master's degree	30.6	23.3	74.6	14.0
Doctorate	34.1	68.1	13.9	1.2
Other	16.5	-	-	-
Total	100.0	100.0	100.0	100.0

Note: (a) Not in survey for these countries.

By virtue of their qualifications and experience they are predominantly in high technology areas of manufacturing such as biotechnology and microelectronics, within the services sector in universities, hospitals, government and NGOs and overwhelmingly occupy professional or managerial positions. The employment sectors they occupied in Bangladesh and Vietnam are shown in Table 7.2.

Table 7.2 Employment sectors

Sector	Bangladesh %	Vietnam %
Government	9.4	13.0
Research or university	31.1	42.0
NGO	15.1	5.0
Business services	14.2	20.0
Industry	15.1	5.0
International/UN organisations	(a)	3.0
Not stated	15.1	12.0
Total	100.0	100.0

Note: (a) Not in survey.

As Table 7.3 indicates across three of the four case studies, where comparable data are available, 85 per cent of return migrants in the study occupied managerial; administrative; professional or para-professional positions.

Table 7.3 Employment positions

Employment level	Bangladesh %	Taiwan %	Vietnam %
Managerial or administrative	36.4	45.8	31.0
Professional or para-professional	61.7	39.0	61.0
Not stated	1.9	15.3	8.0
Total	100.0	100.0	100.0

Note: Comparable data not available for China.

These figures highlight the potential of these migrants to significantly shape processes of nation-building and socio-economic transformation. However, the extent to which this potentiality can be realised seems likely to be affected by the extent to which they are integrated into the domestic socio-economic environment and their capacity to act as agents of socio-economic transformation is facilitated.

The individual country case studies in this report indicate that there is a range of considerations that impinge upon the decision of skilled migrants to return to their own country. These relate to conditions both within the host and the home country. Within the host country they may be compelled to return because of the non-availability of residential status, formal restrictions on undertaking employment and the expiry of entry permits.

Evidence of 'push' factors within the host countries is less clear-cut. Very few indicated job difficulties, but most of the returnees had gone overseas to study and very few undertook employment. Many Vietnamese returnees indicate that they had 'no choice' but the survey results do not make it obvious whether this is an outcome of such matters as the expiry of residence permits or contractual obligations within their home country. There were also a considerable number that cited 'other' reasons. Open-ended responses in the Bangladesh survey suggest experiences of isolation and discrimination in the host countries.

Within the home country they may have a formal contractual obligation to return home and/or to their previous position. Other reasons may include obligations to the immediate or extended family, and the expectation of employment or business opportunities. For instance, for both Vietnam and Bangladesh the home country factors of family ties, employment opportunities, government policies and, in the case of Bangladesh, business opportunities, were appreciably nominated as reasons for return.

The data suggest that returnees are generally satisfied with their employment and socio-economic circumstances. On the other hand the data also suggest that they are confronted with adjustment problems on their return. In Bangladesh 23 per cent of respondents agreed that they had suffered from 'culture shock' on their return compared with 20 per cent in Vietnam. In Bangladesh and Vietnam respondents indicated that although they saw their remuneration as inferior to their overseas colleagues, they generally saw themselves as better off than their domestic colleagues, see Table 7.4.

Table 7.4 Remuneration of respondents

	Compared with overseas colleagues		Compared with colleagues at home	
	Bangladesh %	Vietnam %	Bangladesh %	Vietnam %
Much lower	36.1	35.0	8.7	7.0
Lower	24.7	22.0	18.3	23.0
Same	10.3	22.0	44.2	53.0
Higher	22.7	18.0	24.0	15.0
Much higher	6.2	3.0	4.8	2.0
Total	100.0	100.0	100.0	100.0

Although in an overall sense these issues of adjustment may not appear to be particularly significant, by most of the indicators that have just been discussed nearly 30 per cent of the returnees report some dissatisfaction with their integration into the local socio-economic environment. As has already been noted women appear to be under-represented in the sample populations so that the aggregate results tend to over-represent the experiences of men. When the results are disaggregated with respect to gender, the data suggest that women have contradictory experiences of adjustment, integration and satisfaction, at least in the cases of Bangladesh and Vietnam where relevant comparative data are available (see Table 7.5).

Table 7.5 Problems faced by respondents

	Bangladesh		Vietnam	
	Males %	Females %	Males %	Females %
Employment adjustment problems	53.2	50.0	28.0	44.0
Satisfied with current position	74.3	70.4	80.0	62.0*
Role on work place decisions	87.2	68.0*	n/a	n/a
Living adjustment problems	40.3	46.4	20.0	38.0*
Culture shock	16.9	37.0*	16.0	28.0

Note: * Significant at better than 95 per cent confidence level.

The results suggest that in Vietnam, in particular, women are less satisfied with their current employment and experienced greater problems than men in readjusting to living conditions in their home country. There is also a suggestion, although the sample size was insufficient to fully substantiate the point, that women experience greater employment adjustment problems and cultural shock on return as well. In Bangladesh, although the other indicators don't provide clear evidence, over twice as many women as men reported experiencing cultural shock on return and felt marginalised in the work place, despite their administrative and managerial responsibilities.

These results show that women are confronted with a range of specific problems associated with tensions and disjunctures between their own aspirations and what they can achieve. Also, migrants find it difficult to participate in nation-building and socio-economic transformation within their own country because of local gender expectations and modes of discrimination. It is possible that these specific gender concerns are symptomatic of a broader issue of tensions between local and globalised sectors.

This next section will discuss a possible staged approach to examining the phenomenon of the 'brain drain'. The remainder of Chapter 7 will incorporate a broad comparison across the four case studies. This is not statistically based, but emerged from the more qualitative aspects of the research.

FACTORS IN THE COUNTRY OF ORIGIN AFFECTING SKILLED RETURNEES

The results demonstrate a wide discrepancy in the range of issues facing 'possible' skilled returnees to Bangladesh, China, Taiwan and Vietnam. Table 7.6 summarises the situation for professional migrants in each case and the general impact of their return.

In general, for 'unsuccessful' migrants, return migration is partly a result of lack of success in the country of immigration and partly a perception of the prospect of better opportunities back home – even if it means returning to their old job. Thus Bangladeshis, for example, do not move home having accomplished what they set out to achieve and they return reluctantly, feeling a sense of failure. The decision is often made in the context of family obligations but without a deep sense of commitment to 'solidarity' with the nation-state. Some returnees in our study joined the NGO sector as this provided some hope of changing the politico-social environment in Bangladesh. There was a sense among those interested more in economic aspects that they would fall behind in their profession on their return and some intended to remain only as long as it took them to migrate elsewhere.

Table 7.6 Summary of macro factors affecting return skilled migration

Factor	Bangladesh	China	Taiwan	Vietnam
Rate of return skilled migration	low	increasing	high – both permanent and temporary	high for students
State of high skilled labour market	oversupply, low wages	rapidly improving, high wages in foreign companies and joint ventures	high unmet demand, highly valued	demand increasing but wages low
Major motivation for return	failure elsewhere, little choice, little impact of TNCs	increasing opportunities, TNCs growing, barriers to advancement in o/s countries,	economic growth high since 1970s, dynamic economic climate, family and other networks	social, nationalistic, increasing importance of economic factors
Government policies	none	some science parks, other incentives and policies	wide range of policies and incentives	none, except commitment to organisations
Impact of returnees	little, except in NGOs	significant in private sector	crucial in high-tech sectors and general economic growth	limited – lack of reward for merit, rigid environment
General impact on social transformation	no noticeable effect due to structural problems	noticeable change in private and public sectors	very strong effects – economic, social and political	little to date but future prospects seen

Successful professional migrants return home on a quite different basis. There is a strong commitment to social units in the country of origin – not only in terms of the strength of social ties but also in terms of the content. Chinese returnees were mostly students and they encompassed some of the feelings and experiences of the Bangladeshis, of having achieved less than they would have liked overseas. But they were buoyed by the prospect of expanding economic opportunities in China. Political inertia concerned them but they were optimistic that they could take advantage of the opportunities provided by rapid economic growth and be at the forefront of exciting developments in China. They felt that the technology infrastructure in China was advanced enough to ensure that they could keep up with developments overseas, even after their return.

The Taiwanese have been the most highly motivated to return home. Highly skilled returnees were able to utilise their skills and knowledge and they were 'valued' in Taiwan. The policies that have been put in place to try to attract them home, ranging from travel subsidies, job seeking advice, higher salaries, special housing and attractive working conditions to sponsoring trial visits, have been very influential. They have helped the Taiwanese to remain attached to Taiwan and to feel strong nationalistic feelings that have encouraged them to assist with the development of Taiwan. Back home in Taiwan, they are able to maintain excellent links with Taiwanese people who are still overseas, especially in the US. Moreover, the Taiwanese in the US have formed strong associations among themselves and they have also been 'increasingly building professional and social networks that span national boundaries and facilitate flows of capital, skill, and technology'. The networks that now operate between Silicon Valley and Taiwan are described as a 'two-way bridge' between the technology communities (Saxenian 2001, p. 220).

The Vietnamese were under a more social/political obligation to return and most were overseas students. Nevertheless, there seems to be more optimism about the future of Vietnam, and to be able to contribute to this future provides a stronger motivation to return home. The Vietnamese who fled in the late 1970s and 1980s were forced migrants and few are returning for economic reasons. Most returned intermittently to assist with social reconstruction through non-bureaucratic mechanisms.

FACTORS IN THE COUNTRY OF ORIGIN AFFECTING BUSINESS RETURNEES

The return of business migrants was much less easy to capture as the samples contained relatively few of this cohort. This was mainly because these people were not returnees. Table 7.7 summarises the business climate in each situation and the reasons why there were few returnees to date in this sector.

Taiwan was the only case so far where there was significant evidence of business migrants being attracted back home. In the 1960s and 1970s, the relationships between Taiwan and the US was a 'textbook First World-to-Third World relationship', according to Saxenian (2001, p. 222). American businesses invested in Taiwan to take advantage of low wages, and Taiwanese postgraduate students were part of the 'brain drain', and remaining in the US after their studies, because of better professional opportunities. By the late 1980s, engineers had begun returning to Taiwan – drawn by government policies and economic growth. The Taiwanese began establishing IT businesses in Silicon Valley in the late 1980s, using venture capital and capital from Singapore and Taiwan.

Table 7.7 Summary of macro factors affecting return business migration

Factor	Bangladesh	China	Taiwan	Vietnam
Business climate	little change, inefficient, red tape, little globalisation	opening up, increasing globalisation & reducing red tape	rapid economic growth since 1980s, highly globalised	starting to change since 1995, increasing global focus
Rate of business return	low	rising	high, especially circular	low
Major motivations	few – undeveloped business landscape	rapidly increasing economic opportunities	rapid economic growth, dynamic business networks, proximity to China and SE Asia	increasing importance of economic growth
Government policies	none	some	many	none
Impact of returnees on business climate	little	significant in private sector	high rate of setting up SMEs	limited by red tape, politics
Impact on social transformation	little noticeable effect due to structural problems	dramatic impact in private sector practices	very strong economic impact, political and social effects	little impact to date due to short time frame

These businesses expanded and with the assistance of the Taiwanese government they established manufacturing partnerships with Taiwan's 'state-of-the-art semiconductor foundaries and incorporated in the Hsinchu Science-Based Industrial Park to oversee assembly, packaging, and testing' (Saxenian 2001, pp. 222–3). Returnees played a key role in developing local customers in Taiwan.

The growing integration of the technological communities of Silicon Valley and Hsinchu, which started in the 1980s, offers substantial benefits to both economies. It provides opportunities for US firms to invest and manufacture in Taiwan and increasingly the Taiwanese are providing access for US firms to customers and markets in China and Southeast Asia (Naughton 1997). None of this would be possible without the 'reciprocal and decentralized nature' of the relationships between Taiwan and the US.

> The Silicon Valley–Hsinchu relationship ... consists of formal and informal collaborations between individual investors and entrepreneurs, small and midsize firms, and divisions of larger companies located on both sides of the Pacific. In this complex mix, the rich social and professional ties among Taiwanese engineers and their US counterparts are as important as the more formal corporate alliances and partnerships (Saxenian 2001, pp. 224–5).

The return of Taiwanese business people, in contrast to the Indian situation, mentioned in Chapter 1, where few return home other than temporarily, is a function of both the higher standard of living in Taiwan but also the more favourable and open business climate. Close relationships between Taiwan's policy makers and US-based engineers from Taiwan have been an ongoing feature and this has worked in favour of both encouraging greater return and reducing   red tape in the business environment.

Saxenian (2001, p. 230) reports that Mainland Chinese engineers in the Silicon Valley are poised to follow the trajectories of their Taiwanese predecessors. With encouragement from Chinese bureaucrats and universities and the incentive of the expanding Chinese market, they have already started their own companies and are building ties back home. Whether they will emulate the Taiwanese model will depend largely on political and economic developments in China. Other issues, such as governance and political climate, are also important as business people will not set up in China if the level of red tape is overwhelming and the system is inefficient.

CONCLUSION

This chapter has discussed the difficulties and limitations of comparative research. At the same time, it has described four quite different economic, social and political systems and their impact on the phenomenon of return skilled and business migration. The insights that emerge from this comparison far outweigh the difficulties with the method and show the merit of looking across different contexts.

The concluding chapter will draw out the theoretical elements and address the four hypotheses that were posed in Chapter 1.

8. Conclusion

Robyn Iredale, Fei Guo, Santi Rozario and John Gow

Chapter 1 argues that knowledge workers are the modern source of economic growth and development and for this reason countries are competing for highly skilled immigrant workers. These skilled and business migrants bring skills and knowledge but more importantly they bring positive externalities in the form of increased technological and economic networks, in and between the sending and the receiving countries. These networks stand to benefit both the sending and receiving countries.

Consequently, countries that have lost skilled emigrants are increasingly turning their attention to methods and policies for encouraging them to return in order that some of the benefits may accrue to them. This book has focused on the case of four regions in Asia and the level, characteristics and impacts of return skilled and business migrants. The research encompassed people who moved both temporarily and permanently in the first instance although we see a high degree of crossover in current times.

Most skilled and business emigrants went overseas originally as students (especially from China, Taiwan and Vietnam) and this is contiguous with skilled emigration. Some out-migration from Vietnam was intended to be permanent but was different in that it was forced. Generally, skilled emigration was not part of an 'overt' strategy, as in the Caribbean, though doubtless many students went abroad to study with the intention of remaining permanently. Perhaps the distance from the US, the great 'mecca' for skilled migrants, nationalism and politics made for a different situation in some parts of Asia.

Most skilled emigrants from Asian countries come from privileged upper classes. They most certainly have more choices than the less educated. They also have more choices as a result of the increasing trend towards the internationalisation of professions. Internationalisation is not proceeding evenly in all professions but the IT, finance and business professions have become relatively open and universal in terms of their knowledge content (Iredale 2001). The demand for 'knowledge' workers in many developed and developing countries is now making the range of possible destinations much wider.

STAGES IN RETURN SKILLED AND BUSINESS MIGRATION

This research has shown that it is important to make a clear distinction between skilled and less skilled migrants in terms of many factors, but especially when discussing the concept of emigration being replaced by immigration or return migration – what is often called the 'migration transition'. The four case studies show that:

- Bangladesh is still at the predominantly 'brain drain' stage (Stage 1). Bangladesh at this point in time is what may be referred to as an 'anti-globaliser' (Kelly 2002, p. 28) or perhaps a 'non-globaliser'.
- A 'reversal of the brain drain' started tentatively in Vietnam in the late 1990s but the sluggishness of the economy, the impact of the Asian financial crisis and the slow rate of reform of state-owned enterprises and the bureaucratic sector have all worked to discourage potential returnees (early Stage 2).
- A 'reversal of the brain drain' started to occur in China in the mid-1990s so that return skilled migration occurred as China's open door policies gained momentum, the economy took off and entry to the WTO became a possibility and then a reality (Stage 2).
- Taiwan entered Stage 2 in the 1980s as the economy took off and Taiwan became a newly industrialising country (NIC). The return did not equal the outflow but became substantial in actual numbers. The openness of the Taiwanese economy and its globalisation has taken it into Stage 3 in the 1990s. Stage 3 is characterised by skilled outflows and return inflows and an increasingly high level of temporary and intermittent circulation of nationals and expatriates.

The 'skilled migration transition' is quite different from the 'overall migration transition'. There is no point at which skilled emigration stops and is replaced by skilled immigration but the two may come to co-exist. The 'brain drain' in one period may come to be accompanied, but not replaced, by a 'brain reversal' at a later stage. It may also lead, in the current global context, to a 'brain circulation' or many short-term movements. That is, both emigration and immigration may co-exist and be supplemented by short-term, circulatory movements as an economy becomes more integrated into the global economy. But this movement through the 'stages' is not automatic and a country may become stalled at Stage 1 or 2. This makes it even more important to understand the reasons and to put in place appropriate policies or development and other strategies. But before discussing this, the gender dimension requires a special focus.

THE GENDER DIMENSION

Specific issues have emerged for women returnees that need to be considered further. The inference that can be drawn from the results is that women are confronted with a range of specific problems associated with tensions and disjunctures between their own aspirations as highly skilled and educated return migrants seeking to participate in nation-building and socio-economic transformation within their own country, and local gendered expectations and gendered modes of discrimination which inhibit the articulation of those aspirations. It is possible that these specific gender concerns are symptomatic of a broader issue of tensions between local and globalised sectors.

Both the Bangladesh and Vietnam findings suggest that women face more hurdles on their return than men, not just in their employment but also in society generally. How they cope with this depends on many factors but there were instances where major changes to living arrangements ensued and female returnees in Bangladesh, in particular, became very active in civil society and in trying to overthrow practices that discriminated against women.

Further research needs to be done into how women construct or reconstruct their gender identity within the country to which they migrated and how they renegotiate this when they return to their home country.

FACTORS AFFECTING HOST COUNTRIES

This project intended to examine the impact for host countries, especially Australia, of returning or circulating skilled and business migrants. Because we interviewed a sample of potential rather than actual returnees in Australia we have only been able to posit some of the possible future benefits to Australia, in Chapter 2. But it is clear that Australia stands to benefit from returning Taiwanese and the incorporation of Australia into the Taiwanese diaspora. The Chinese who are returning to China also provide an opportunity for Australia to be better linked to opportunities and institutions in China. Anecdotally, we know from the return of academics that they provide a bridge to universities and research institutes in China.

This aspect has received little coverage in Australia and the 'network' value of returnees has not been capitalised upon. The US has seen much greater obvious benefits (from skilled migrants' networks) and some have been measured. Moreover, Saxenian states that the US needs to maintain open boundaries so that Silicon Valley and other parts of the US 'continue to both build and benefit from their growing ties to the Asian economy' (Saxenian 2001, p. 231). In the light of 11 September 2001, this warning carries even more weight.

Similar attempts at quantifying the 'benefits' to Australia of skilled emigrants/astronauts and networks have not been undertaken and there is much less acknowledgement of the possible benefits. This is a sphere for future research.

FINDINGS IN RELATION TO HYPOTHESES

Finally, this research was conducted in line with four major hypotheses and each of these will be taken and discussed in turn. These findings represent the first attempt at evaluating the impacts of return migration in the Asia Pacific region.

(1)   The 'brain drain' is no longer a major problem for countries as return migration and brain circulation have started to become more significant

This was found to hold for Taiwan and increasingly for China, but China is a long way from repatriating the number of skilled overseas Chinese that it needs or would like. The hypothesis does not hold for Bangladesh or Vietnam at this point, although Vietnam is placing less emphasis on the negative aspects of the 'brain drain' and more on the potential advantages.

Temporary return has become a more common phenomenon in recent years and is more readily undertaken as part of a long-term strategy – to re-migrate, to come and go – with specific goals and strategies in mind. For example, sending someone abroad for education has become part of a family strategy for gaining a foothold in another country. The growing ease of converting from a student visa to a permanent resident visa in countries such as the US, Canada and Australia will undoubtedly lead to an increase in this phenomenon.

On balance, therefore, it appears that this currently popular view applies to some countries and regions but not others. Taiwan is probably the best example of an economy that has been networked into the global sphere largely as a result of skilled migration. But many other regions are not in this position and experience most of the losses of the 'brain drain' without receiving any or many benefits. Connell's (2001) work on the Pacific shows that most parts are now being negatively affected by skilled emigration with outcomes such as low productivity and morale, and declining health and education services. Pellegrino (2001, p. 119) concludes that 'circulation migration', or 'brain exchange', is not the predominant model for Latin America and evidence from Africa provides a similar understanding.

(2)   The stronger the commitment of migrants to social units in the country of origin, the more likely it is that return migration of successful migrants takes place

Individual decisions to return home, for professionals and business people, are made in response to a careful weighing up of many factors – especially personal factors, career-related prospects and the economic/political/environmental climate. Social/family factors remain important for some but the growth of transnational communities, better communication and ease of travel are changing the impact of this element. Returning home for family reasons still carries weight but it is only one factor. It may become more important when successful integration does not occur in the host country, as for Bangladeshis, or when the emphasis on extended families and national pride is still very strong, as for the Vietnamese.

In terms of commitment to the wider society, what is very clear is that returnees cannot 'drive' change – they start to return following change. Unless there is overall development or social transformation, skilled and business emigrants are reluctant to return. As Meyer states (2001, p. 104), in order to achieve the repatriation of foreign trained professionals emphasis must be 'placed on science and technology as well as educational policies that could provide incentives and conditions for effective returns'.

(3)   The stronger the economic growth and the more 'globalised' the economy, the greater the rate of return migration as skilled émigrés will not feel that they will drop out of the loop of their profession

This hypothesis was found to be largely true and the notion that professionals do not want to get out of touch with changes and developments in their profession is strong. The study found that skilled returnees place great emphasis on being able to stay in touch with professional colleagues overseas. For those who returned and felt hampered by overly bureaucratic environments, poor equipment and working conditions, there was a level of frustration that may in the future lead to re-migration.

(4)   The role of the government in facilitating return migration is as important as the economic, social and political environment of the country

This was definitely found to be true. Factors affecting the movement of professionals are closely linked to science and technology policies. Policies aimed at encouraging entrepreneurship, training, education and research are all important. Centres of excellence, research and higher education institutes act as 'meccas' for attracting people and many become part of their elite and stay.

National policies cover the whole gamut of general and specific policies. Science parks in Taiwan and China are performing the role of being hubs of innovative, cutting-edge technology and manufacturing. China recently launched a programme aimed at turning 100 universities into world-class centres. Other policies have been documented throughout this study, including scholarships tied to returning home and various incentives and subsidies to encourage people to come home for a visit. The two case study countries that do not have specific policies, Bangladesh and Vietnam, are urged to turn their attention to developing them.

Other studies have produced similar findings. For example, a study conducted by the Committee on Science and Technology in Developing Countries (COSTED 2001, p. 55) in Bangladesh, India and Sri Lanka called for the establishment of joint research institutes with overseas partners and a whole range of policies to provide incentives for people to stay or return. Conversely, weak public research which involves too little money, an inflexible environment, etc. can 'push' people, especially the young, out.

Interviews with returnees highlighted the importance of the overall context within the economy/country. Policies that improve civil society, the level of democracy, environmental amenity, security and other aspects of the quality of life are all necessary to encourage the retention and return of skilled personnel. Basic services, such as health and education, and adequate infrastructure are all needed to improve the general living conditions.

One way of getting around the generally poor living conditions that prevail in many developing countries has been to encourage the development of enclaves for the 'elite'. While this runs counter to arguments about social equality, the reality is that this type of housing and special policies in terms of higher wages and other advantages for returnees, have been one way of encouraging people to return.

Theorists of the social consequences of globalisation, such as Bauman (1998) and Beck (2000), argue that one of the major consequences of the way that processes of globalisation have destabilised the economic and geo-political boundaries of nation-states is to establish new sociocultural, economic and sometimes physical barriers that increasingly separate local populations from the globalised elite within countries. At the same time, open economies, open borders, air travel and global telecommunications constitute a cosmopolitan economic and sociocultural space that transcends countries. Within the cosmopolitan space, the globalised elite associate with each other and decreasingly associate with locals. Practices of demarcation may be as overt as the establishment of special economic zones, gated housing estates and the cachet of overseas qualifications, or as subtle as the pervasive impact of cultural capital and networking.

The return migrants are complicit in these processes irrespective of their desires in the matter and, although they may wield some influence to redress the development of divisions between the elite and the rest of the population, they are not really the major players in this situation. To participate in nation-building and economic transformation, skilled return migrants need employment that matches their aspirations to local economic and social priorities and sufficient economic and physical security to ensure that their commitment to their own country is not compromised in the face of the exigencies of everyday life.

In the short term, and perhaps even in the medium term, it is possible that these objectives may be consistent with an enclave model of development. But this is not a strategy for long-term stability or security. Where strategies of nation building and transformation can link the skilled and educated elite to the needs and aspirations of the broader population then long term stability is a more likely possibility. How this may be achieved in practice is a matter of the implementation of appropriate policies.

INTERNATIONAL DIMENSIONS

There is an increasing level of debate about international policies to manage the costs and benefits of the 'brain drain'. The General Agreement on Trade in Services (GATS) that was adopted in Uruguay in 1994 recognised the importance of such movements as a critical factor in the expansion of world trade in services and the global economy. In *Managing Migration,* Ghosh (2000, p. 232) discusses the possible benefits for the world economy of a freer and more orderly circulation of labour and argues that 'this implies a fuller exploitation of current and potential comparative advantage of different countries'. He contends that developing countries will be able to benefit more from being able to export more knowledge and information-intensive services in which they have a comparative advantage and that this is a major way in which they can increase their export income.

The OECD's *International Mobility of the Highly Skilled* (2002, p. 7) calls for greater co-operation between sending and receiving countries to ensure a fair distribution of benefits. One possibility is the establishment of the Intellectual Resource Management Fund (IRMF) that was recommended by COSTED (2001). The IRMF would 'fund actions at regional and international levels augmenting national efforts to produce and develop world class human resources in S&T', particularly in Asia, Africa and Latin America (COSTED 2001, p. 51). The recommendation put to UNESCO in November 2001 was that the IRMF be a 'Corpus fund in partnership with UNDP, World Bank, EC and other interested donors and governments'. It is anticipated that it would help developing countries to expand their training capacity of S&T professionals, encourage mobility of S&T professionals into developing countries and assist developing country S&T professionals to undertake exchanges and training attachments in more developed countries.

While cooperation between sending and receiving countries is the absolute minimum necessity if sending countries (essentially the poor developing ones) are to gain anything from a hierarchically subordinate position, we need to bear in mind the political hurdles in this process – in spite of much debate and even formal agreement at the level of international policies. As Castles has pointed out, there is an:

> inherent interest conflict between sending countries and receiving countries. The former want access to the labour market of richer countries, adequate pay, conditions and protection for their citizens, and long-term benefits through remittances, training and orderly return. All too often, the latter just want cheap, flexible labour and care little about the human rights and social well being of the migrants (Castles 1999, p. 16).

Castles goes on to argue that if they:

> combine to take a longer term view, both types of country could have an interest in orderly migration and regulated conditions for migrants, combined with strategies that would support the sustainable development of the sending country. If migration helps contribute to more productive economies and more prosperous societies, that is likely to benefit everybody through greater international trade, security, as well as through social cultural interaction (Castles 1999, p. 16).

While Castles makes an important point about the potential outcome of cooperative efforts for the developing economies, it is difficult to imagine that the developed nations, lacking the necessary political will, will come to the party. As Appleyard (1992, p. 23) argues, although the general background described so far has been well known for years, there has been a 'dearth of systematic thinking at the international level on the linkage between large-scale migration, population increase, racial inequality and global insecurity'.

For Appleyard, the four essential aspects of a development package that would address the issues of both the income and demographic differentials between the developing and developed countries are trade, debt relief, investment and effective aid. The burden of accumulated foreign debt in developing countries is probably one of the most fundamental obstacles to human development (Appleyard 1992, p. 24). Recent widespread public support and pressure on the relevant governments and organisations, including the World Bank, IMF, etc, in favour of debt relief has indeed been impressive. However, it is all too noticeable that even such powerful public pressure has failed to move the relevant bodies in taking steps to remedy the situation which would begin to make a difference to the developing countries. Despite a lot of noise about substantial debt relief for many of the developing countries, so far little or nothing has actually happened. Exploitative relations/conditions continue to feature in both trade and investment relations and these are integrally related to debt problems between richer and poorer nations.

Genuine cooperative aid and development assistance with a view not only to enhancing economic growth but also to the redistribution of wealth (both internationally, and internally within the developing nations) has an important role to play. However, the lack of political will is the fundamental obstacle at both the international level and within individual developing countries. The challenge is to somehow go beyond the talking and protesting and bring about a genuine desire to eliminate exploitation and to ensure a more equitable distribution of the world's resources.

For this change to begin to take place within a particular country, politically motivated return migrants can play a significant role by liaising with 'change agents', as discussed in Chapter 3, in their own countries. They may be instumental in facilitating change, though this research has shown that they cannot necessarily be the 'drivers'. They can serve as 'navigators' in a system that has already begun to address its basic economic, social and political problems.

References

Ahmed, Imtiaz (2000), *The Construction of Diaspora: South Asians Living in Japan,* Dhaka: The University Press Ltd.

Ahmed, Shamsun Naher (1998), 'The Impact of the Asian Crisis on Migrant Workers: Bangladesh Perspectives', *Asian and Pacific Migration Journal,* 7(2–3): 369–93.

Amin, Ruhul (1998), 'Enhancing the Capabilities of Emigration Countries to Protect Men and Women Destined for Low-skilled Employment: The Case of Bangladesh', Paper No. VI/2, *Technical Symposium on International Migration and Development,* The Hague, Netherlands, 29 June–3 July 1998.

Ammassari, S. (2000), *'Intercontinental Mobility and Return of Elites to Ghana and Côte d'Ivoire',* Ph.D. Research Proposal, University of Sussex.

Appleyard, R. 1962, 'The return migration of United Kingdom migrants from Australia', *Population Studies,* 15: 214–25.

Appleyard, R.T. (1992a), 'Migration and Development: A Global Agenda for the Future', *International Migration, Special Issue,* 30(1): 17–32.

Appleyard, Reginald (1992b), 'International Migration and Development–An Unresolved Relationship', *International Migration,* 30(3–4): 251–66.

Appleyard, Reginald (1995), 'Emigration Dynamics in Developing Countries', *International Migration,* 33(3–4): 293–309.

Asian Migrant Yearbook (1999), *Migration Facts, Analysis and Issues in 1998,* Hong Kong: Asian Migrant Centre Ltd.

Baker, M., J. Sloan and F. Robertson. (1994), *The Rationale for Australia's Skilled Immigration Program,* Canberra: Australian Government Publishing Service.

Barrett, A. (2002), 'Return Migration of Highly Skilled Irish into Ireland and their Impact on GNP and Earnings Inequality', in OECD, *International Mobility of the Highly Skilled,* Paris: OECD, pp. 151–60.

Bauman, Z. (1998), *Globalization: The human consequences,* Cambridge: Polity Press.

Beine, M., F. Docquier. and H. Rapoport. (2000), 'Brain Drain and Economic Growth: Theory and Evidence', *Journal of Development Economics,* 64(1): 275–89.

Bilsborrow, R. E., Graeme Hugo, A.S. Oberai and Hania Zlotnik (1997), *International Migration Statistics: Guidelines for Improving Data Collection Systems,* Geneva: International Labour Office.

Branjgan, W. (1995), 'Importing Skills Needed, or Cheap Labor?',*Washington Post*, 21 October.

Castles, S. (1999), 'International Migration and the Global Agenda: Reflections on the 1998 UN Technical Symposium', *International Migration, Special Issue: Migration and Development*, **37**(1): 5–20.

Central Census Steering Committee (CCSC) (2000), *Census Vietnam 1999. Sample Results*, Hanoi: The Gioi Publishers.

Chakravartty, Paula (2001), 'The Emigration of High-Skilled Indian Workers to the United States: Flexible Citizenship and India's Information Economy', in Wayne A. Cornelius, Thomas J. Espenshade and Idean Salehyan (eds), *The International Migration of the Highly Skilled*, San Diego: Center for Comparative Immigration Studies, University of California, pp. 325–50.

Chang, Shirley L. (1999), *Taiwan's Brain Drain and Its Reversal*, Taipei: Lucky Bookstore.

Chen, Bin-Hua (1995), *Comparative Study of the Employment Status between the Individuals Returning from Overseas with a Master's or Doctor's Degree and the Locally Trained Degree Holders*, Taipei: National Youth Commission, Executive Yuan.

Cheng, X. (1999), 'Chinese Students Abroad and the Strategy of Chinese Government', *Historical Research on Overseas Chinese*, Volume 2.

Colton, N. (1993), 'Homeward Bound: Yemeni Return Migration', *International Migration Review*, **27**(4): 873–86.

Committee on Science and Technology in Developing Countries (COSTED) (2001), International Mobility of S&T Professionals: Demands and Trends, Impact and Response, Chennai: COSTED.

Connell, J. (2001), *The Migration of Skilled Health Personnel in the Pacific Region*, Study commissioned by the WHO Western Pacific Regional Office, School of Geosciences, University of Sydney.

Cornelius, Wayne A., Thomas J. Espenshade and Idean Salehyan (eds) 2001, *The International Migration of the Highly Skilled*, San Diego: Center for Comparative Immigration Studies, University of California.

Dunn, A. (1995), 'Skilled Asians Leaving U.S for High-Tech Jobs at Home', *New York Times*, 21 February.

Engardio, P. (1994), 'The Skills Explosion: High-Tech Jobs All Over the Map', *Business Week*, 18 November.

Faist, T. (1997), 'The crucial meso-level', in T. Hammar, G. Blockmann, K. Tamas and T. Faist (eds), *International Migration, Immobility and Development. Multidisciplinary Perspectives*, Oxford: Berg, pp. 187–217.

Gardner, David (2000), 'Comment and Analysis, India's Plans to Plug the Brain Drain', *Financial Times*, 24 April.

Gardner, Katy (1995), *Global Migrants, Local Lives: Travel and Transformation in Rural Bangladesh*, Oxford: Clarendon Press.

Ghosh, Bimal (2000), 'New International Regime for Orderly Movements of People: What Will It Look Like?, in Bimal Ghosh (ed.), *Managing Migration*, Oxford: Oxford University Press, pp. 220–47.

Glaser, W. (1978), *The Brain Drain. Emigration and Return*, UNITAR Research Report No. 22, London: Pergamon Press.

Glick-Schiller, N., L. Basch and C. Szanton-Blanc (eds) (1992), *Towards a Transnational Perspective on Migration: Race, Class, Ethnicity, and Nationalism reconsidered*, New York: New York Academy of Sciences, Vol. 645.

Gmelch, G. (1980), 'Return Migration', *Annual Review of Anthropology*, **9**: 135–59.

Gmelch, G. (1987), 'Work innovation, and investment: the impact of return migrants in Barbados', *Human Organization*, **46**(2): 131–40.

Gray, P. (1994), 'Looking for Work? Try the World', *Time*, 19 September.

Guo, F. (2001), *School Attendence of Migrant Children in Beijing, China: A Multivariate Analysis'*, Presented at the *Rural Labour Migration Forum*, 3–5 July 2001, Beijing, China.

Hamilton, Nora and Norma Stolz Chinchilla (1996), 'Global Economic Restructuring and International Migration: Some Observations based on the Mexican and Central American Experience', *International Migration*, **34**(2): 195–231.

Huang, Kun-fei (1979), *A Survey Analysis of the Employment of the Returned Scholars and Students*, Taipei: National Youth Commission, Executive Yuan.

Hugo, G. (1994), *The Economic Implications of Emigration from Australia*, Canberra: Australian Government Publishing Service.

Hugo, G. (2002), 'Introduction', in OECD (ed.), *International Mobility of the Highly Skilled*, Paris: OECD, pp. 7–12.

Huguet, Jerrold W. (1992), 'Future of International Migration within Asia', *Asian Pacific Migration Journal*, **1**(2): 250–77.

Iredale, Robyn R. (1997), *Skills Transfer: International Migration and Accreditation Issues*, Wollongong: University of Wollongong Press.

Iredale, Robyn (2000), 'Migration Policies for the Highly Skilled in the Asia-Pacific Region', *International Migration Review*, **34**(3): 882–906.

Iredale, Robyn (2001), 'The Migration of Professionals: Theories and Typologies', *International Migration, Special Issue*, **39**(5): 7–26.

Kanjanapan, Wilawan (1992), 'White-Collar Foreign Workers in Taiwan', *Asian and Pacific Migration Journal*, **1**(3–4): 569–83.

Kee, P. K. and R. Skeldon (1994), 'The migration and settlement of Hong Kong Chinese in Australia', in R. Skeldon (ed.), *Reluctant Exiles: Hong Kong Communities Overseas*, Hong Kong: Hong Kong University Press, pp. 183–96.

Kelly, John (1987), 'Improving the comparability of international migration statistics: contributions by the Conference of European Statisticians from 1971 to date', *International Migration Review*, **21**: 1017–37.

Kelly, Paul (2002), 'Anti-globalisers lag behind', *The Weekend Australia*, 13-14 April, p. 28.

Khadria, Binod (1999), *The Migration of Knowledge Workers: Second-Generation Effects of India's Brain Drain*, New Delhi: Sage Publications.

Khadria, Binod (2001), 'Shifting Paradigms of Globalization: the Twenty-first Century Transition towards Generics in Skilled Migration from India', *International Migration, Special Issue*, **39**(5): 45–72.

Khoo, S. E. and A. Mak (2000), 'Career and Family Factors in Immigrant Adjustment', *Conference on Immigrant Societies and Modern Education*, 31 August – 2 September, National University of Singapore, Singapore.

Kim, J.-Y. (1995),'Korean Émigrés Return to Chase Economic Dreams', *Bangkok Post*, 17 October.

Kraly, Ellen Percy and K.S. Gnanasekaran (1987), 'Efforts to improve international migration statistics: a historical perspective', *International Migration Review*, **21**: 967–96.

Kraly, Ellen Percy and Robert Warren (1991), 'Long-Term Immigration to the United States: New Approaches to Measurement', *International Migration Review,* **25**: 60–92.

Kraly, Ellen Percy and Robert Warren (1992), 'Estimates of Long-term Immigration to the United States: Moving US Statistics toward United Nations Concepts', *Demography*, **29**: 613–28.

Kulu, H. and T. Tammaru (2000), 'Ethnic Return Migration from the East and the West: The Case Study of Estonia in the 1990s, *Europe–Asia Studies*, **52**(2): 349.

Kunz, E. (1975), *The Intruders: Refugee Doctors In Australia*, Canberra: ANU Press.

Kunz, E. (1988), *Displaced Persons: Calwell's New Australians*, Canberra: ANU Press.

Larmer B. (2000), 'Home at Last', *Newsweek International*, 31 July, p. 32.

Li, J. and D. Liu (1999), 'Analysis of Demand for Foreign Education in China', *Consumer Demands and Economy*, **5**: 20–28.

Liao, Chi-ching and Ming-yueh Tang (1984), *Research and Analysis on the Employment of the Returned Scholars and Students*, Taipei: National Youth Commission, Executive Yuan.

Lim, L. L. (1996), 'The migration transition in Malaysia', *Asian and Pacific Migration Journal*, **5**(2–3): 319–37.

Lindstrom, D. (1996), 'Economic Opportunity in Mexico and Return Migration from the United States', *Demography*, **33**(3): 357–75.

Logan, Ikubolajeh Bernard (1992), 'The Brain Drain of Professional, Technical and Kindred Workers from Developing Countries: Some Lessons from the Africa–US Flow of Professionals (1980–1989)', *International Migration*, **30**(3–4): 289–303.

Lowell, B. Lindsay (2001), 'The Foreign Temporary Workforce and Shortages in Information Technology', in Wayne A. Cornelius, Thomas J. Espenshade and Idean Salehyan (eds), *The International Migration of the Highly Skilled*, San Diego: Center for Comparative Immigration Studies, University of California, pp. 131–62.

Mahmood, Raisul Awal (1995a), 'Emigration Dynamics in Bangladesh', *International Migration*, **30**(3–4): 699–726.

Mahmood, Raisul Awal (1995b), 'Data on Migration from Bangladesh', *Asian and Pacific Migration Journal*, **4**(4): 533–41.

Mahroum, Sami (2002), *The International Mobility of Academics: The UK Case*, Ph.D. Thesis, USA: DISSERTATION.COM.

Mak, A. (1997), 'Skilled Hong Kong Immigrants' Intention to Repatriate', *Asian and Pacific Migration Journal*, **6**(2): 169–84.

Massey, D. and K. Espinosa (1997), 'What's Driving Mexico–US Migration? A Theoretical, Empirical, and Policy Analysis', *The American Journal and Sociology*, **102**(4): 939–1000.

Meyer, J-B. (2002), 'Migration of Skilled and Highly Skilled Workers in South Africa: A Case Study', in OECD, *International Mobility of the Highly Skilled*, Paris: OECD, pp. 213–24.

Meyer, Jean-Baptiste (2001), 'Network Approach versus Brain Drain: lessons from the Diaspora', *International Migration*, **39**(5): 91–110.

Miller, M. (1998), 'New Gold Mountain', *Far Eastern Economic Review*, 9 July.

Moore, R. (1994), *An Administrative History of the Assessment of Skills and Qualifications of Migrants of Non-English Speaking Backgrounds and Equal Opportunity – From the Second World War until 1990*, Working Paper No. 111, Department of Economics, Murdoch University, Western Australia.

National Youth Commission (various years), Data for Taiwan, Taipei.

Naughton, B. (ed.) (1997), *The China Circle: Economics and Technology in the PRC, Taiwan and Hong Kong*, Washington, DC: Brookings Institution Press.

Ong, A. (1999), *Flexible Citizenship: The Cultural Logics of Transnationality*, Durham, NC: Duke University Press.

Ong, Paul M., L. Cheng and L. Evans (1992), 'Migration of Highly Educated Asians and Global Dynamics', *Asian and Pacific Migration Journal*, 1(3–4): 543–67.

Ongley, P. and D. Pearson (1995), 'Post-1945 International Migration: New Zealand, Australia and Canada Compared', *International Migration Review*, 29(3): 765–93.

Organization for Economic Cooperation and Development (2002), *International Mobility of the Highly Skilled*, Paris: OECD.

Pal, Mariam S. (2001), *Women in Bangladesh: Country Briefing Paper*, Asian Development Bank, Programs Department (West).

Pellegrino, A. (2001), 'Trends in Latin American Skilled Migration', *International Migration*, 39(5): 111–32.

Pe-Pua, R., C. Mitchell, R. Iredale and S. Castles (1996), *Astronaut Families and Parachute Children: The Cycle of Migration between Hong Kong and Australia*, Canberra: Australian Government Publishing Service.

Pires, Jose (1992), 'Return and Reintegration of Qualified Nationals from Developing Countries Residing Abroad: The IOM Programme Experience', *International Migration*, 30(3–4): 353–75.

Rogaly, Ben (1996), 'Micro-finance Evangelism, "Destitute Women", and the Hard Selling of a New Anti-Poverty Formula', *Development in Practice*, 6(2): 100–12.

Rosenblum, Marc (2001), 'Immigration and the US National Interest', in Wayne A. Cornelius, Thomas J. Espenshade and Idean Salehyan (eds), *The International Migration of the Highly Skilled*, San Diego: Center for Comparative Immigration Studies, University of California, pp. 373–400.

Rozario, Santi (1995), 'Dai and Midwives: The Renegotiation of the Status of Birth Attendants in Contemporary Bangladesh', in J. Hatcher and C. Vlassoff (eds), *The Female Client and the Health-Care Provider*, Ottawa: International Development Research Centre (IDRC) Books, pp. 91–112. Also available in electronic form at http:/www.idrc.ca/books/focus/773/rozario.html

Rozario, Santi (1997), 'Development and Rural Women in South Asia: the Limits of Empowerment and Conscientization', *Bulletin of Concerned Asian Scholars*, 29(4): 45–53.

Rozario, Santi (2001), *Purity and Communal Boundaries: Women and Social Change in a Bangladeshi Village*, Dhaka: University Press Ltd.

Russell, Sharon Stanton (1992), 'Migrant Remittances and Development', *International Migration,* 30(3–4): 267–87.

Saxenian, A. (2001), 'Silicon Valley's New Immigrant Entrepreneurs', in Wayne A. Cornelius, Thomas J. Espenshade and Idean Salehyan (eds), *The International Migration of the Highly Skilled*, San Diego: Center for Comparative Immigration Studies, University of California, pp. 197–234.

Schiller, N. G., L. Basch and C. S. Blanck (1995), 'From Immigrant to Transmigrant: Theorizing Transnational Migration', *Anthropological Quarterly,* **68**: 48–63.

Shah, Nasra M. (1995), 'Emigration Dynamics from and within South Asia', *International Migration,* **30**(3–4): 559–626.

Shenzhou Xueren (1999), 'Zhongguo guojia ziran kexue jijinwei guanyu zizhu liuxue renyuan duanqi huiguo jiangxue zhuanxiang jijin shishi banfa de buchong guiding (Additional Provision of Special Funding for Short-term Visiting Scholars from Overseas, National Science Foundation)', Vol. 12.

Siddiqui, Tasneem (2000), *On the Margin: Refugees, Migrants and Minorities,* Dhaka: University of Dhaka Refugee and Migratory Movements Research Unit (RMMRU).

Solinger, D. (1999), *Contesting Citizenship in Urban China: Peasant Migrants, the State, and the Logic of the Market,* Berkeley: University of California Press.

Stalker, Peter (2000), *Workers Without Frontiers: The Impact of Globalisation on International Migration,* Boulder, Colorado: Lynne Rienner Publishers.

Stark, O. (1984), 'Migration Decision Making: A Review Article', *Journal of Development Economics,* **14**: 251–9.

Stark, O. (1991), *The Migration of Labor,* Cambridge, Mass: Basil Blackwell.

State Statistical Office (2001), Chinese Census, Beijing, China.

Straubhaar, T. (2001), 'Globalization, Internal Labour Markets and the Migration of the Highly Skilled', *Intereconomics,* Sept/October, **5**: 221–22.

Taylor, J. E. (1995), *Micro Economy-Wide Models for Migration and Policy Analysis: An Application to Rural Mexico,* Paris: Development Centre Studies, OECD.

Taylor, J. E. (1999), 'The New Economics of Labour Migration and the Role of Remittances in the Migration Process', *International Migration, Special Issue: Migration and Development,* **37**(1): 63–88.

Thomas-Hope, E. (1999), 'Return Migration to Jamaica and Its Development Potential', *International Migration, Special Issue: Migration and Development,* **37**(1): 183–203.

Thornton, P., J. Devine, P. Houtzager, D. Wright and S. Rozario (2000), *Partners in Development: A Review of Big NGOs,* Dhaka: DFID.

Thornton, P., S. Rozario, D. Griffith, J. Herm, S. Ward, R. Regmi and F. Khalil (2001) , *DFID Support to HPSP (Health and Population Sector Program): Mid-Term Review,* Dhaka: DFID.

Thurow, Lester (1999), *Building Wealth: The New Rules for Individuals, Companies, and Nations in a Knowledge-Based Economy,* New York: Harper Collins.

Tsay, Ching-lung (1987), 'Status of Women in Taiwan: Educational Attainment and Labour Force Development, 1951–1983', *Academia Economics Papers*, **15**(1): 153–82.

Tsay, Ching-lung (2000), 'Trends and Characteristics of Migration Flows to the Economy of Chinese Taipei', Paper presented at the *APEC-HRD-NEDM Workshop on International Migration and Human Resource Development in the APEC Member Economics*, Chiba, Japan, 19–22 January.

Tsay Ching-lung and Tai Po Fen (2001), 'Trends and Impacts of the Reversal of Brain Drain to Taiwan: The Case of High-Tech Industries', in Gee San and Ming-Chung Chang (eds), *Human Resources and the Development of High-Tech Industries in Taiwan*, Chung-Lih, Taiwan: Research Center for Taiwan Economic Development, National Central University, pp. 21–50.

Tseng, Yen-Fen (2000), 'The Mobility of Entrepreneurs and Capital: Taiwanese Capital-linked Migration', *International Migration*, **38**(2): 143–68.

Tzeng, R. (1995), 'International Labor Migration Through Multinational Enterprises', *International Migration Review*, **29**(1): 139–54.

United Nations (1980a), *Improvement of Statistics on the Outflow of Trained Personnel from Developing to Developed Countries: A Technical Report*, Series F, No. 30, New York: United Nations.

United Nations (1980b), *Recommendations on Statistics of International Migration*, Series M, No. 58, New York: United Nations.

United Nations (1986), *National Data Sources and Programmes for Implementing the United Nations Recommendations on Statistics of International Migration*, Series F, No. 37, New York: United Nations.

United Nations (1998), *Demographic Yearbook 1996*, New York: United Nations.

Visweswaran, Kamala (1997), 'Diaspora by Design: Flexible Citizenship and South Asians in US Racial Formations', *Diaspora*, **6**(1): 5–29.

Waldorf, B. (1995), 'Determinants of International Return Migration Intentions', *The Professional Geographer*, **47**(2): 125–37.

Wilhelm, K. and D. Biers (2000), 'No Place Like Home', *Far East Economic Review*, 15 June, pp. 72–75.

Wong, S. L, J. W. Salaff and E. Fong (1994), 'Network Capital: Emigration from Hong Kong', Paper presented at the *Conference on Tansnationalization of Overseas Chinese Capitalism: Networks, Nation-States and Imagined Communities*, Singapore, 8–12 August.

Wood, Geoffrey D. (1994), *Bangladesh: Whose Ideas, Whose Interests?*, Dhaka: University Press Ltd.

Wood, G. (1999), *'Prisoners and Escapees: Towards Political and Administrative Improvement'*, National Institutional Review, Dhaka: World Bank/ Bangladesh.

World Bank (1996), *World Development Report*, Delhi: Oxford University Press.

World Bank (2000), *Entering the 21st Century, World Bank Development Report 1999/2000*, New York: Oxford University Press.

Xiang, Biao (2001), 'Structuration of Indian Information Technology Professionals' Migration to Australia: An Ethnographic Study', *International Migration, Special Issue*, **39**(5): 73–90.

Xinhua News Agency (1999), 'Most Government-sponsored students return to China', 22 December.

Zhao, Z. (2000), *Community Profiles: 1996 census. 'China Born'*, Canberra: Department of Immigration and Multicultural Affairs.

Zweig, D. (1997), 'Return or not to return? Politics vs. Economics in China's Brain Drain', *Studies in Comparative International Development*, **32**(1): 92–125.

Appendices: Programmes to Facilitate the Recruitment of Highly Educated Professionals by Different Government Agencies

1. NATIONAL YOUTH COMMISSION (NYC)

1a. Assisting overseas students to return and work

Application:	By individuals directly to NYC or through government representative offices overseas.
Qualification:	Person who earned a university degree or higher in a foreign country.
Assistance:	1. Reimbursement of airfare and travel allowance.
	2. Employment services.
Implementation:	Since 1978 but reimbursement of airfare and travel allowance was terminated at the end of 1995.

1b. Employment service for doctorate or master degree holders

Application:	By individuals directly to NYC or through government representative offices overseas.
Qualification:	Person with a Master's degree or higher, below age 50 and currently unemployed.
Assistance:	Various kinds of employment services.
Implementation:	Since 22 December 1995.

1c. Short-term research programme for doctorate or master degree holders

Application:	By public and private universities, government agencies and research institutions to NYC.
Qualification:	Person with a Master's degree or higher and looking for their first job since being awarded the degree.
Assistance:	Salary for one year.
Implementation:	1996 to 16 September 2000.

1d. Post-doctorate research in private enterprises

Application:	By private enterprises wishing to strengthen R&D, improve management or upgrade production technology.
Qualification:	Person with a doctorate degree and looking for their first job after receiving the degree or after returning to Taiwan from abroad.
Assistance:	Salary for up to one year at NT $55 000 ($1800) per month.
Implementation:	Since 16 August 1996.

1e. Short-term professional training programme for doctorate or Master's degree holders

Application:	By vocational training institutions to NYC.
Qualification:	Person with a Master's degree or higher, below age 40 and currently unemployed.
Assistance:	1. Partial support to cover the training cost.
	2. Services of employment placement.
Implementation:	Since 26 July 1995.

1f. Short-term visiting research programme for overseas senior scholars

Application:	By individuals to NYC or to the agency in charge.
Qualification:	1. Senior professionals with distinguished achievement.
	2. Person with a doctorate degree and adequate experience in high-tech professions.
Assistance:	Comparative salary for a short period of time.
Implementation:	Since 1 March 1977
	Expanded to cover Master's degree holders in 1992.

2. MINISTRY OF ECONOMIC AFFAIRS

2a. Assisting private enterprises to recruit Taiwanese experts from abroad

Application:	By contracted agencies.
Qualification:	1. Doctorate degree and over 5 years' work experience.
	2. Master's degree and over 7 years' work experience.
	3. Bachelor's degree and over 10 years' work experience.
Assistance:	Monthly salary of NT $50 000 to $80 000 for up to one year.
Implementation:	Since 17 January 1995.

2b. Recruiting professionals and technicians to work under contract with the Ministry of Economic Affairs

Application:	To Ministry of Economic Affairs
Qualification:	n/a
Assistance:	Travel allowance and salary
Implementation:	28 May 1975.

3. MINISTRY OF EDUCATION

3a. Recruiting Taiwanese scholars from abroad for teaching jobs

Application: By universities and colleges.

Qualification: Qualified as a professor or associate professor, below age 65 and has researched continuously over the past three years overseas in his or her area of specialisation.

Assistance: 1. Same salary and benefits as local professors of the same rank for a period of one year, with possible extension of another year.
2. Allowances for relocation, housing and research (terminated on 29 November 1994).
3. Priority of being admitted to be a permanent faculty member.

Implementation: May 1989 to 31 December 2000.

3b. Assisting private universities and colleges to upgrade the quality of faculty members

Application: By private universities and colleges.

Qualification: Below age 65 and having a certificate of professor or associate professor or having a doctorate degree.

Assistance: Award to be determined by teacher–student ratio, and the number of additionally recruited faculty members.

Implementation: Ongoing

3c. Facilitating children of returned scholars and scientists to enrol in primary and secondary schools

Application: Individual families.

Qualification: Under any government programme of assisting returned schools.

Assistance: Priority to enter bilingual or other prepared schools.

Implementation: 25 May 1992 to 31 December 2000.

3d. Assisting returned scholars to purchase housing units

Application:	Individual Families.
Qualification:	Under any government programme of assisting returned schools.
Assistance:	Low interest rate of housing loans.
Implementation:	21 June 1978 to 1993.

4. NATIONAL SCIENCE COUNCIL (NSC)

4a. Recruiting research scientists

Application: By universities, colleges or research institutions to NSC.

Qualification: (1) Chair research scientist

Professor at a famous university, and having well-recognised publications from the past 3 years.

Internationally well-known scholar, having high academic reputation in a field in which Taiwan does not have any experts.

Distinguished achievement in applied sciences or technology.

(2) Specific research scientist

Professor at a famous university and having valuable publications from the past 3 years.

Associate professor at a famous university for over 4 years and having valuable publications from the past 3 years.

Doctorate degree from a famous university and conducting a profession or continuously doing research in an institution for over 8 years.

No doctorate degree but having distinguished ability in specific technology and having performed well in the profession for over 10 years.

(3) Specific associate research scientist

Associate professor at a famous university and having valuable publications from the past 3 years.

Assistant professor at a famous university, for over 4 years and having valuable publications from the past 3 years.

Doctorate degree from a famous university and conducting a profession or continuously doing research in an institution for over 4 years.

No doctorate degree but having distinguished ability in specific technology and having performed well in the profession for over 6 years.

(4) Post-doctorate researcher

Taiwanese nationals with research potential.

Foreign nationals whose areas of specialisation are lacking among Taiwanese nationals.

Assistance: Travel expenses, insurance cost and monthly salary based on these scales:

Chair research scientist NT $120 000 to $160 000

Specific research scientist NT $100 000 to $150 000

Specific Associate research scientist NT $70 000 to $100 000

Post-doctorate researcher NT $48 000 to $70 000

Implementation: Since 24 October 1973

From 1993 the programme applied to both overseas and domestic scholars.

4b. Encouraging research cooperation between private enterprises and academic institutions

Application: Proposals to be submitted by research institutions under NSC or by private enterprises.

Qualification: Collaborating research institutions and enterprises involved in key national development and construction projects.

Assistance: (1) Research cost for the principal investigator.

(2) The first year salary of a 3-year contract for a post-doctorate associate research fellow in a research and development department within an enterprise.

Implementation: Since 3 September 1991.

4c. Assisting new faculty members

Application: Individuals.

Qualification: Newly appointed research or teaching staff in higher education.

Assistance: Salary, travel expenses, insurance and research costs.

Implementation: Since 24 March 1992.

5. ACADEMIA SINICA (AS)

5a. Post-doctorate research

Application:	By any of the 23 institutes under AS on behalf of the individual to be recruited and with recommendation for the individual.
Qualification:	A person who received the doctorate degree in the past three years and who is less than 40 years old.
Assistance:	Monthly salary of NT $61 000 to $68 000 for up to four years.
Implementation:	Ongoing.

5b. Inviting foreign consultants, experts and scholars

Application:	Any of the 23 institutes of AS.
Qualification:	(1) Nobel Laureate.
	(2) Chair professor.
	(3) Professor.
	(4) Associate professor.
Assistance:	Highest work reward set by the government, international transport costs, local transport costs and insurance.
Implementation:	Ongoing.

6. THE INDUSTRIAL AND TECHNOLOGY RESEARCH INSTITUTE (ITRI)

6a. Employing Taiwanese nationals from abroad

Application:	Initiated by an institute of the ITRI based on long-term needs.
Qualification:	(1) Doctorate degree holders with valuable publications applicable at the ITRI.
	(2) Master's degree holders with over 3 years' work experience and outstanding performance in professions related to the research areas of the ITRI.
	(3) An individual with a qualification specified in (1) or (2) who also meets the requirements of a research fellow at the ITRI.
	(4) The qualified individual's area of expertise is uncommon in Taiwan.

Assistance: (1) Tickets for the recruited expert, spouse and two children under age 18.
(2) Housing allowance (NT $8000 to $10 000 per month).
(3) Moving expenses.
(4) Salary

Implementation: Ongoing.

7. THE SCIENCE AND TECHNOLOGY ADVISORY GROUP FOR THE CABINET (STAG)

7a. Enhancing the utilisation of highly educated professionals in sciences and technology

Application: By government agencies, research institutions and state enterprises.

Qualification: (1) Senior professionals with excellent credentials, or
(2) Doctorate degree holders with an adequate amount of professional experience.

Assistance: Salary for a year.

Implementation: 8 August 1995–1997.

Sources: *Handbook for Studies Returning from Abroad to work in Taiwan.* Taipei: National Youth Commission. April 1995.
Handbook of Employment Services for Scholars with Master Degree or Higher. Taipei: National Youth Commission, March 1996.
Communications and Clarifications with National Youth Commission, Ministry of Education, Ministry of Economic Affairs, and National Science Council.

Index